The Philadelphia Irish

The Philadelphia Irish

Nation, Culture, and the Rise
of a Gaelic Public Sphere

MICHAEL L. MULLAN

RUTGERS UNIVERSITY PRESS

NEW BRUNSWICK, CAMDEN, AND NEWARK,

NEW JERSEY, AND LONDON

Library of Congress Cataloging-in-Publication Data

Names: Mullan, Michael L. (Michael Leigh), author.
Title: The Philadelphia Irish : nation, culture, and the rise of a Gaelic
    public sphere / Michael L. Mullan.
Description: New Brunswick : Rutgers University Press, [2021] |
    Includes bibliographical references and index.
Identifiers: LCCN 2020043924 | ISBN 9781978815452 (paperback) |
    ISBN 9781978815469 (cloth) | ISBN 9781978815476 (epub) |
    ISBN 9781978815483 (mobi) | ISBN 9781978815490 (pdf)
Subjects: LCSH: Irish Americans—Pennsylvania—Philadelphia—Ethnic identity. |
    Irish Americans—Pennsylvania—Philadelphia—Social life and customs—
    19th century. | Irish—Pennsylvania—Philadelphia—HIstory—19th century. | Irish
    language—Social aspects—Pennsylvania—Philadelphia | Irish Americans—
    Pennsylvania—Philadelphia—HIstory—19th century. | Community life—
    Pennsylvania—Philadelphia—HIstory—19th century.
Classification: LCC F158.9.I6 M85 2021 | DDC 305.8916/2074811—dc23
LC record available at https://lccn.loc.gov/2020043924

A British Cataloging-in-Publication record for this book is available from the British Library.

☉ The paper used in this publication meets the requirements of the American National
Standard for Information Sciences—Permanence of Paper for Printed Library Materials,
ANSI Z39.48-1992.

www.rutgersuniversitypress.org

Manufactured in the United States of America

*I dedicate this book to the anonymous, the ordinary
Irish Americans of a not-too-distant past who rose above conditions
in a northeastern American city to make a history of their own,
a revival of a cherished culture. And to readers who might appreciate
the accomplishments of their Gaelic ancestors now rendered
less obscure by the contents of this work.*

Contents

The Philadelphia Irish

Introduction

The hunger ended but it never went away; it was there in silent memories, from one generation to the next.   —*Inscription, Philadelphia's Irish Memorial*

In the decade of the 1890s the Irish community of Philadelphia, a group that was Catholic, nationalist, and now more comfortably settled in their diaspora city of commerce and industry after the mid-nineteenth-century crisis and exodus from Ireland, cast a gaze back in time across the Atlantic, to native Ireland and its cultural revival. The collective silence that had been induced by decades of Irish mobility and emigration and been made more poignant by the trauma of the Famine was broken in the cultural awakenings that were motivated by events in native Ireland. This is a story of a people's ascent and arrival in a distant and initially inhospitable urban location, a northeastern American city, Philadelphia. It was an expansive urban center that the Irish Americans made their own in the late nineteenth century, which became the home of a renaissance of Irish remembrance and discovery of cultural meanings that had long been dormant, but now, near the turn of the twentieth century, were alive again.

A Gaelic Public Sphere

What follows is indeed a history of ordinary people ascending to unanticipated heights. It is also backed, in part, by sociological considerations, an understanding of the "public sphere," a typology made widely known by Jürgen Habermas in his study of emerging bourgeois sub-societies in the 1700s to early 1800s in Europe, which coalesced in public meeting places for conversation and thought. The classic bourgeois public sphere, for Habermas, was a category of social order imbedded alongside the state, the economy, and the private realm of the family. Habermas's nascent publics were ideal sites for face-to-face interaction and discourse, products of enlightenment and the freeing of thought from suspicion and religious influence.

In essence, the rich associational life of the Irish Americans of Philadelphia represents a late historical arrival of a public sphere, a Gaelic colony organized

around ethnic closure and a certain opposition to existing norms and integrative pressures. The communicative centers of the Irish Americans were the meeting rooms of their many voluntary associations, which were equivalent to
Habermas's coffeehouses, and which served as an Irish forum that housed an
egalitarian culture outside the eyes of the state, wedged between private and civil
society.[1]

The Gaelic public sphere was not a perfect replica of the original type, in which
abstract, free citizens moderated experience and life through analysis and reason; it was a "counterpublic" that required group agreement on certain topics,
such as the sanctity and special meaning of Irish heritage and the moral and
emotional commitment to Ireland and its impending freedom from British rule.[2]
Joanna Brooks writes, "Counterpublics foster political and cultural activities that
allow working-class and other disenfranchised persons to reclaim a measure of
subjectivity," an analytical frame that captures a good part of the resurgent spirit
of Irish Americans in the 1890s.[3] The Gaelic public in Philadelphia was a specialized zone within a fragmented social order, influenced by modern practices
and means of communication yet traditional in tone and content and ever loyal
to the popular Irish narrative of victimhood. The world the Irish built in the years
around the turn of the twentieth century was replete with public rituals, festivals on Celtic culture, and forays into Gaelic literature, theater, language, and
sport; it was developed and bound by communicative practices, with a burgeoning ethnic press that produced pamphlets of Irish content with a national circulation that were distributed and consumed in neighborhood meeting halls,
through lectures, oratory, and conversation.

A public sphere was formed, first around the physical locations that gave rise
to communicative practices, row homes converted into a meeting space for associations, the cavernous confines of the Academy of Music for a weekend's folk
festival of Gaelic culture—an Irish *feis*—or a day-long picnic at Washington Park
along the Delaware River, which provided an escape from the industrial city and
an emotional excursion to old Ireland and its traditional dance and music. The
public sphere of the 1890s was also of the mind and heart, a consciousness defined
by sentimental remembrance, renewed understanding and appreciation for an
ancient Celtic past, and allegiance to the cause of Ireland as a republic.

Those Irish Americans who were active in Gaelic affairs and causes in the
1890s were a sizable minority of the substantial population of Philadelphians of
Irish descent, a committed cohort living side by side in industrial neighborhoods
with a majority population driven by the normative demands of work and family,
many of whom found comfort and meaning in the neighborhood parish and its
many community programs. The legacy of nativist oppression in Philadelphia
was still prescient in the 1890s, and the memory of the anti-Catholic street violence formed a permanent imprint as a potential threat to all of Irish Catholic
Philadelphia. Gaelic activism required a minor digression from the pull of assim-

ilationist instincts and practices; for other Irish Philadelphians, assimilation was a calling card for acceptance and upward mobility.

In essence, two Irish Americas existed side by side in Philadelphia, connected by Irish descent but separated by contrasting modes of allegiance, a normative collection of Irish Catholic Philadelphians tied together by the demands of the Church and the varied community programs of the parish, familial in loyalty and pursuing industrial employment as a tool of survival. The socialization of Irish American Catholics of the nineteenth century into the inherited refrain of Irish nationalism was simply an ideology bequeathed at birth; Irish American Catholics in late-nineteenth-century Philadelphia could not ignore some form of the redemptive fervor to right the Irish past and reclaim the future for a free Ireland of Gaelic content. And yet, for the mass of Irish Americans, a total commitment to Irish nationalism would have seemed out of place, given the demands of life, family, and labor; instead, a passive nod to the nation-building tenor of the times substituted for a commitment to Irish national rebirth.

Habermas gave us the ideal type, freeing others to expand and liberate the original from its restrictive descriptive elements, and thus sprouting public spheres everywhere.[4] The Gaelic public sphere was imperfect when laid next to Habermas's original heuristic, but there were many overlapping elements of commonality: the setting aside of work-related and even family-oriented problems, the casting away of status implications, and the use of discussion and reason in the running of the ethnic organizations. There was a mutual subjectivity of Irish awareness and belonging that bound those who were invested in the Irish public of Philadelphia and who approached the ideal of the abstract individual acting in liberated, modern settings; however, the Irish often rejected reason when it came to interpreting and applying Irish nationalism and British culpability for past wrongs.

To claim Irish American status in the 1890s in Philadelphia required the citizen to confront and accept an ideology that contained certain truths about heritage and dislocation, a documented guilt of foreign agents responsible for the Famine, the greed of landlords in the homeland, and the unfortunate necessity of emigration. The Gaelic public of the 1890s was suspicious of an urban modernism, strictly controlling the boundaries of its influence to Irish men and women of a certain religious heritage, in an example of what Harold Mah describes as "the narrow expression of social particularity."[5] The Irish of Philadelphia achieved much in their late-century community but failed to reach the high pinnacles of universalism and rationalism consistent with Habermas's original model, failed to shed their minds and hearts of ethnic content and symbols, and were resistant to opinions and arguments that threatened a specific interpretation of Ireland's historic mission.

The Gaelic civic world flourished within the disinterested control of the powerful Catholic Church of Philadelphia, outside the control of the state and minimally influenced by the Archdiocese of Philadelphia, a diaspora community whose identity was closely aligned with Catholic heritage but also a people who had assembled in an urban landscape driven by the demands of industrialism and the need to find work. Gaelic activism often overlapped with parish identity, extending a respectful nod to the mainstream Catholic world and even mimicking the style and structure of Church-sponsored societies, but it was careful not to lock horns with the Church, and in return it received a benign neglect of its multiple forms of associationalism, which allowed the resurgence of Irish culture and the murky shadow of a persistent Irish nationalism to bind and flourish side by side with Church influence, with neither seriously attempting to challenge the other. Nationalism filled the devotional void of Irish Americans in the 1890s as Peter O'Neill notes: "Catholicism, when applied to the Irish subaltern, was a signifier of Irish nationalism rather than signifier of devoted allegiance to Rome."[6]

A steely resistance to the legacy of Catholic bigotry in Philadelphia and an allegiance to nationalism for their departed small island defined the communicative means of the Irish in Philadelphia and the resurgent late-century moment in Gaelic culture, a worldview that elevated emotion, nostalgia, and historical redress into meaning and action. Irish nationalism was a persistent and powerful backdrop for the Irish Americans of Philadelphia of the period, an inherited communicative component of Irish American citizenship, which constituted a serious social, cultural, and political movement but also a comfortable rhetorical touchstone of unchallenged authenticity.

ECONOMY AND SOCIETY IN THE INDUSTRIAL CITY

This study also takes into account the structure of late-nineteenth-century industry in Philadelphia, the assembly of material forces that affected the life chances and labor and housing opportunities of Irish Americans. Philadelphia's vast urban spaces combined with its diverse and diffused economy to spread the Irish Americans all over the city. Philadelphia was still a walking city for the working class in the 1890s, and the Irish followed work, settling in row-home neighborhoods close to industry, eschewing the pull and emotional security of all-Irish blocks for a chance to live within a walking commute of life- and family-sustaining work. This spatial fragmentation of an ethnic community did not undermine the formation of a collective consciousness on Irish meaning; however, living some distance from an ethnic heart or urban center of Irish concentration required adaptation, the use of communicative networks, detailed organizational practices, and the occasional use of public transport to come together for Irish events. The capillary framework of the ethnic associations, with their many branch associations, was another adaptive tool that built Irish consciousness across the wide urban landscape of Philadelphia.

The spatial configuration of Philadelphia's urban territory and the fixed landmarks of its industrial architecture presented a dualism representative of Foucault's heterotopia, the Irish American city a juxtaposition of locations that defied "the normal order of things," urban spaces and ingrained practices that reflected and at the same time deviated from and opposed the established edifices of the city and its cultural codes of modernity.[7] Philadelphia's vast space restricted the facile and convenient option of close communication in all-Irish neighborhoods, but at the same time it opened other opportunities for communicative networking and outreach across urban space that catered to an expanding Irish nationalism and imaginary Irish nation in wait and, ultimately, the creation of a Gaelic public sphere.

Social Discipline among the Irish of Philadelphia

In encountering the historical lives and experiences of the Irish Americans of this period, the pipe fitters, brick layers, pub owners, and grocers, one is struck by the heights of organizational efficiency and self-sustaining practices evident in the small democracies of the Irish societies; the control required to originate, staff, and manage associations is also evidence of a people who had acquired a level of personal and social discipline long denied in public caricatures of Irish competence. As E. P. Thompson notes, industrial society required an adjustment in discipline for all its members: "without time-discipline we could not have the insistent energies of industrial man."[8]

The demands and necessities of running a practicing mutual aid society organized around Irish heritage and meaning invoked a social efficacy of its own, which required members to pay dues on time, attend meetings, sign up for committees, and contribute to the collective. The ethnic societies of late-nineteenth-century Philadelphia were depositories of Irish knowledge and education; they were primers on democratic order, on the keeping of financial records and sober, calculating control of the public gathering—in many forms, they were models of bourgeois propriety. The efficacy of operation and control in the Irish American associational record applied to societies organized around the imagery and content of Irish nationalism as well as those inspired by an association with the Catholic Church, involving mutual aid support distributed and followed by ordinary Irish American Catholic men and women in the many parishes of the city.

This work suggests that the origins of this Protestant-styled rationality were located in hidden zones of native Irish life, buried in the social practices of rural and urban Ireland, the friendly societies of Ireland, farmers cooperatives, political organizations, and even Gaelic football clubs, all of which were small democracies, mainly Catholic, of civic self- and group control. As an instrumental rationality developed to support the vast network of Irish ethnic mutual aid societies in late-nineteenth-century Philadelphia, a public sphere was simultaneously forming around Gaelic culture, tapping emotional cores, releasing an expressive Irish nature, and endorsing a reading of an Irish history of the heart, fed by various communicative networks that ranged between rare moments of cosmopolitan reportage and a standard primitive diatribe.

MAGNIFYING THE GAELIC CONTEXT: COMPARATIVE HISTORY

Part of the meaning aspired to in this study is a process of transnational historical comparison; while the primary historical universe is Irish Philadelphia in the 1890s and its embrace of Irish cultural nationalism, greater understanding is achieved by a methodology that also references institutions and practices in ancestral Ireland. This method follows Peter Kolchin's advice of using a "soft" approach to comparative thinking in historical studies, involving a focus on the dominant historical case in concert with observations with another location in history and an analytical pairing of the associated, structural elements of two social orders. In this context, it is two aligned nations separated by an ocean united in history in order to explore "common patterns," enhance perspective, and, ultimately, produce a "reduction of parochialism."[9]

This work argues that the diaspora Irish of Philadelphia created a separatist subsociety within a dynamic and tough industrial city out of a drive for preservation and the need for communal protection. The Philadelphia Irish faced discrimination early on—the 1844 nativist street violence was a prime example—and they relied on themselves and their own stock of accumulated knowledge, as first encountered in Ireland and then on coming to North America, to create a separatist urban Catholic community and a Gaelic public sphere.

A singular focus on the American context to explain the civic achievements of the Irish Philadelphia in the 1890s might posit American democratic instincts and associational practices as primary influencers in the growth of an Irish American civic mentality in Philadelphia. The case for a Gaelic public sphere, however, employs a comparative method to challenge assumptions and uncover a broader historical context, the transnational connection between the lasting imprint of cultural knowledge in Ireland and the organizational dynamism of a working-class ethnic group in a northeastern American city.

This study states and concludes that the Irish of Philadelphia followed a model they first encountered in Ireland and adapted it to their diaspora location. Trading on the surplus of industrial wages supplied by Philadelphia's industrial economy, the Irish Americans extended the social supports of mutual aid and made their associations more humane and more prosperous repositories for preserving and promoting Irish nationalism and, ultimately, more democratic ones. Thus, the case for the Gaelic public sphere in Irish Philadelphia is presented as a dyad of comparison with Ireland, and the two historical examples are often presented in close textual proximity in correlated expression and excursions in time and location across the Atlantic, connecting cultures and context for a deeper explanation of the Irish Philadelphia of the 1890s to 1920s.

SOCIAL CLASS AND IRISH MEANING

The Irish men and women of the industrial network of Philadelphia entered into a relationship, inside and outside work, that positioned them to come to grips with their position in society, as workers with particular interests opposed to those of others, such as owners, managers, and bosses. The marker of social class as an element of differentiation in addition to Irish heritage was a prominent and problematic element in the public consciousness of Irish meaning and experience in the 1890s and early 1900s; the relationships of work and labor, forming a singular identity around familiar concepts of social class, were largely buried as a topic of discussion and awareness in the broad associational life that the Irish constructed in Philadelphia, making it a secondary identity trait mutually shared and recognized but not often mentioned or acted on, and not a constituent element of the public setting.

Irish culture and remembrance crowded out social class as a singular unifying agent; class allegiance and the troubles of finding and maintaining work in industrial Philadelphia did, at times, combine with the more explicit commitment to Irish heritage and nationalism, but the contours of labor solidarity, even among the working class, did not often define the Irish American public life in 1890s Philadelphia. Instead, a cult of opposition existed in the place of an explicit militant working-class consciousness: opposition to social forces, to the resurgence of a reactionary Protestantism, the memory of British rule, and, at times, cosmopolitan modernism.

NATIVE ORIGINS OF IRISH AMERICAN CIVIC ACHIEVEMENT

In hierarchical societies, the upper tier represents the standard to which others ascribe, forming a social setting in which cultural symbols and modes of expression secure order without the use of state force. The network of Irish American ethnic associations has been conceived as such a system, in which the means of bourgeois hegemony motivate compliance, modeling behaviors to encourage subordinates to accept and copy the practices of the leading social groups. The modeling of hegemonic symbols is an attractive thesis to explain the rush of the Irish to their civic institutions in Philadelphia in the late years of the nineteenth century, a movement commensurate with the social arrival and begrudging acceptance of the Irish in the city.

This work accepts bourgeois hegemony as a partial explanation for the rise of Irish American civic action in the nineteenth century, but it also states that the instincts and inherited cultural traditions of associational life were already

implanted in the Irish on native soil, the immigrant cohort, which were ultimately transferred to the landed second and third generations in Philadelphia
in addition to the many recent immigrants of the late 1800s and early 1900s. The
lessons of friendly societies in Ireland, rural organizations, Gaelic sport clubs,
indeed of societies of all stripes, were part of the experience of living, and it mattered little on which side of the Gaelic Atlantic the lessons were first encountered; the content, even the language of the pocket-sized rulebooks handed to
members on initiation in an Irish society in Philadelphia, were standard and
Irish, practically identical whether the text originated in a workers' tontine in
Dublin, the Philo-Celtic Society of Philadelphia, a parish beneficial society of
the archdiocese of the city or a branch of the Ancient Order of Hibernians (AOH).
The social discipline, rational calculation, and planning evident in the financial
rendering of the organization, the organization by society members into committees for financial support, all of which were traits of serious business acu-
men and communal cooperation, became part of the lives of ordinary working
Irish men and women without interference and influence from more elite models or quarters.

The impetus for the Gaelic revival was the preservation of what was considered a dying Irish language in the tumultuous years after the Famine in a rural
Ireland stripped of its economically vulnerable people, its rural traditions, its
collective pastimes, and even its Gaelic tongue. Emigration became a way of life
in the regions of native Gaelic speakers—the west—characterized by an inherited expectation of almost certain migration into the Irish Diaspora, to Britain,
America, and Australia, and thus English became the required language of
mobility.

Philadelphia's committed Irish Americans responded to the call of language
preservation, with the Gaelic Leagues in Ireland and America serving as the original organizing bodies of active support for rescuing the Gaelic language. In
concert with many other Irish American organizations of similar conviction, the
Philo-Celtic Society of Philadelphia, whose language school welcomed and
recruited all comers with free grammar texts and instruction in Irish on week-
nights and weekends, was one of the cultural centers of late-century Irish cultural nationalism in Philadelphia.

THE BURDEN OF HISTORY

The Irish were a people consumed and burdened by history, with their long periods of conquest and foreign occupation, the Catholic Penal Laws, revolts, and
civil war all tilting toward an understanding of history as tragedy. In Philadelphia, urban ecology, the mix of labor opportunities, the expansive structure of
industry and commerce, housing, neighborhoods, and the nature of urban transportation all combined to influence the life chances of the Irish; material condi-

tions both limited and propelled the Gaelic public sphere as the Irish took advantage of their numbers and their employment in a volatile and spatially diverse industrial economy and worked to overcome the logistical obstacles that might have limited a far-reaching ethnic consciousness in late-nineteenth-century Philadelphia.

The facts of urban transportation, and especially the expense and inefficiency of the steel rails of urban streetcar transportation in Philadelphia, molded the life choices of the Irish American working-class community, motivating men and women to find home residences in ethnically heterogeneous neighborhoods near work. But when it came to the singular mission of Irish identity, the Irish Americans of the Gaelic public sphere extended themselves, digging into their shallow pockets to take the trolley out of their neighborhood to share an evening in a friend's Irish society or attend the summer Irish festival in North Philadelphia's Pastime Park, an all-day event that featured jigs and reels, political oratory, Gaelic sport, and the annual tug-of-war contest among the city's many AOH branch societies.

Stock assumptions about a distinct national personality, a social type, plague the Irish even among historians who have devoted many pages to the growth of Irish Americana. On the one hand, the Irish are portrayed as a communal people with a missing achievement ethic, content to labor on jobs of short duration, unable to plan, and devoid of the social discipline to construct institutions. In this view, the parochialism of Philadelphia's neighborhoods define the ethnic group, with the comforts of the neighborhood taproom, grocery store, and street corner conversation all new world extensions of a village left behind, an example of traditional social practices carried forward. In the village interpretation of the Irish Diaspora, to join an Irish association was to move up in status, a transition to a more ordered life that was an extension of the surrounding urban village.

This narrative of the Philadelphia Irish rejects the calculus that equates Irish identity with urban neighborhoods and states that neighborhood in Philadelphia was more often a casual and meaningless social unit selected by Irish men and women for its proximity to work. The real substance of Irish life in the late nineteenth century was in the public sphere created around and through print media, ethnic association meetings, intimate gatherings, and mass cultural events. The Irish of the Catholic Gaelic public sphere ignored neighborhood, traveled around the city to events, read newspapers, met friends at their home association meeting and deliberated in formal settings in their voluntary associations. The message of this work on Philadelphia's Irish departs from historical writings and depictions of the Irish as hard-working animals, perennial premoderns incapable of a sophisticated institutional life; the Gaelic public sphere the Irish created in Philadelphia was a factual counter to these inherited images.

LEISURE IN THE GAELIC PUBLIC

The life world of Irish Philadelphia was also an outlet for leisure, an expressive fraternalism in which humor, song, and poetry filled the meeting halls at the end of formal deliberations, sometimes with drink, but often without. The expressive personality existed alongside the instrumental in the Irish public, with the rituals and humor of Irish remembrance an emotional part of the required structure of social interaction.

Philadelphia was home to militant nationalist Irish American organizations, with the Clan na Gael the most prominent and active among the many groups vying for attention at century's end. The organizational skill of the Clan na Gael allowed the society to establish branch associations all over the city, leaving the local "camps" free to run their own association as long as they paid dues to the Central Board of the Clan na Gael. The Clan na Gael purchased a prominent building on Spruce Street as its headquarters, named it the Irish American Club of Philadelphia, and turned it into something of a gentlemen's club, complete with pool tables, waiters, and service for food and drink.

IRISH MASCULINITY ON DISPLAY

Modern Victorian athleticism originated in nineteenth-century Britain but soon spread around the world wherever British influence planted itself, in the colonies, across the Channel to northern France, Germany, Italy, and beyond. In Ireland, however, the initial forms and styles of British sport were resisted by Catholic Ireland and the forces of Gaelic revival in the late decades of the nineteenth century, and were recast and re-formed in the shape of native, Gaelic games. The Irish sports club had arrived by the 1890s, and the Catholic population seized on its popularity to support the Gaelic Athletic Association, embracing Irish football and ancient Irish hurling and eschewing British rugby and soccer.

In the 1890s and early decades of the twentieth century in Philadelphia's Irish community, hurling and Irish football emerged as part of the landscape of cultural revival as Gaelic sport teams there. Philadelphia's Limerick Guards Hurling Club was formed in 1889, and it was soon joined by other Gaelic-styled sport clubs from around the city with colorful, revolutionary names: the Celtic Sons, the Charles Stewart Parnells, the Charles J. Kickhams, and the James Stephens Club.[10]

The Gaelic sport movement in Philadelphia also emerged with the renewal of Catholic Irish paramilitarism in the form of Hibernian Rifle brigades, units from the city that turned up to perform in military style at festivals, Gaelic Games, formal winter balls, and parades and symbolized the revived and defiant Celt in full-dress defiance. The AOH formed Hibernian Rifle Divisions in the 1880s, and soon rifle divisions sprouted across the city and in Frankford and Manayunk, mill towns within the industrial colossus of late-nineteenth-century Philadelphia. The rise of these oppositional Irish Catholic institutions, both the hurling and the paramilitary Celtic rifle clubs, expressed an Irish version of Social Darwinism in a Gaelic reordering of the late-nineteenth-century racial landscape, an equation that positioned the Celt as the masculine warrior and the Anglo-Saxon as a modernist of less martial bearing.

The Gaelic public sphere in Philadelphia was formed by ordinary Irish men and women in search of their own voices and social world, who created a separate zone of thought and action that focused on culture and Irish nationalism. It was plebian, populated by men and women of modest means and achievement who relied on their own cultural influences of Irish origin, adapting reasoning and planning in the running of their many voluntary associations.

This study certainly reflects the contents and debates on Irish American history, with the focus on Irish urban life a replication of the traditional Irish American theme, yet it uncovers an adaptive and creative set of historical actors, bound to a traditional past yet willing to overcome obstacles and eager to create a world of their own, a Gaelic public sphere in which mutual aid flourished as well as self-education and self-government. The Irish of the public sphere were primarily Catholic by heritage and practice, but this appellation, when set against their worldly actions and achievements, was more often a surface representation, a cultural marker, and not a restrictive religious loyalty. Philadelphia's dynamic late-nineteenth-century industrial economy dispersed its historical Irish actors, offered them jobs in manufacturing enterprises, supplied wages that were funneled into societies of mutual aid, and provided the means and supports for an Irish cultural awakening in the 1890s; the city had conditions that promoted as well as restricted ethnic inclusion, but it also unleashed a set of motivated historical agents who were willing to act.

CHAPTER 1

Outlines of a Gaelic
Public Sphere

A GAELIC PUBLIC EMERGES IN
LATE-NINETEENTH-CENTURY PHILADELPHIA

The Irish American community in Philadelphia had matured by the 1890s, coinciding in time and mentality to welcome the voices of a resurgence of Gaelic cultural awareness in Ireland. The Philadelphia Irish were a sizable ethnic group that was still eager to exercise its voice, having endured the mid-nineteenth-century Famine and a decades-long exodus from their native Ireland, and now poised in Philadelphia to flex their muscles at the end of the nineteenth century. It was a subsociety that might have espoused a more integrationist strategy and a focus on American conditions in the 1890s; instead, a substantial segment of Irish Philadelphia sealed off its surrounding borders, turning its gaze inward and eastward and looking across the Atlantic to the changes occurring in Ireland.

This late-nineteenth-century Philadelphia communal network, which was a micro-public of Irish Americans, was linked by a number of available and exploitable mechanisms, all bound by what Jürgen Habermas called "communicative action."[1] The forms of communication in the 1890s ranged in content and style, a collection of memoirs and reminders of exile and nationalist sentiment distributed through print media; the ethnic press in Philadelphia; circulating pamphlets and broadsides on history, politics, culture, and sport; these were expansive, separatist texts whose meaning always returned to Ireland as an aggrieved land.

The Gaelic public that emerged in the 1890s was populated by the men and women of the various neighborhoods of Philadelphia, but it was more than simply a community of the resettled looking for work. Thomas Bender describes community as "an aggregate of people who share a common interest in a particular locality . . . a network of social relations marked by mutuality and emo-

POVERTY AND ITS CAUSES IN IRELAND

A LECTURE

BY

F. J. MᶜGRATH,

AN IRISH NATIONALIST

THURSDAY EVE. JULY 11th, 1889

AT KELLY'S HALL

CHRISTIAN ST. BELOW 8TH AT 8 O'CLOCK.

TICKETS · · · · · · · 50 CTS.

Public notice to Philadelphia's Catholic community in the wake of an 1844 nativist riot. Source: CHRC.

tional bonds."[2] The Irish in Philadelphia went beyond neighborhood and its convenient relations to reach a higher state of concern and awareness on ethnic meaning; this late-century consciousness was achieved through the production and consumption of texts supplemented by an urban mobility of ordinary Irish Philadelphians moving around the city to attend meetings, lectures, and Irish sporting events in their precious moments of leisure to accompany their interest in the resurgence of Irish culture and nation

A public sphere first consisted of the material locations of communicative action, spaces in which people came together in a determined manner to retain Irish meaning or coalesced in more casual ways, pulled along by a family member, friends, or colleagues from work to attend the Irish National Games and political oratory at Rising Sun Park in North Philadelphia. The public sphere sprouted in association meeting rooms, the Irish American Club on Race Street (relocated later to Spruce Street), and the building owned by the Philadelphia Ancient Order of Hibernians (AOH) on 8th Street in Center City; in evening Gaelic classes of the Philo-Celtic Society of Philadelphia and in neighborhood grocery stores and taverns; on street corners where copies of *The Hibernian* or *The Freeman and Irish American Review* were available every Saturday morning. The Gaelic public occupied the streets for the St. Patrick's Day Parade and in more formal places like the splendorous settings of patrician Philadelphia for fancy winter balls and formal dinners at the Academy of Music, or a festival of Irish culture, a feis, at Philadelphia's Convention Hall.

The Philadelphia Gaelic public occupied spaces of subterranean existence, a heterotopia of counterurban centers that held meaning for those Irish Philadelphians who occupied and claimed citizenship of these other spaces that were, as Marco Cenzatti writes, "public only for the social groups that produced them."[3] The Irish American Club in Philadelphia was a centrally located sanctuary for Irish meetings, gatherings, leisure, and retreat from urban reality, a place for serious thought and discussion, and, ultimately, an Irish American convivial club. It was the halls of the neighborhood Irish association, however, that formed the backbone of a peoples' public sphere in the 1890s, whether in back rooms or store fronts, rooms on the second floor, or, increasingly, row houses purchased and turned into association houses by members' careful saving and investment in Philadelphia property. It was in these urban locations that a public of the people emerged as ordinary Irish American men and women gathered for mutual aid in a tough industrial city.

The people of this late-nineteenth-century explosion of interest in Gaelic essence were a diverse lot. They were mainly working men and women, the second and third generations of Famine migrants supplemented by the steady pace of Irish migrants to Philadelphia throughout the nineteenth century. Philadelphia was a prominent port that was part of the migratory network triggered by the mid-century Famine, receiving exiles (who were mainly Catholic) from ports in Ireland or from England, with the firm of H. & A. Cope with its five vessels sailing Liverpool to Philadelphia on the twelfth of each month in 1848.[4]

The subsequent surviving generations of the Famine exodus were overwhelmingly Catholics, who were freer in America than in Ireland from the formal constrictors of religious allegiance to embrace an urbanity defined by secular bonds; to endorse and live the life of hope, support, and nationalist activism for Ireland's emancipation also required a certain separation from the Church and yet, for all of the newer freedoms and worldly influences of a bustling urban center, the distant surveillance and shadow of the Church was ever present.

The Gaelic public in Philadelphia was a slice of the broader Irish population, ordinary members of the AOH, with their many branches scattered across the city, and joining one of the fifty-one "camps" of Philadelphia's Clan na Gael in 1903, men on a hurling team or Hibernian militia troop, or women in auxiliary branches of Irish American societies, in supporting roles of men's associations or working women running their own mutual aid associations. They were working men and women, mainly, people like Michael Brady, who was elected president of the Cavan Society in 1913; Brady was Irish-born, from Cavan's Killinkere parish, a saloon keeper from the Delaware River district of Kensington known as "Fishtown," and, at age forty, older than most members of Irish American associations. Brady was elected president of the Cavan Society for twelve straight years. They were people like Patrick O'Neill, born in County Mayo, Ireland, who made his way in 1871 to Philadelphia and rose to become president of the Philadelphia AOH in 1893, and newspaper editor Edward O'Meagher Condon of the Irish American weekly *The Freeman and Irish American Review*, who seemed to be everywhere in the later decades of the 1800s, covering Irish events in Philadelphia and lecturing Irish American crowds on his version of Irish history and its meaning.[5]

The impetus for a Gaelic public sphere was not intellectual in the tradition of Habermas's historical agents cultivating the realm of discourse and debate operating in a liberated zone between state authority and private concerns. Reason was not a complete guide for the Irish Americans, yet it did surface and intervene in important moments of public action, in meetings, in associational debates, in the strategies and plans of committees gathered to commemorate Irish patriots, for fundraising, and in the financial planning required for the subsistence and expansion of ethnic societies and cultural events.

Reason and the speedy resolution of problems were paramount in the Irish associations; the reminder to members to "confine themselves to the question under consideration, and avoid personality" was a typical stricture inscribed in the association rule book of the ethnic society.[6] Intellectualizing, or the play of ideas, could be of minor substance and often was, but the democracy of the meeting and the equality of voice allotted each citizen of the Gaelic world comprised a sacred value of special Irish devotion.[7] Neighborhood, local issues, and the necessity to find work defined everyday life for the Irish of Philadelphia, but the proliferation and popularity of print media in the form of the Philadelphia Irish American weeklies provided the connective tissue for a broader consciousness of nationalism and Irish culture and an urban network of men and women committed to those ends.

The flourishing of Irish American media, reading, and lectures, accompanied by an all-consuming interest in Irish history, language, and conversation, all reinforced a late-nineteenth-century Irish enlightenment based on communicative means commensurate with Habermas's hope for modernity, a community based on rational discourse and reasoned action.[8] Yet, for the Irish, communication reached into and tapped emotional cores of expression and meaning, an affective realm of cherished, traditional, and sometimes stifling beliefs about Irish victimhood at the hands of others—British colonialism, landlords, American Protestantism, and industrial bosses. This ideology of regret and suspicion bound the Gaelic network; it naturally undermined communication based on an objective reading of the past and present and deviated from Habermas's original intention, but it informed an ethnic public sphere and motivated the men and women of Irish Philadelphia.

Michel Foucault writes about heterotopias and their influence on the nexus of space and people, and about the nineteenth-century city as a collection of "counter-sites, a kind of effectively enacted utopia in which the real sites, all the other real sites that can be found within the culture, are simultaneously

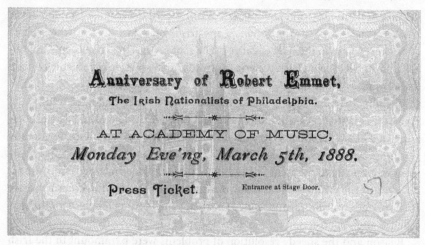

Press ticket for an 1888 celebration of Robert Emmet. Source: CHRC.

represented, contested, and inverted."[9] The writings of Dennis Clark have left us with his portrait of the Irish neighborhood in Philadelphia as a self-contained, static ethnic enclave with a distinct "social heritage . . . [an] array of symbols, usages, and attachment," bound by memories and conceptions of "a place, a people, and a legacy of recollections."[10]

A committed core of Irish Americans of the late nineteenth century contested the conditions of their adopted city, acknowledged its industrial configuration, and adapted to its disciplinary codes, and at the same time inverted their identity as a neighborhood people into a mobile ethnic group. They employed the one ideology they inherited and knew well, British colonial responsibility for Ireland's malaise, and reconstructed it as a communicative mantra, a sacred history, a utopia of remembrance that sustained an intense drive for redemption of the Gaelic nation. In June 1916, Philadelphia's Clan na Gael, reacting to the executions of the leaders of the Easter Rebellion, Patrick (Padraig) Pearse, James Connolly, and Thomas Clarke, wrote in its journal, "the eternal agony of our race will make a consuming blaze that will destroy the last vestiges of the British Empire."[11]

Robert Emmet, who was Anglo-Irish by birth, sympathetic to Catholic emancipation, a United Irishman and leader of the 1803 rebellion in Ireland, and later tried and executed, was a particular icon of remembrance for the Philadelphia Irish. His speech from the dock was often recited and extolled, as one Philadelphia Hibernian noted in 1895, referring to the place "where the brave and youthful Emmet hurled defiance at . . . the personification of all that was cruel and bloodthirsty in England's misrule."[12] The Gaelic public sphere was a space of educational enlightenment for the ordinary Irish men and women of Philadelphia,

TABLE 1.1

IRISH-BORN POPULATION IN AMERICAN CITIES, 1870

City	City Population	Irish-Born Population	Irish-Born Share of City Population
1. New York	942,292	201,999	21%
2. Philadelphia	674,022	96,698	14%
3. Brooklyn, N.Y.	396,099	73,985	19%
4. Boston	250,526	56,900	23%
5. Chicago	298,977	39,988	13%
6. St. Louis	310,864	32,239	10%
7. San Francisco	149,473	25,864	17%

Source: Susannah Ural Bruce, *The Harp and the Eagle: Irish-American Volunteers and the Union Army, 1861–1865* (New York: NYU Press, 2006), 234.

but it was not an open forum of reasoned interaction; it had its own requirements and codes of consensus on vital issues of Irish importance, nationalism, a binding heritage, and the mission to restore a lost culture.

PHILADELPHIA: A NINETEENTH-CENTURY IRISH CITY

Philadelphia was the exception in terms of ethnic social development; it was a city whose industrial structure scattered the Irish in distant urban neighborhoods only to have them reach out to discover themselves and their cultural heritage in communicative practices and institutions of their own making. Philadelphia was indeed a tough, gritty city, but also one with rich resources for the settling of an immigrant population, a place of plentiful labor opportunities and affordable homes, a location that spawned an Irish awakening in the 1890s linking local with national networks of Irish news and meaning that incited a renaissance of Irish culture and historical experience.

Philadelphia may not enjoy the reputation of other urban centers as a location of Irish awareness in America, but it was a city with a large Irish population in which the Irish-born came to exert a sizable presence in the city in the latter half of the nineteenth century (see Table 1.1). It differed in its construction of its Irish identity because its urban ecology, its diverse industrial structure, spatially diffused the Irish so that no single location turned into an exclusive zone of Irish influence, as in Irish urban ghettos such as New York City's Five Points, Boston's Fort Hill, and Chicago's Bridgeport.[13] Instead, as the working classes sought housing close to labor opportunities, the Irish would share city blocks with German Americans and native white Americans in heterogeneous urban settlements as all these groups positioned themselves to find work in a walking city.

Philadelphia had its major enterprises, including the Baldwin Locomotive Works, which shipped its locomotives all over the world, and the Cramp Shipyards, located along fifty acres of the Kensington shoreline of the Delaware River, which constructed merchant and war ships in the late nineteenth and early twentieth centuries.[14] Kensington and Manayunk were the locations for textile mills of various sizes, mill towns within the city that employed English and Scottish weavers as well as Irish workers specializing in wool.[15] Other smaller craft operations and diversified manufacturers dotted the city's landscape, shipping finished products of all kinds along the East Coast, to the Midwest interior, and all over the world.

The Structure of Philadelphia's Irish American Neighborhood

The Irish confronted the industrial colossus of Philadelphia in the latter half of the nineteenth century, entering the workforce as laborers and settling in already established urban neighborhoods where they could find housing. By 1860, according to the U.S. census by wards, the distribution of the emigrating Irish had begun to show and the dock areas just south of the central city on the Delaware River exhibited high concentrations of Irish settlement in the neighborhoods of Southwark and Moyamensing; however, the Irish never constituted more than 26 percent of the population in these areas. On the other side of William Penn's city, its second river, the Schuylkill, with its own set of docks, received river traffic from upstate Pennsylvania and unloaded the coal, lumber, stone, and other materials for the construction and contracting industries of Philadelphia as well as agricultural goods, and an Irish concentration emerged in neighborhoods contiguous to the commerce of the rivers.

Philadelphia's Irish neighborhoods in the late nineteenth century acted less like urban villages than assembly points around Philadelphia industries. Port Richmond employed the Irish in unskilled labor on the Reading Railroad wharves, unloading the coal barges and relocating the material to the railroad terminal in Port Richmond.[16] Kensington was a polyglot of ethnic identity, marked by early generations of German settlement and the many English immigrants who monopolized the textile weaving trades, with the Irish filling in the neighborhoods of working-class row homes sandwiched between and among warehouses.[17]

A Mobile Irish American Working Class

The Irish American population in late-nineteenth-century Philadelphia moved often in search of work, making the neighborhood an urban unit given to rapid turnover and change. Stuart Blumin states of Philadelphia, "only one out of every four or five adult male inhabitants (and probably their families) remained in a given neighborhood as long as ten years."[18] He concludes that in late-nineteenth-century Philadelphia, "men follow[ed] jobs" which provided the dynamism of the years of industrial expansion, a mobility that militated against the concentration of the Irish in ethnic enclaves.

Analysis of membership rolls over various Irish associations in the late nineteenth century also reveals mobility, with the Irish American association bound to a fluid structure and its citizens moving on to other locations and dropping from the rolls of the original society. The Irish societies were always searching for new members, and cash incentives provided for society recruiters to fill the vacant positions; a healthy, constantly replenished membership was always a top agenda in the monthly meeting, a reflection of the geographic instability of Philadelphia's Irish population. The Cavan Society of Philadelphia offered incentives in a search for new members—"25¢ be put in a pool and given to the member bringing in the most members."[19]

Industry brought Irish workers together, but the spatial diffusion of Philadelphia's industry, which was spread out in smaller factories and manufacturing sites all over the city, undermined the facile connection of work with tradition and ethnic identity.[20] As industry dispersed, so did labor and its immigrant newcomers, and the result was an initial fragmentation of Irish tradition, resulting in competing world views amid the pressures of the practical choices demanded every day by an immigrant ethnic group. The Irish found housing close to work, wherever they could, squeezing into blocks already settled by other ethnic groups.

By the 1890s, the second or third generation, the American-born of Irish immigrants of the Great Famine era, had adjusted to Philadelphia's industrial structure and expansive housing opportunities and established their imprint on the city. Table 1.2 demonstrates a continuation of the geographic dispersion of ethnicity by the end of the nineteenth century as well as the persistence of early patterns of urban settlement and reflects the new mobility of the higher-status Irish away from the previous areas of residential settlement. While the Irish did not dominate any neighborhood—they were never more than 40 percent of a ward—they had a presence in every neighborhood in Philadelphia in the early 1900s.[21]

Malcolm Campbell, in his study of Irish diasporas, confirms the ascendance of the Irish in the 1890s, saying they were now "widely dispersed across the socioeconomic scale . . . a more confident, settled, and imperious force in American life than at any time since the 1820s."[22] While Campbell acknowledges a persistent occupational concentration at the "lowest reaches" of the work hierarchy, the Irish of Philadelphia at the end of the nineteenth century constituted a different type of diaspora, one more secure in specific economic niches for the flowering of Irish culture in Philadelphia.[23]

TABLE 1.2

IRISH RESIDENTIAL PATTERN IN PHILADELPHIA, 1900–1910

Ward	Neighborhood	Irish Share of Population[a]
8	Southwark/Schuylkill docks	20.0%
9	Schuylkill docks	15.0%
15	Schuylkill docks	24.5%
22	Germantown/Chestnut Hill	15.7%
25	Port Richmond	15.6%
27	West Philadelphia	15.7%
30	Schuylkill docks	24.7%
44	West Philadelphia	18.6%

Source: U.S. Census Bureau, 1910, National Archives at Philadelphia.

[a] The ethnic content of these neighborhoods includes both Irish immigrants and the second generation in which both parents were Irish-born. If we had considered the intermarriage possibilities of the second-generation American-born Irish, the imprint of Irish ethnicity in these neighborhoods would have been greater.

A PLEBIAN PUBLIC SPHERE

While Habermas asserts that his classic empirical universe was that of a floating, ascending bourgeois realm, meeting in coffeehouses and salons in Germany, France, and England in the late 1700s and early 1800s, where they arbitrated their public sphere using reason and deciding questions based "on the best argument,"[24] the model for the Philadelphia Irish community of the 1890s came closer to a "plebian" public sphere, a "counterpublic" consisting of working people, its message distributed by a minor but vocal and active intelligentsia of journalists, cultural commentators, neighborhood leaders, traveling orators, priests, and nationalists of many stripes.[25] Typical of the style of educational missionizing was a lecture delivered in 1876 at the Academy of Music by Reverend F. E. Doyle and titled, "Irishmen of the American Revolution."[26]

This popularized vernacular of Irish identity invited Irish Philadelphians into a public; it organized men and women into associations, enticed them to read newspapers and handbills, to attend Gaelic festivals, summer river or beach excursions, and fancy winter balls; it made lives more connected and literate, and it gave life experiences to a mass that might have remained fragmented, isolated, and forgotten. The Gaelic public of the 1890s ranked low in an occupational hierarchy but did not approach the rougher versions of plebian culture, the Philadelphia Irish firehouse gangs Dennis Clark describes so well, which were street gangs that roamed and ruled through physical force and intimidation the dockside neighborhood of Ramcat as well as in Moyamensing, just south of the old city in Southwark.[27]

To say that the Irish Americans emerging in the 1890s were plebian is to say that they were of the lower orders, mostly working-class people occupying a diverse hierarchy of positions in the industrial economy, in niches from laborers to skilled workers, publicans, shop owners, clerks, and salesmen.[28] The economy the Irish inherited and helped to build in nineteenth-century Philadelphia reflected the small-scale industry of Philadelphia's colonial past as well as the vast, open spaces of the incorporated city, which provided room for commerce and industry. Industrialism and its attendant cultural commands and codes defined the nineteenth-century city and its immigrant workers; labor rhythms, time disciplines, skill requirements, and an economic system of "increasing rationalization in the service of economic growth" shaped the nature of the Irish American experience in Philadelphia.[29] Economic life chances brought the Irish to Philadelphia in the nineteenth century, creating a plebian diaspora community of a distinct Irish nature, a distribution of Irish men and women scattered across the urban landscape in search of labor, and a rising communicative collective of industrial workers.

The Irish in Philadelphia in the 1890s consulted all the resources of ethnic meaning but essentially relied on themselves and their traditions of small group organization and cooperation to frame and support an ideology of cultural separatism even as they found themselves more integrated in Philadelphia's economy and society. Typical of this fundamentalist approach of Gaelic activism was a winter lecture by Father McSweeney, "Ireland Today," which was delivered to the Moriarty Branch of the National League of Philadelphia in 1889; it was noted that the members were "all wearing green badges."[30]

THE ETHNIC ASSOCIATION: HOUSING THE GAELIC PUBLIC SPHERE

The late 1800s and early 1900s were the era of voluntary associations in the United States, a time of civic expression, as Robert Putnam writes, featuring a "burst of social-capital investment" evident in the explosion of societies and associations.[31] And, as Geoff Eley states, a public sphere assumes the "voluntary association and associational life as the main medium for the definition of public commitments."[32] Habermas also recognized the voluntary association as a harbinger of modernity, a location in emerging public spaces freed from state control and separate from family and the world of commerce and work.

For the Irish in Philadelphia, their public meant first organizing the means of supplying subsistence support, the mutual aid society, which doled out workingman's insurance in exchange for monthly membership dues. Mutual benefit societies, according to Kaufman and Tepper, involved "interlocking financial obligations, unmitigated by a larger 'bonding' mechanism" such as elaborate initiation rites or sacred oaths.[33] For all its focus on culture and sociability, the necessary support for working men in an industrial city was the spirit of mutual aid, which supplied material benefits. In 1893, Martin P. Moroney, an officer in one of the many Kensington branches of AOH, described his members as "progressive, and fully alive to the requirements of the times. To be a member of such an organization is a valuable provision in case of sickness, and, under the watchful eyes of a good staff of officers, one can feel assured that he will receive a generous share of brotherly sympathy and assistance in a time of sickness or trouble."[34]

Voluntary associations were long associated with forming publics in America, as historians have noted. Howard Wach writes, "Associational practices, the worldly orientation of privately generated individuality and ideologically charged bourgeois values were strong presences in late eighteenth- and early nineteenth-century England and the United States."[35] The vast web of Irish American associations in Philadelphia at the turn of the twentieth century has been portrayed as a network of schools for bourgeois mentalities; the Philadelphia story exposes a dualism to this assumption, suggesting that the experience of associational life reinforced middle-class discipline in its operational practices, leaving working-class and ethnic oppositional attitudes in place.

For workers faced with the destabilizing influence of industrialization, the association was an organization of defense against the pressures of modernization and the hegemony of capital. Ira Katznelson notices that defense became a priority for workers as "they formed a variety of self-help organizations such as insurance and friendly societies."[36] Roland Bertoff describes an identical historical trend in workers' associations; he writes, "whole new orders were created expressly to provide the working man's family with cheap, reliable insurance such as commercial companies did not offer."[37]

The Philadelphia Irish constructed many types of associations by the 1890s. These were workers' mutual aid societies mainly identified with an Irish nationalist theme or neighborhood Catholic parish. These Irish Catholic workers' institutions held regular meetings for business, debate, and leisure; organized committees and divided the labor required for communal subsistence; kept exact records of member residence and dues; and managed the financial details. Officers were elected, stewards for the investigation and care of members on sick leave were either appointed or elected, and members were expected to assume a role on the multiple committees, from fundraising to consciousness-raising, that kept the organization flowing. The arrangements and expectations for the individual were outlined in a rule book, which was handed over as a rite of initiation. These were guides for sober, orderly behavior in a public setting, in the form of the brief, printed, pocket-sized texts common in Irish societies of all ideological bearings in the 1890s and that bore a striking similarity to rule books distributed in native Ireland.

The Irish American voluntary association did not let just anyone of Irish descent into its doors; rather, its entrance rules outlined a private citizen of some financial stability—a job and the means to pay dues—a history of decent health, a promise of sobriety and the temperament to tolerate and engage in the back-and-forth of debate and discussion in public settings. While the Irish American voluntary society protected the privacy of its members and elevated the stature of citizen responsibility in democratic settings, it also laid out a singular vision of Irish group identity that individuals adhered to without much resistance. A distinct cultural message was shaped in public gatherings, and it was most poignantly and consistently nurtured in the casual conversation and formal discussions of the meetings of the Irish voluntary association and mutual aid society. David Shields notes an identical penchant for sociability in and out of the formal settings of early America, clubs, and coffeehouses, all bound by "modes of discourse necessary to the creation of the public sphere."[38]

Philadelphia's Gaelic moment was several decades of vibrant energy and independent action, although it was ultimately of short duration, and while it deviated from the original ideal type, it bound and shaped a formidable historical presence of ordinary men and women in an industrial outpost of Irish influence. As clubs, meeting rooms, and voluntary associations housed bourgeois aspirations in the late 1700s and early 1800s in France, Britain, or Germany for Habermas's historical agents of change, derailing the authority and status derived from state and nobility, in Philadelphia in the 1890s the ethnic society was a zone of emancipatory possibilities for an ethnic group of modest status in its moment of ascendancy.

TRACING THE ROOTS OF A GAELIC PUBLIC

An interesting question of causal association invades this exploration of Irish Philadelphia: how did American modernism and traditions associated with civic publics, which were derived from more elite groups of higher literary and financial standing, influence more plebian publics like the Irish Americans of late-nineteenth-century Philadelphia? The answer proposed by this study is that American traditions had minimal initial influence over Irish American civic institutions; the hostile welcome and Philadelphia's aggressive nativism produced a defensive response from Irish Catholics, who surrounded themselves with their own institutions.

Instead, the Irish of Philadelphia relied primarily on what cultural heritage and social learning was passed on from a history of associationalism in old Ireland: the workingman's tontine, for example, or town and rural friendly societies and all types of fraternal and civic societies in all regions of the native nation.

The Diaspora Irish in Philadelphia had many more opportunities and freedoms in their public settings than the Irish in Ireland, including more financial security from industrial wages, less interference from a suspicious state, and conditional disinterest from the Catholic Church, and the Philadelphia Irish came closer to the classical ideal model of reasoned discussion and debate.

The influence of American values and small group democratic traditions was not far off. Alexis de Tocqueville's enthusiasm and energetic defense of American democracy was postulated on the American voluntary association and its role as a buffer between state and society. As he described it: "Americans of all ages, conditions, and all dispositions constantly unite together. Not only do they have commercial and industrial associations to which they belong but also a thousand other kinds, religious, moral, serious, futile, very general and very specialized, large and small."[39] Tocqueville's endorsement of voluntary associations is derived from his observation of small-town America, and the American traditions extolled by the visiting French aristocrat existed alongside, somewhat insulated from, the cultural traditions of civic practices belonging to Irish immigrants in the bustling American cities.

CONFLICT AS UNITY

Conflict and the perception of enemies tended to instill feelings of unity for the Irish Americans, and the men and women of Irish Philadelphia drew boundaries around their identity, making the bonds of fraternity closer and more durable. Max Weber writes of the binding energy of conflict among social groups, whose subjective awareness is made more salient by the invention of enemies, opponents who "are linked to some antagonism against members of an obviously different group."[40]

Among the Diaspora Irish in Philadelphia, an ethic of generalized conflict and mutual defense mobilized group formation for civic action, sustained by unchallenged Irish folklore beliefs, transferred to America, of the Catholic Irish as historical victims; the memory of the violence of the 1844 Philadelphia street confrontations, in the Kensington and Southwark districts, over Catholic immigration, primarily Irish, and nativist defense was not far removed from an 1890s reality of renewed questions about Irish Catholics in America. Conflict that was social, political, and historical defined the Gaels of Philadelphia and differentiated their civic institutions from normative American voluntary associations. Catholic Philadelphian John Doyle, president of AOH Local 49 at 8th and Fitzwater in the river district of Old Philadelphia, rose at his association meeting in 1895 and reminded the assembled brothers of their ancestral bonds in the easily recognizable vernacular of Irish discontent that "it [was] incumbent on every manly, honorable man of our grand and ancient race to firmly resolve to continue the glorious fight for freedom until the last vestige of English tyranny had

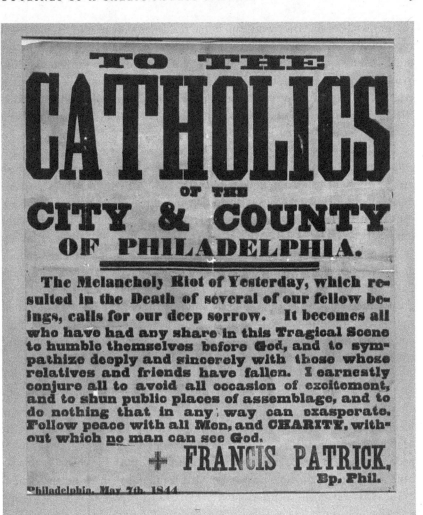

TO THE
CATHOLICS
OF THE
CITY & COUNTY
OF PHILADELPHIA.

The Melancholy Riot of Yesterday, which resulted in the Death of several of our fellow beings, calls for our deep sorrow. It becomes all who have had any share in this Tragical Scene to humble themselves before God, and to sympathize deeply and sincerely with those whose relatives and friends have fallen. I earnestly conjure all to avoid all occasion of excitement, and to shun public places of assemblage, and to do nothing that in any way can exasperate. Follow peace with all Men, and CHARITY, without which no man can see God.

✝ FRANCIS PATRICK,
Bp. Phil.

Philadelphia, May 7th, 1844.

Admission ticket for a lecture on Ireland, 1889. Source: Digital Library@Villanova University.

been forever obliterated, and until the last red-coated myrmidon had ceased patrolling the land of St. Patrick's Shamrock."[41]

It is worth noting that an Irish public was based on decades of hostility toward outsiders, those located above in the social hierarchy (white Protestants) and those ranked below (other ethnic groups struggling for existence in Philadelphia). Dennis Clark writes of the structured enmity between African American Philadelphians and the Irish in the mid-decades of the nineteenth century that it was an "Irish-Black vendetta [that] amounted to an accepted communal pathology."[42] Philadelphia was a city of many emigrating groups in the nineteenth century, and conflict over work and home residence were part of the historical record. African Americans and the Irish competed for labor opportunities for much of the 1800s, and the influx of African Americans from the South during World War I increased the tension.[43] In 1917–18, Black strike breakers exacerbated ethnic cleavages, and in summer 1918 public disorder by white Philadelphia, which was associated with Irish heritage, broke out in South Philadelphia at a home purchased by an African American woman.[44]

The Irish Americans also borrowed from traditional, rural methods of closure from past conflicts over land, adopting Ireland's village boycott to impose on its Protestant enemies in Philadelphia. The Irish American Catholic associations bought their supplies from their own and, during the height of the resurgence of nativism in the 1890s, eschewed commercial relations with Protestant purveyors.

The public sphere, for Habermas, existed between a state still defined by monarchy and civil society, a zone of freer expression that resisted penetration. Similarly, the Irish American public in the 1890s existed in a social space between greater Protestant American influence and institutions, a largely disinterested state, and a watchful Catholic Church, where it was free to develop a counter-culture around the real and imaginary walls of Catholic Irish repression and emergent Gaelic expression.

IDEOLOGY AND HISTORY

Ideology is a set of myths, half-truths, which are often connected to subterranean interests; as Kevin Kenny describes it, "a series of narratives through which people attempt to make sense of their social worlds."[45] And so the Irish Americans in Philadelphia employed a nationalist frame for their worldview, which by the 1890s was a well-worn and convenient narrative of past wrongs that framed a version of historical knowledge, a hard resurgent monument of meaning and agreement that opened doors of inclusion to a restricted universe of thought and reason. Yet, as much as the emotional discourse of national regret had been planted in the Diaspora Irish by decades of pre- and post-Famine analysis of what went wrong in Ireland, in their formal deliberations in their ethnic associations, the Irish maintained a modernist discipline over proceedings, reserving time for the discussion of public life, all within the highly ritualized expectations for order in formal meetings.

Raymond Williams reminds us of the persistence of cultural indices of knowledge and meaning—once imprinted, the categories of thought and action move forward with a will and life of their own, unchallenged, difficult to dislodge, accepted as tested truths and common wisdom. His comments on Gramsci's concept of hegemony help explain the durability of the historical myths that circulated in the Gaelic zone of the late 1800s and early 1900s: "[hegemony] supposes the existence of something which is truly total . . . but which is lived at such a depth, which saturates society to such an extent, and which even constitutes the substance and limit of common sense for most people under its sway, that it corresponds to the reality of [their] social experience."[46]

The Gaelic discourse of victimhood in the nineteenth and early twentieth centuries was a motivational mantra sustaining Irish American nationalism; it was also in some respects a burden blinding reason and an appreciation of assimilationist options.

The Gaelic public sphere was not a movement of high enlightenment—it often suppressed reason and demanded consent as it followed patterns of thought in texts long considered accurate and essential, reconstructing truths about the culpability of the English for the Famine and other crimes of conquest and colonial management. The Gaelic public sphere became an accepted, inherited accumulation of writings, folk tales, and popular understandings that passed for common knowledge in Irish American communities in the 1890s.

An appeal for funds to rebuild a missionary college in Dublin circulated among the many parish beneficial societies of the city, reminding Irish Philadelphians in 1895 of a not too distant past: "the dark days of the forties, when famine and pestilence were abroad, and the emigrant ship was carrying away from the hearths of their fathers, human cargoes . . . into foreign lands."[47] The burden of the Irish past, of history as tragedy, was an additional weight, a persistent reminder carried forward and acted upon in diaspora settings.

John Mitchel was influential in the post-Famine decades, and once his conclusions about English guilt for the Famine were distributed, they spread among a willing audience in the Irish Diaspora, acquiring a validity that simply became part of Irish Catholic experience in America. Mitchel, the son of a minister, who was educated at Trinity College, Dublin (a bastion of Anglo-Irish ascendancy in Ireland), and leader of the Young Ireland opposition in the late 1840s and early 1850s, changed the tone of Irish nationalism with his harsh words of contempt for the British handling of the Famine. Mitchel writes in his work, *The Last Conquest of Ireland (Perhaps)*, that "the Famine policy of the government was the slaughter of a portion of its people, and the Pauperization of the rest."[48]

Mitchel's pamphlet, *An Apology for the British Government in Ireland*, was an essential text that circulated in the communicative network of Irish Americana in the late 1800s and early 1900s, offering up Mitchel's interpretation of the Famine as a British plot.[49] Mitchel noted that "almighty God sent the potato-blight but the English created the Famine," referring to the mid-century agricultural failure that gave way to the depopulation of the island.[50]

A reprint of an 1847 lecture by John Hughes, bishop of New York, that circulated in Philadelphia Irish societies, "A Lecture of the Antecedent Causes of the Irish Famine in 1847," amplified the message Mitchel delivered on outside culpability for the mid-century agricultural crisis. Hughes stated of Ireland that "since her union with England, commerce followed capital . . . and forsook the sister island. Nothing remained but the produce of the soil. That produce was sent to England to find a better market."[51]

For the Irish in the 1890s, the coming together of a separate Irish identity through communicative means also implied some central ground of agreed-on social meaning and methodology, and in this case, it was an ideology of nationalist intensity and historical half-truths backed by ideas about American freedoms, a collection of cherished beliefs wandering through time with a willing audience. The circulation of pamphlets became a communicative outlet in Irish American associations across the country; they were ubiquitous, inexpensive, and available wherever Irish Americans convened. George Russell's *The Inner and Outer Ireland* cost 5¢ a copy, $4 per one hundred copies in 1920 for Irish American societies eager to distribute them to their members.[52]

The Irish mastered the late-nineteenth-century techniques of communication in an open society and used whatever means available to make their case in defending their Gaelic existence; during the fury of the Anglo-Irish War in the early 1920s Irish American associations sent wires to Congressmen in a campaign of counterpropaganda. The following text was typical of these communications: "I (we) demand our government protest England's violation of Hague Convention by shooting six Irish prisoners of war at Cork."[53]

A pamphlet, *"Oration Delivered at the Request of the Fenian Brotherhood,"* which circulated on the Fourth of July, 1867, also represents the type. The text challenged Irish masculinity in the face of the occupation and colonization of Mother Ireland—"we have seen her for ages rising in the impotence of her anger in fitful bounds against her dungeon bars." The blame was self-directed for the "double crime of weakness and insubordination [for] the fruitless invasion of Canada, and the abortive risings in Limerick and Wexford."[54] The pamphlet, which was typical of the genre of conflict in Irish American texts, completes the circle of recrimination, noting that the oppressor, the English, remained "mean, despicable, degrading—an insult to the Irish character."[55]

The Irish of Philadelphia reconstructed their own history so that it would not die in America; in doing so, they reified the past, adapting sacred texts and creating their own historical interpretations laden with villains and victims, in a language of regret and defiance suited for the Gaelic resurgence of the 1890s. As Herbert Marcuse writes, language has its own mechanisms of control, and its one-dimension frame can represent "a suppression of history."[56] Marcuse warns of the "authoritarian ritualization of discourse," which leaves no room for the refutation of opposing ideas, "no time and space for a discussion which would project disruptive alternatives"; this critique had equal meaning for a suppressed people struggling to define themselves in opposition to their surrounding, changing modern landscape.[57]

The inherited content of the Gaelic public sphere was indeed ideological, its production and consumption passed on as sanctioned truth. David Doolin suggests that the acts of remembrance and reverence for fallen heroes and failed risings, such as Wolfe Tone, Robert Emmet, and the 1866 Fenian invasion of Canada, were a "reflective strategy to help consolidate that sense of Irishness."[58] And yet, for all of their modernism, their adaptation to the pace and rhythms of industrial labor, the Philadelphia Irish in the late decades of the nineteenth century were not yet ready to deflect the influence of sacred traditions.

THE SUBMERGED RITES OF LABOR IN THE ETHNIC PUBLIC SPHERE

The late-nineteenth-century Philadelphia Irish community was also defined by a matrix of classes formed in the industrial era, but the overt expression of labor and class was subverted in the public sphere in favor of Gaelic culture; the resurgence of Irish cultural nationalism on both shores of the Atlantic crowded out the identification of the Irish with a specific location in the industrial division of labor. For the Irish who were coming together in voluntary associations, who were overwhelmingly of the working class, cultural traditions prevailed, but in late-nineteenth-century Philadelphia, the Irish preferred to leave their working clothes at the door, entering a zone free of labor's conflicts, one of pleasant memories, turbulent nationalist visions, and collegial interaction.

If we consult E. P. Thompson's proposition about social class, which "happens when some men, as a result of common experiences (inherited or shared), feel and articulate the identity of their interests as between themselves, and as against other men whose interests are different from (and usually) opposed to theirs,"[59] we can appreciate the complexity of the Irish American position on class, in which multiple signs of conflict, allegiance, and opposition all demanded attention.

A historical treatment of working people in an industrial city demands an acknowledgment of an economic basis of social class, but it is also an unpredictable social process penetrating culture, interaction rituals, language, personal and private relations, and masculine codes of honor, as well as the life opportunities defined by material conditions. This understanding promises to take the historian in new and unanticipated directions; as Sean Wilenz acknowledges, "The history of class relations cannot be deduced by some 'economic' or sociological calculus and imposed on the past; nor can it be ignored if it does not appear just as the historian thinks it should."[60] In Gaelic Philadelphia, in gatherings of chiseled working men in a city of nineteenth-century union heritage, many of whom were recently arrived from Ireland, the finding that the conversation around industrial work was muted in favor of cultural remembrance and attention to the emerging if imaginative Irish nation was an unanticipated conclusion

of the historian's process. Gaelic Philadelphia did not deny Thompson's definition of workers as men who "feel and articulate the identity of their interests as
between themselves, and as against other men"; it was in workers' societies of
mutual aid that were initiated as defense mechanisms against industrial capitalism that Irish men and women opted for ethnic markers of organization and a
leisure of remembrance and sentimental salute to old Ireland.

Taking what evidence is available on occupation from the records of Irish
associations, we discover a mix of occupational groupings at the low end of the
working hierarchy of the industrial city, predominantly working-class, both
skilled and unskilled, small owners of property, and shop owners. The process
of collective organization in voluntary associations behind a singular class identity was blocked by the fog of multiple surrounding influences: American images
of resilient democracy and independent economic action, the materialist impulses
of a rising middle stratum, and the pull of an emerging Irish cultural nationalism, all distracting factors. The mission of creating a public sphere in Philadelphia also involved shifting the weight and content of past ethnic imagery, from
an Irish image described by Friedrich Engels as "wild, headstrong, fanatical
Gaels" to a more respectable, new Irish type able to govern in societies bound to
an unfulfilled national cause.[61]

Having consulted the practices of working-class culture in Ireland, the mutual
aid societies that were the supportive institutions of the working class—the
tontines of Dublin—research showed that divisive politics in that imperial city
were often censured as a topic of discussion, a tradition that worked its way into
Irish thinking in friendly societies across the island nation and into Diaspora
Philadelphia. The transatlantic comparison of cultural forms between Ireland
and an American extension, the norms and dictates of practices and rules in
working-class societies, yields a context to interpret the silent voice of labor activism in Philadelphia's Gaelic public.

Dublin's working-class tontines were careful to avoid seditious politics and
routinely questioned prospective members on their political instincts and
whether they belonged to a "secret society." Religion was another tense topic that
had formally excluded in associational life in native Ireland, the divide between
Protestant and Catholic a raw reminder of the occupational hierarchy and colonial order, a set of differing life chances based on religion. American associations failed to adopt the original Irish model in its totality, such as that of the
Dublin tontines and the friendly societies of Ireland, in which discussions on
"religious, sectarian or political party character" were banned. Ireland's Northumberland Friendly Society restricted divisive public discussion, disallowing
"religious or political discourses, or any matter connected with combination."[62]
The Northumberland Society wanted its worker members to appear at its weekly
meetings clean and dressed with clothes that did not belie their social class,
imposing fines on members who arrived at meetings "intoxicated, or with

unclean linen, face or hands dirty . . . beard of a remarkable length, or wearing an apron.[63] The apron was worn by artisans as they plied their trade, which made it a symbol of working-class status in late-nineteenth-century Dublin. In comparison, by the 1890s in Philadelphia the Irish societies were practically open forums, less restrictive in thought and deed, unlike those driven by militant nationalism like the Clan na Gael, which were more secretive.[64]

The underlying message of mutual aid in Irish Philadelphia was a muted class solidarity. The president of AOH branch 46 in South Philadelphia, John McCoy, in a rare departure from the usual communal Gaelic script, stated to his members in 1895: "In this aggressive age it is necessary that all persons should be associated for mutual aid and support, particularly in this great land where all nationalities are represented, and where class interests are so zealously guarded by powerful, exclusive and well-organized societies and institutions."[65]

The 1893 depression hit working men hard in Philadelphia, exerting pressure on the mutual aid function of divisions; in AOH 55, located in Kensington's textile district, it was recorded that "trade depression had its direct effect upon us, most of our members being employed in the textile industry."[66]

The Irish in Philadelphia had entered the workforce at the bottom, as laborers and new emigrants, throughout the mid- to late nineteenth century and faced challenges and competition in the search for work; these daily reminders of the toughness of the industrial order served only to reinforce a preexisting distrust of outsiders and their institutions, which was offset by a blind faith in the heroic version of Irish heritage, an ideology that was sustained in the meeting rooms of the ethnic associations of turn-of-the-century Philadelphia. As Thomas Brown notes of the late-nineteenth-century Irish in America, "a sense of suffering was the fuel which kept Irish-American organizations going."[67]

The Irish American disdain for labor politics in their civic institutions contrasts with the extant historical example of early British workers, who defended themselves by forming their own voluntary associations, the friendly societies, which became funnels for the sponsoring of mass meetings espousing workers' opposition and the growth and development of a workers' press, which was at times underground but eventually became legal and able to distribute widely. The British friendly societies and other working-class associations were also outlets for an artisan-based program of worker self-education in which reading rooms sprouted up and evening debates were held.

The Clan na Gael, with over forty neighborhood "camps" in Philadelphia in the 1890s, was a secretive, oath-bound association bent on Irish national retribution, but it also revealed a structure and organizational discipline similar to the Dublin tontine, with self-surveillance and self-governance by members all supported by an understanding that the heart of the association was from below, based on the self-initiative of members, who were expected to bond and act together to confront a hostile world. Working-class solidarity penetrated in a voiceless mode the backrooms of the meetings of the Gaelic public sphere—with severe labor troubles the only exception. The Clan na Gael of Philadelphia devoted a meeting in 1889 to develop a strategy to solicit funds for the "Johnstown sufferers" created by the flood.[68]

Support for the victims of Johnstown reached the Irish everywhere in 1889—the branches of the Irish Catholic Benevolent Society (ICBS) were asked to forward donated funds from across the country to the secretary of the Philadelphia ICBS, Martin Griffin, to be dispatched to western Pennsylvania. Griffin appealed to Philadelphia and Pennsylvania ICBS branches, "Now Pennsylvania, the stronghold of the I.C.B.S., is stricken by a calamity, dreadful in its character and extent."[69]

The hundred-odd branches of Philadelphia's AOH in the 1890s were nothing like the conspiratorial, oath-bound organizations of the mid-nineteenth century in Ireland or in Pennsylvania coal country. Kevin Kenny has traced the AOH affiliation, real and imagined, in connection with the Molly Maguires and suggested that a few Schuylkill Valley lodges were organizing centers for violence, but he affirmed that "most A.O.H. members had nothing to do with the Molly Maguires."[70] He concludes that by century's end it was "clearly a peaceful fraternal society rather than a violent conspiratorial one."[71] By the 1890s, the Philadelphia AOH was a mutual aid society, a workingman's leisure club, and an outlet for Irish nationalism and the host of a sentimental remembrance of old Ireland, whose activities were covered weekly in *The Hibernian*.

The ethnic voluntary associations and the order required for behavior in public settings were small schools for the absorption of American bourgeois values, and since many of the officers of the associations were recruited from an Irish petty bourgeoisie, a preference for leaders with status at the top of a modest Irish American occupational hierarchy in Philadelphia was established. To be an association man was to enter a world of bourgeois order, gaining an acquired respectability not always associated with Irish street society.

Association meetings were also moments for education, discussion, and debate about political and social events in Ireland and the condition of Irish Americana. It was said of AOH Division 67, at 25th and York in North Philadelphia, that "the rank and file are composed of a fine lot of young and intellectual Irish-Americans, who discuss in a true brotherly spirit every question before the house."[72]

The Irish mutual aid societies of Philadelphia were initially defense organizations intended to support working-class subsistence; by the 1890s, however, the Irish Americans turned their societies into vehicles of communication, self-education, and consciousness-raising, depositories for excursions into the resurgence of Gaelic culture and history. These societies were populated by men of labor, an allegiance not easily discarded, but labor concerns were more often set aside by the attention to Irish culture and nationalism that defined the Irish in Philadelphia in the 1890s. Outside events naturally broke through this steely ethnic shield—for example, the Cavan Society would formally acknowledge and offer support to its many members on strike against the Baldwin Locomotive Works of Philadelphia in 1911.[73]

Finally, Irish American associationalism in Philadelphia was supported by industrial wealth—the wages from labor and profits from small enterprises that were poured into the cultural societies and associations that were well established by the 1890s. In Ireland the stalled nineteenth-century industrial economy spawned the proliferation of workers' mutual aid societies that allowed for minimal health and injury benefits, a subsistence level with high rates of failure and instability among the many voluntary associations.[74] In contrast, the Irish Americans were able to distinctly reject this model from across the Atlantic, preferring to save funds and purchase property to house their cultural associations and support the small democracy and communicative expression that defined their formal gatherings; in essence, surplus derived from working-class wages in Philadelphia supported Gaelic ideals and produced a more dynamic Irish in the diaspora, involving support for an expansive vision and for a public sphere.

By the 1890s, the Gaelic public was a volatile mix of competing voices, and, at least in Philadelphia, nationalism and culture crowded out an overt sensibility to labor as the defining label of identity. Dennis Clark's assertion that the ideal Irishman "sought participation in the life of the country as working citizens, and except for a tiny minority, not any socialist solutions" might explain the penchant for culture over class.[75]

Thus, there came to exist certain taboos and required allegiance to status symbols operating on the working-class members of the Gaelic public sphere, and the Irish in Philadelphia in their gatherings took pains to refrain from class analysis, preferring Irish culture, remembrance, and nationalism to class solidarity. The public realm of the Irish in the 1890s offered much to its mass of working-class participants, who were a hierarchy of men in industrial positions that ranged from experienced machinists to the unskilled, but it seems not to have carved out a defiant and expressive identity for working men; rather, Gaelic expression and culture pushed aside the potential for any meaningful manifestation of working-class consciousness.

The Connective Tissue of Print Media

By the 1890s there was an array of inexpensive and available Irish American newspapers in Philadelphia supplemented by Patrick Ford's *Irish World* from New York. This plebian literature shaped and connected the Irish among the dispersed neighborhoods of the city and suburbs, forming an ethnic network of words and images in a popular culture defined by oral traditions and scarce texts.

Irish associations nationwide existed off the newspaper as well; public events such as parades were required postings in the ethnic press—"all members must be notified through a city newspaper, at least twenty-four hours before the time of the fixed parade" was written into the bylaws of one Irish American association.[76] In Philadelphia's diverse industrial economy, the Irish, although fragmented by space and an industrial division of labor, were brought together by texts. Thomas Brown writes, "The Irish-American press was the chief instrument of nationalist influence. It was to the newspapers that the immigrants turned when in their newly awakened consciousness they sought knowledge of Ireland and the Irish."[77] The ethnic newspapers helped the Irish overcome the spatial separation of distant towns and neighborhoods in the nineteenth century, as the following report from an AOH gathering in 1893 reflected: "the greatest auxiliary to civilization, the newspaper, should be established in order that we should keep with the march of progress. . . . We must circulate the schoolmaster, the newspaper, and instruct our people in the necessity of cohesion, disparage dissension, and propagate the imperishable spirit of Irish Nationality."[78]

In Philadelphia, *The Hibernian* was the outlet of the AOH, its newsprint covering the content of branch meetings and Irish gatherings, with whole pages devoted to promoting Irish Gaelic Games in the summer or autumn, summer river excursions on the Delaware, winter fancy dress balls, the life and death of Irish men and women. In addition to *The Hibernian* there were *The Freeman and Irish American Review* and *The Irish American Review and Celtic Literary Advocate*, popular weekly journals covering Philadelphia's Irish events and gatherings and national debates within Irish America, complete with treatises and essays on Irish history; the latter weekly proudly announced its journalistic contract with Irish Philadelphia as "devoted to the interests of the Irish race . . . Irish in every fibre—American to the core."[79] The ethnic press in Philadelphia was robust in its coverage and its range of topics, inexpensive (5¢ a copy) and available at the neighborhood grocery store every Saturday morning.

It has been stated that the Irish Americans in Philadelphia engaged in a separatism that insulated the people from outside scrutiny, making them impervious to any sense of criticism yet often leaving them respectful of bourgeois propriety and the norms and rules of communication. The board of the ultranationalist Philadelphia Clan na Gael debated a resolution brought forward by a branch in 1889 that sought to protest the mainstream journal, the *Public Ledger* of Philadelphia, for its "attitude on Irish affairs in general and its hostility to this organization [Clan na Gael] in particular."[80] The assault on Gaelic purity noted, the resolution was defeated, and the higher modernist value of an open press was thus affirmed.

Enriched by the explosion of communicative methods and publications in the 1890s and augmented by the extraordinary mobility of the Irish when it came to Irish matters, a Gaelic voice with a citywide, at times national, network of meaning emerged and spoke to Irish Americans in the 1890s. In essence, a new urban ethnic subculture was created around the expanding, late-nineteenth-century networks of ethnic communication that found a home in the voluntary associations and gathering places of Irish Philadelphia.

LEISURE IN THE PUBLIC SPHERE: CONVERSATION IN PUBLIC PLACES

As noted, the Gaelic zone was plebian, of the laboring classes, and within the meeting rooms of the ethnic associations, the art of conversation flourished, supplemented by reasoned argument practiced in certain setting-specific topics. Even though the societies followed a script of ordered business and discussion in strict formulas, the monthly meeting or the bimonthly meetings of action committees were also opportunities for face-to-face interaction and conversation among neighbors, fellow members, and visiting friends; within the cracks of the formal proceedings, the informal content of these gatherings flourished, making this a ritual of association that further cemented the communicative role of the association in the Irish community.

At the end of formal business, a ritualized time was set aside for leisure at the close of the monthly meeting. It was a moment for Irish songs and ballads or poems, brief oratory, a welcome to guests outside the local (who were obliged to then reciprocate with a few words), the sharing of a joke, refreshments, and conversation among the exiles of Erin. Songs such as "Our Land Shall Be Free," "Paddies Evermore," "Green Old Flag," and "Erin Weeps Forsaken" were favorite ending notes to an evening's meeting.[81] Other ballads, such as "Gems of the Emerald Isle," "Joe Hardy," "Darby Maguire," "Emmet's Grave," "Heroes of the Past," and "Poor Pat Must Emigrate," punctuated the evening air in 1890s Irish Philadelphia.[82]

The expressive Irishman thus found his outlet within the confines of the ordered meeting, remaining careful in avoiding a communal emotionalism that verified unflattering nineteenth-century images of the Irish at home and abroad, yet able on occasion to lampoon himself and his colleagues. The social discipline displayed by ordinary members of these associations has been attributed as a derivative of bourgeois influence, but the Philadelphia Irishman of the 1890s was well-schooled in the imagery of the premodern, child-like caricature he had inherited and determined to refute this tired label. No less a critic of English modernity than John Mitchel reminded his compatriots of the Irish reputation and the need to oppose it, a legacy he defined as "incorrigible idleness, vice, drunkenness, violence, ignorance and barbarism."[83]

The Philadelphia meetings of ethnic associations also attracted men from branch associations from all corners of the city, work colleagues from outside the host association who dropped by to share an evening with a friend and extend Gaelic good will across the industrial landscape. An AOH meeting of Kensington's Division 9 in 1899 attracted guests from five other divisions; business was dispensed with, and the meeting finished with the usual rituals of poems and songs: "Brother Lynch recited in fine form 'For Ireland's Sake,' [and] Brother Sheerin sang, amid cheers, 'Who Fears to Speak of '98,'" a reference to the United Irishmen.[84]

Irish Philadelphia had a social calendar, with summer a time for excursions along the Delaware River or to Atlantic City and the mass Irish American picnics, cultural festivals in Philadelphia devoted to Irish music, dance, oratory, and sports. The Philadelphia AOH took a riverboat excursion down the Delaware River to Bay, Delaware, in August 1893; it was reported that "a good piper rolled out the jigs, the reels and the hornpipes."[85] When it came to the public display of Gaelic pride, the working-class Irish always seemed to have resources to spend—for the ride to the July Fourth picnic and summer sport festival, AOH Division 34 rode up Broad Street in "tally-ho [coaches] decorated from front to rear with the colors of 34, the Stars and Stripes and the green flag floating proudly in the breeze."[86]

ALCOHOL AND PUBLIC BEHAVIOR

For the Irish, certain codes emerged that were specialized and catered to their reading of their place in American society—a behaviorism that determined that the expressive Irish, its Paddy image, had to be supplemented by the instrumental actor. Thomas Brown captures the image the second and third generations detested, "Paddy, the hapless, witty Irishman, given to drink and quick to tears and laughter, who loved nothing more than 'rows and ructions.'"[87]

Alcohol could be a topic of intense debate within the public discussion of the societies of Philadelphia; if the Dublin society could meet in the backroom of a pub, with members calling for drinks and building up a bar tab, the American Irish either banned alcohol for meetings or allowed it only in strict time frames and in controlled doses, accepting yet careful, on special occasions and at times often at the end of the meeting as voices were lifted in Irish song. In Manayunk, a textile mill town inside the Philadelphia city limits along the Schuylkill River, AOH Division 5 celebrated its twentieth anniversary in 1894 with a series of guest speeches and, afterwards, "Refreshments were then served and adjournment did not take place 'til the 'wee sma' hours."[88]

When formal affairs were concluded at an 1895 meeting of AOH 29 in South Philadelphia, "President Egan ordered the stewards to do their duty which they cheerfully and promptly did." Drinks and snacks served, sentimental voices were lifted for "Emmet," "The Valley Lay Smiling Before Me" and "Brother O'Brien . . . concluded by reciting in fine form a new and unpublished poem by Annie Kingstown, entitled, 'An Eventful Dream.'" On it went, song after Irish song, until it was time to rise and sing together the "National Anthem of Ireland."[89]

Where alcohol was not prohibited at balls and purely social gatherings, it was treated with respect, as a potential threat to this particular ethnic group and its attempts to purify its image in Philadelphia. All these self-imposed constraints conformed to a pattern of self-discipline in public gatherings, a commitment to avoid any confirmation that the Irish in the 1890s bore any resemblance to a caricatured past. As an example, the 1872 Constitution of the AOH stipulated that "any member coming into the Lodge in a state of intoxication, and annoying the members, shall be fined in the sum of $1.00 and leave the Lodge room that night," a stern reminder of the self-discipline and control required of Irish American gatherings in the 1870s.[90]

Thus, the civic life of the ethnic associations required and produced a rational, calculating approach to maintain and expand the organizations, but just as a business model of worker mutual aid emerged, so too did the expressive, emotional core of Irish meaning and identity. The staying power of a public sphere is in its communicative development: the Irish in Philadelphia achieved a vibrant, ethnic community through communication, using the many forms and props available to them, in essence forming a subnation with its own language and codes, anthems, and symbols of unity. The Gaelic public sphere came close to the Habermas idyllic hope for communication based on reason, but the Irish filtered their plebian consciousness through their own lens, using fraternity, heritage, nation, and humor as guides.

CHAPTER 2

Inserting the Gaelic
in the Public Sphere

In the closing decades of the nineteenth century, Ireland gazed backward on its winding path toward modernity and nationhood to rediscover and reconstruct what was ancient in its national identity. The reclaiming of indigenous Irish culture became a catalyst for change to create the Gaelic revival of the 1890s, a short-lived movement of high intensity that would help propel its people into and through the Irish wars of independence in 1916–1923.

The Gaelic revival was a reconstruction of the origins of a past civilization identified with multiple markers of national pride and primordial origin, symbols, myths, scholarly traditions, fallen nationalist heroes, and renewed ambitions of nationhood, backed at the turn of the century by an invigorated and more confident Catholic opposition to Protestant leadership and influence both inside and outside the native country.

The opening round of the Gaelic language revival in Ireland can be traced to Douglas Hyde's "de-Anglicization" speech in 1892 in Dublin; he stated, "this awful idea of complete Anglicization . . . has been making inroads upon us for a century. . . . The Ireland of today is the descendant of the Ireland of the seventh century: then the school of Europe and the torch of learning."[1]

Language preservation was prominent in the catalogue of Gaelic options, with the Gaelic League an organizing force on both sides of the Atlantic. But the revival found expression in varied yet connected Gaelic mementos of a past, in industrial arts, theater, leisure, sport, and the legacy of Irish nationalism; the perpetual iconization of Wolfe Tone's eighteenth-century martyrdom is an example. As Úna Ní Bhroiméil states, the revival in the diaspora was "a badge of ethnicity that indicated an ancient and glorious past rather than a demeaned and debased one."[2]

The Gaelic revival would land in Philadelphia's Irish community in the 1890s, which was a period of relative stability for the city's Irish after decades of survival existence and resistance to nativist pressure, which made them a receptive ethnic group eager for the redemptive message of Irish cultural rebirth. Philadelphia's definition of ethnic boundaries in the 1890s was bound to be influenced by the city's own troubled past of ethnic and religious conflict, including the anti-Catholic Riots of 1844, which resulted in a defensiveness born of street violence directed at minority peoples, especially Irish Catholics. The lingering memory of vulnerability created barriers of protection around Irish Philadelphia and motivated an ethnic and religious separatism and the building of Irish Catholic protections and institutions.

And yet, a network of communicative activists in Irish Philadelphia confronted the city's past and emerged to drive the spectacle of Gaelic remembrance; this nucleus of an Irish public sphere would assume responsibility for the city's late-century turn to Irish culture and would take on a messianic tone in its commitment to varied cues of Gaelic content. Philadelphia's Gaelic core would welcome and replicate the movement of cultural nationalism as it organized and expanded in native Ireland from its roots as language education to a Gaelic populism expressed in mass folk festivals, the Gaelic feis.

The language movement and the cultural initiative in Irish America were always connected to the ever-present, at times subterranean but nonetheless consistent, mantra of Irish nationalism inserting its calling in the affairs of its diaspora audience. Úna Ní Bhroiméil notes that the rise of the Gaelic League in Ireland and America was always "allied to other aspects of nationalism."[3] For all its spotlight on the material and conceptual interpretations of Gaelic culture, support for language classes, and festivals of Gaelic arts, the movement in Philadelphia was surrounded and influenced by an adherence to traditional and unfolding forms of Irish nationalism.

For other Irish Philadelphians of the period, dropping in on a reading in Gaelic, a feis at the Academy of Music or taking in one of the many Sunday outings in Washington Park along the Delaware River, the echoes of a deep past, now alive in music, dance, and oratory, may have been instances of longing for identity but were not a motivating life force associated with a Gaelic public sphere.

This majority Irish population of normative integrationist tendencies had much in common with the committed population of Gaelic activists, a mobile working class occupying the same Philadelphia neighborhoods: an attraction to the communal props of neighborhood parish existence and, naturally, Irish ancestry. The social life surrounding Catholic parish identity, its many programs of education, and its opportunities for leisure were more persuasive to many Irish Philadelphians than the reverberations of the active Gaelic revival sweeping across the Atlantic.

Language was the guiding focus of the Irish cultural revival but, as Timothy McMahon points out, saving the Irish language was "a meta-concept, open to multiple understandings."[4] There were also multiple and varied means of communicating the various forms of the cultural revival in Philadelphia, from newspapers and circulating handbills to formal lectures and, as always, casual conversation wherever the Irish gathered at the turn of the nineteenth century.

The message from those active in the language preservation movement of the 1890s and early 1900s was a combination of assorted content, opposition to the intrusion of the language of urban modernism and commerce—English—and a subtle shaming of the Irish who voluntarily let their tongue disappear. The Philo-Celtic Society of Philadelphia admonished its own Irish community for their sloth, warning that native Gaelic was "slowly and surely perishing through the neglect and carelessness of the Irish people."[5] This self-critical lament of a casual disregard of the Gaelic language by its own people, so many of whom were being forced to contend with English as the tongue of commerce required for emigration, was a constant in the discourse of the language preservation movement of the era.

The Philo-Celtic Society of Philadelphia confronted this dualism of language preservation, its impulse to reclaim an ancient past in a bustling diaspora city and the reluctance of its own people to recognize the crisis. In 1903 Philadelphia's Philo-Celtic Society secretary McFadden "recalled the days of the foundation of the Philo-Celtic Society about twenty years ago at a time when Gaelic was treated with indifference almost bordering on contempt even by its own people."[6]

Appeals to Irish Philadelphians to remember their Gaelic were distributed from all directions in the early 1900s. The Clan na Gael of Philadelphia called for "language bigots, for aggressive language propagandists . . . to go out into the highways and byways and speak the language . . . learn the language, make your children learn it, stand up for it . . . the Irish nation depends upon it."[7]

Philadelphia's Rev. Maurice Wilson addressed a crowd at the 1902 Gaelic feis at the Academy of Music in Philadelphia on the leadership of Douglas Hyde and the slow loss of Gaelic, especially in "the hillsides of Connaught and Munster." His words were retrospective, a recalibration of Irishness in the first years of the twentieth century, an excavation of "the buried history" and the unearthing of a "vast Celtic empire over the western and southern portion of the Continent."[8]

The revival's ideological core was language but could not be contained to that one medium as it would, at times, combine with traditions of nineteenth-century Irish nationalism and the simultaneous appearance of the urbanized literary and theater movement surrounding W. B. Yeats. The revival assumed many faces and attached itself to various social forms—Irish American associationalism, popular forms of leisure, industrial arts, music, dance, sport—all supported by the transatlantic initiative of Gaelic substance at the end of the nineteenth century.

The Philo-Celtic Society of Philadelphia Asserts Leadership

The Philo-Celtic Society of Philadelphia was formed in 1882 to preserve the Irish language and Ireland's cultural heritage, and it backed this ambitious agenda by offering evening and weekend classes in Gaelic language instruction to all comers. Its constitution defined its mission as "the preservation and extension of Irish as a spoken language"; it also promised the "establishment in Philadelphia of an Irish Literary Institute."[9] Meetings were weekly, monthly dues were 25¢ and the following rule singled out the Philo-Celtic Society as an organization with a special mission in an already overcrowded urban landscape of Irish civic commitments—"as far as is practical, the Irish language only shall be used at the sessions of the society."[10]

Language classes in Gaelic were held each Sunday evening at Philopatrian Hall in Center City—"instruction free" was promised to all comers.[11] A circulating letter of appeal and encouragement to Irish Philadelphia noted, "We would again respectfully invite all who desires to learn the language . . . to join our classes. Courage to begin is the only thing wanting . . . every member of the Philo-Celtic Society will be most happy to assist all who have the patriotism to learn and assist in preserving our language."[12]

The Philo-Celtic Society followed the norms of nineteenth-century associationalism as detailed in its rulebook. The final business and discussion meeting of the Philo-Celtic Society in June 1899, before a summer break of four months, with classes resuming in October, was held at its temporary home on 16th and Arch Streets. It was recorded that "the members seemed anxious to congratulate each other on their success in the classes." President Francis O'Kane chaired the business portion of the season's final meeting, reporting that the society had $175 left in the treasury; O'Kane also noted that $25 "had been sent to Patrick Ford of the 'Irish World' for the Irish language fund."[13]

The society would move its quarters wherever space could be found before eventually settling on the Center City location near Philadelphia's Parkway. Its rooms at 12th and Arch were open every evening for language study, with Saturday evenings "devoted to the study of Irish history."[14] Irish history and language education were often combined in the curriculum of the society, and a meeting in 1894 was devoted to the memory of Archbishop MacHale of Tuam from the west of Ireland, a figure of nationalist sympathies and an activist for land reform who conversed with his people in Gaelic. At that meeting, Philo-Celtic Society president Francis O'Kane gave a brief lecture on "the life and works of the great Archbishop of the West."[15]

In 1894, Sunday meetings opened at 7:30 P.M. with the business of running the society, with classes starting at 8:00 in Industrial Art Hall, 314 North Broad Street. President O'Kane usually chaired the meeting. Francis O'Kane seemed

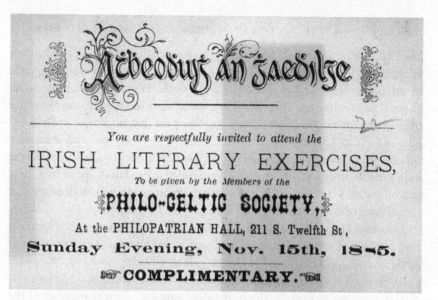

Announcement of an 1885 Philo-Celtic Society event. Source: CHRC.

to manage everything in the early years from teaching and fundraising to event preparation and publicity. In 1899, in a letter to the city's Irish American press, he reminded Irish Philadelphia that fall classes were resuming in October after the summer break and pointed out that the "free instruction" was "an opportunity that all lovers of Ireland should avail themselves of."[16]

The Center City headquarters of the Philo-Celtic Society was not the only location in the city for Irish language instruction as Gaelic League branches in Philadelphia would also offer Irish language classes. In industrial Manayunk, a branch of the Philadelphia Gaelic League opened in 1899 at St. John's Catholic Church. Philo-Celtic Society president Francis O'Kane was again on hand, assisted by Father Brehony, who promised the use of the schoolroom and library for weeknight and Sunday afternoon classes. Close to a hundred new students signed on that evening in Manayunk for classes—"books were distributed and classes formed at once."[17]

In June 1903 at St. Edward's Church in the industrial port neighborhood of Kensington, a branch of the Gaelic League of Pennsylvania, the Sarsfield Gaelic School (named after one of Ireland's aristocratic rebels, Patrick Sarsfield), held its annual gathering at the close of its academic year of Gaelic language classes. The Germantown Gaelic chorus joined the festivities at St. Edward's, providing music and song by "white-robed little choristers who transformed the floor space into a fairy scene."[18] In 1903 the Germantown Gaelic School also celebrated the end of its academic year for its forty students taking Gaelic language classes, with the "Kerry Dance" presented as "lads and lasses danced against a scenic background of Irish woodland."[19]

But the Philo-Celtic Society was the epicenter of Gaelic language resurgence in Philadelphia. It was a grassroots organization seeking ordinary Irish men and women to commit and submit to the discipline of language instruction outlined in Gaelic grammar texts, in an extension of the Gaelic League approach in native Ireland. The Philo-Celtic Society welcomed newcomers but always encouraged native Irish speakers to come forward, reporting constantly that Philadelphia was an Irish town with a hidden subculture of people who were fluent in Gaelic; one of its broadsides proclaimed that "Philadelphia, with an Irish-born population of over one hundred thousand, of whom ten thousand can converse in the Irish language," was an ideal location for a renaissance of the Gaelic language.[20] Úna Ní Bhroiméil estimates that there were 40,000 Gaelic speakers in the 1890s in Philadelphia, with recent arrivals also fluent in English.[21]

In 1888, orator Patrick Murphy finished his speech to the Philo-Celtic Society of Philadelphia by conjuring up Ireland's common enemy: "John Bull came to the 'The Noble Island,' the original Celtic name of Ireland, with the bull in his pocket and the 'devil' in his heart, and tried to suppress the ancient language, but it was still in existence . . . modern Babylon must be destroyed and an empire after the grand old Celtic order, be erected in its ashes." Note that in the report of this event, "Babylon" referred to the "British Empire."[22]

Marking the Years: Philo-Celtic Longevity in Philadelphia's Gaelic Revival

In 1888 the Philo-Celtic Society of Philadelphia celebrated its sixth year in existence in spacious Philopatrian Hall with an address in Gaelic, by John Lyons, followed by "recitations, songs and solos" by association members. To cap the occasion, Rev. Peter Murphy "delivered a lively oration on the Celtic language"; he stated in the hyperbolic style of cultural redemption that the Irish language was "the most ancient in existence . . . spoken by the ancient Persians two thousand years before Hebrew was known."[23]

The notation of the society's origins in Philadelphia and its ongoing years was always cause for a celebratory gathering at the close of the academic year, and the June 1903 event at St. Joseph's College consisted of "songs, recitations and readings in both English and Irish."[24] In May 1890 a similar academic year-ending gathering of the Philo-Celtic Society offered a program of Irish songs and poetry readings in Gaelic and a closing speech by Reverend Murphy of St. Teresa's Catholic Church first in Irish, then English, with the event described as a "grand success."[25]

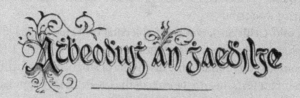

Thirty-third Anniversary
CELEBRATION
OF THE
Philadelphia Philo-Celtic Society
FOR THE
Preservation of the Irish Language
HORTICULTURAL HALL
Broad Street, below Locust

THURSDAY EVE'G, MAY 6th, 1915

LECTURE
"THE TWO IRELANDS"
BY THE
Celebrated German Celtic Scholar
KUNO MEYER, Ph. D.
Of the University of Berlin

CELEBRATION OPENS AT 8.15 P. M.

Circulating handbill of the Philo-Celtic Society of Philadelphia, 1915. Source: CHRC.

Murphy's theme reflected the popular ideology of Celtic longing that circulated among the cultural nationalists of Philadelphia at the turn of the nineteenth century, a retrograde exploration of a past Celtic civilization for a settled diaspora people in a gritty, now culturally vibrant, industrial city. This combination of mystic nostalgia and deep search for a past of distinction, a mythic source of long-buried pride for a people with ambitious, modernist hopes, defined the times—the 1890s—and the idealistic energy of a cadre of Irish Philadelphians committed to multiple visions, one of the past, another of the future. The Philo-Celtic Society celebrated its existence in Philadelphia again in 1892: "a well-attended literary and musical entertainment was given by the Philo-Celtic Society of Philadelphia."[26]

We can thus detect the dualistic missionary zeal of the language movement as it was organized in late-nineteenth-century Gaelic Philadelphia—the espoused public mission of the Philo-Celtic Society of Philadelphia was to "preserve and cultivate the Irish language," but its broader appeal was often phrased in traditional nationalist imagery. The Philo-Celtic Society of Philadelphia, whose motto was "Revive the Irish language," railed against the cultural colonialism of the English language, proclaiming that "to enlarge the English and extinguish the Irish has been the steady and consistent aim of the English government for centuries."[27] In an open letter to Gaelic Philadelphia, the Philo-Celtic Society reminded readers that language revival also required an opposition to British hegemony and made Thomas Davis and his record of revolt an icon—"a nation," said Thomas Davis, "without a language is only half a nation."[28]

John Hutchinson posits "cultural nationalism as a distinctive form of nationalism . . . articulated by secular intellectuals."[29] The sustaining pulse of the Philo-Celtic Society was an intelligentsia of the Catholic Irish and existed in its administration, a slate of seven officers, a librarian, and an executive council of nine committed to student education in language classes; twenty-four students were counted for the fall term in 1894.[30] The leadership of the Philo-Celtic Society of Philadelphia in 1890 was male dominant but also included women on its board, with Lizie McSorles as treasurer and Ellen O'Leary and Mary Mahoney as council members.[31]

The search for students was constantly on the minds of the association's leaders; secretary Bernard McGillian appealed for more students in the mainstream Catholic press in 1900, challenging Irish Philadelphia, "Are you men and women of Irish birth or blood satisfied that your families should grow up in ignorance of that grand old tongue?" McGillian also reached out to the Irish speakers of Philadelphia to come back, take classes, read literature, and "bring your sons and daughters with you."[32] The fall term in 1900 welcomed fifteen new students, all "beginners" starting classes for the first time at Industrial Hall.[33]

LEISURE AND LANGUAGE EDUCATION

Learning the Irish language from grammar texts in evening classes offered by the Philo-Celtic Society of Philadelphia may have been tedious and demanding, but there was time for leisure imbedded within the more serious demands of the curriculum. For example, on a winter's evening in December 1903 the Philo-Celtic Society invited "the entire population of the Irish race in Philadelphia" to its fundraising evening of games with prizes at Odd Fellows Temple in Center City. Those attending were to "be treated to Irish music galore, including the harp and bagpipes."[34]

St. Patrick's Day in 1903 was celebrated in the Philo-Celtic Society with "songs and recitations in both Gaelic and English," with society president Francis O'Kane welcoming those in attendance.[35] The Philo-Celtic Society also managed to put together a Gaelic chorus, holding rehearsals and performances at its home location and neighborhood locations in the city.[36]

Humor, the status-leveling elixir of Irish Americans in their primary groups, also penetrated and enlivened the assembly rooms of the Philo-Celtic Society. The weekly meeting of the society in fall 1900 presented J. J. Lyons forward who delivered a "very interesting story in the Gaelic tongue . . . which was productive of much amusement."[37]

BRANCHES OF SUPPORT: PHILADELPHIA'S GAELIC LEAGUE

The active language movement community in Philadelphia was bolstered by the Philadelphia wing of the American Gaelic League, the city's branch society, which dated from 1881 and had a membership reported to be 1,000 in 1902.[38] Philadelphia's language activists would join hands and collaborate to sponsor and support many cultural events surrounding language preservation and Gaelic revival in the late 1800s and early 1900s. Tom Garvin notes that it was "exotic Gaelic cultural materials" that captured the attention of the turn-of-the-century population on both sides of the Atlantic, offering them a retrograde gaze in the face of modernizing social forces.[39]

Irish-language classes offered after work hours and on weekends were going to be difficult for Gaelic Leaguers to maintain on a consistent basis, as the small population of committed students comprised an insufficient nucleus for a movement of mass circulation. To supplement the language classes and promote the cultural revival, Irish cultural fairs and festivals were organized and penetrated the Gaelic sphere in the early 1900s, sponsored by the Philadelphia Gaelic League in concert with the Philo-Celtic Society and other organizations sympathetic to Gaelic revival. These festivals served to popularize the turn toward culture and featured contests with prizes in various categories, written essays in Gaelic, poetry, storytelling, music, dance, and industrial arts.

Irish Philadelphians were peppered with various interpretations of the mission of the Gaelic League. An interview reported in the city's mainstream press in 1903 with an elder from Ireland suggested that the work of the Gaelic League was "to keep the Irish from excitement and from hectic politics; to work for temperance and anti-emigration . . . to foster honesty and direct thinking." The Irish language was a vernacular of "sentiment" fixed to the "character and temperament of the Celt," and supported "chiefly by the farthings of the poor."[40]

The cultural revival in Philadelphia spawned associations besides the Philo-Celtic Society and the city's branches of the National Gaelic League of America; the Celtic Association of Philadelphia appeared in 1901 inspired by a feis in Philadelphia. The Celtic Association aimed to redress the buried contributions of Celtic culture, exposing authors of "material progress, arts, education, science, literature, philosophy." This was a society of some means as yearly dues were set at $5, with individual monthly dues also $5.[41]

Celtic Association President Thompson delivered a lengthy lesson in Celtic history in Witherspoon Hall on a November evening in 1901. "Europe between 500 B.C. and 300 B.C. was Celtic territory," he explained, and reminded his audience that its language resonated in "the great rivers and mountain ranges, from Italy to the Baltic coast, and from the Vistula to the Atlantic."[42]

Thompson went on to deliver an address at the 1902 December feis at the Academy of Music. President Thompson promised to form a library of Celtic literature and to welcome Celts from all lands, Bretons, Welsh and naturally "Irishmen from the green island." Philadelphia and indeed the whole of America were special places for the Celt "to refute the slanders which charged him with being an unpractical dreamer, a willing idler, a dependent on abler stocks, ever rampant."[43] Purging the floating imagery of the wandering Irish given to short bursts of intense physical labor and lacking in the ethic of sustained production and achievement was on the minds of Irish Philadelphia during the years of culture regeneration.

The Gaelic revival in Philadelphia went to great lengths to elevate its diaspora citizens and arm them with a proud historical record. Gaelic language and culture mixed easily with more militant brands of nationalism, forming a united front of nationalist opposition in which aligned concepts and associated people mingled freely. An excerpt from an 1893 circulating pamphlet, the *Irish Echo*, which was devoted to the cultural movement, established the inner connection of nationalisms as it made reference to the Young Ireland rising of 1848: "I wondered at those men of Forty-eight, those young men to whom everything must be forgiven, they were so purely and sincerely Irish—often I have marveled how it never occurred to them, gifted and brilliant as they were, to study and write the language of the Celt."[44]

Philadelphia's Irish culturists bound themselves with other elements of nationalist content and naturally mingled with the many Irish American associations

Sheet music to "The Star-Spangled Banner in Irish," 1900. Source: Digital Library@ Villanova University.

in the city, a constellation of groups of various agendas coalescing around the disparate yet connected facets of revival. During the height of the Irish war of independence a meeting was held after the race convention of the United Irish-American Societies of Philadelphia, an umbrella organization of Irish America associations in Philadelphia; the gathering was reported to have drawn 30,000 members.[45]

In addition to the leading groups, the meeting included the Clan na Gael, the Ancient Order of Hibernians, the Irish Foresters, and the Irish Catholic Benevolent League, as well as representatives of the cultural movement, St. Enda's Gaelic School of Philadelphia and the Gaelic League of Philadelphia.[46] In these years of Gaelic import, a constellation of forces with cultural overtones often found reason to cooperate in disseminating the message of Ireland and its past.

Transatlantic Connections of the Irish-Language Movement

Philadelphia's Irish-language activists replicated aspects of Gaelic League events staged in Ireland during the early 1900s, the model a transnational replica of an Irish feis, an interactive festival that promoted language education within an assembly of associated activities and enterprises of Irish content. The Gaelic League and its program of education and promotional festivals was established in Ireland by the 1890s. The diffusion to Philadelphia's community of the Gaelic League program, including language classes after work hours and mass folk festivals, was gradual but decisive in setting a similar pattern for Gaelic revival in the Irish Diaspora. The Philadelphia Irish absorbed the content and promotional style of the Gaelic revival, employing communicative methods such as the ethnic newspaper with weekly updates on Gaelic events in Ireland, circulating pamphlets and reprints of lectures, Sunday oration from parish priests, and conversation in society meeting halls.

The comparative context of communication and cultural diffusion across the Irish Atlantic explains the rapid growth of the spirit of revival in North American ethnic communities; the Irish in Philadelphia would put their own stamp on local events influenced, at times, by Gaelic League agents dispatched to the city, but essentially they replicated a cultural form that first appeared in Ireland. There was naturally a minor time lag between the Irish/Ireland movement in Ireland and its transfer to the diaspora, and yet the Gaelic League both in Ireland and in Philadelphia followed similar patterns of growth and expansion, in an ideological drift to a movement singularly Catholic, educational, and entertaining in the evolved style of Gaelic populism.

In Ireland, the Gaelic-language feis could attract huge crowds in a festive atmosphere spanning several days, an example of the return of a pre-Famine rural leisure in a post-Famine land devoid of joy. The serious agenda of language preservation would eventually share space with the entertainment attraction of public gatherings designed to attract crowds and attention to the original mission of the Gaelic League.

In Ireland, at the 1904 feis of the Nine Glens of Antrim, Protestants and Catholics in this northern area of Ireland combined to observe "120 competitions" in "language proficiency, dancing, singing, athletics" as well as "industrial exhibitions," an extensive array of options designed to maximize the size of the crowd.[47] In 1902 in O'Meath, just north of Dublin, it was reported that "about 7,000 with bands" turned out for the feis, while in Newcastle, County Down, it was estimated that "upwards of 10,000" were in attendance for its version of popular Gaelic culture.[48]

In Philadelphia's Gaelic community, festivals attracting massive crowds gathered in sport arenas and urban parks that had been converted for the day's mass Irish "picnic," a similar spectacle of moving cultural parts, Irish music, jigs, oratory, sport, and games accompanied by one or more bands continuously pouring out Irish tunes. The Clan na Gael Games of 1914 in Philadelphia's Central Park featured "two large dancing platforms, with three pieces of music on each, to consist of bagpipes, piccolo, and fiddle [that] will play all afternoon and evening." The event also included a hurling match, with the Wolfe Tone and the Sarsfield Hurling Clubs in competition.[49]

In 1895 Philadelphia Hibernians eschewed the Fourth of July festivities at Independence Hall and instead celebrated at Washington Park a few miles north at the Irish National Games sponsored by the city's branches of the Ancient Order of Hibernians (AOH). Over 40,000 Irish Americans turned up for a summer day of sport and games and an excursion into Irish culture and entertainment. Similar to the tests of Gaelic proficiency and essay competitions seen in Ireland's Gaelic League gatherings, the summer picnic events offered competitions and prizes in the Irish jig and reel, with two bands of music working the grounds all day.[50]

IRELAND'S LANGUAGE DIPLOMATS ARE DISPATCHED TO PHILADELPHIA

The Gaelic festival format in Philadelphia expanded with the assistance of Gaelic League agents dispatched from Ireland. In October 1912, the Gaelic League's Daniel O'Connor of Kerry made his way to Philadelphia to help organize a folk festival around various Gaelic arts. He partnered his efforts with local Irish American associations and mutual aid societies, as well as those devoted to language restoration, a strategy that promised more inclusion from a wider swath of Irish Philadelphia—it was announced that the 1912 feis at Convention Hall would be "under the auspices of the Gaelic League of Ireland in conjunction with the Philadelphia Philo-Celtic Club."[51]

This three-day Philadelphia event featured thirty-five competitions in various disciplines associated with Gaelic pastimes and language. Promotional

Clan-Na-Gael Games

(SANCTIONED BY THE A. A. U.)

WILL BE HELD

SATURDAY, JULY 4, 1914

AT

CENTRAL PARK - 4400 N. 5th ST.

Games Commence at 1 P. M. Sharp.

Prizes Are Handsome Silver Cups

for First, Second and Third Places, in each event, except Five Mile Race, for which Large Cups will be awarded for First Place, and Smaller Cups for Next Four Places. Six Gold, Silver and Bronze Medals will be awarded in Boys' Race.

SPECIAL LARGE CUP FOR CLUB SCORING THE MOST POINTS IN THE MEET

Events Open to Registered Amateur Athletes

HANDICAP

100 YARD DASH	440 YARD DASH	FIVE MILE RUN
220 YARD DASH	880 YARD DASH	ONE MILE RELAY
220 YARD HURDLES	ONE MILE RUN	HIGH JUMP
BROAD JUMP	POLE VAULT	HOP, STEP AND JUMP
	SHOT PUT	

SCRATCH
BOYS' RACE (UNDER 15 YEARS,) SACK RACE

ENTRANCE FEE, 25c   **$1.00 for RELAY TEAM**

Send Entries and Fees to EUGENE J. O'KEEFFE, Irish-American Club, 726 Spruce St., Phila.

Irish Jigs, Reels, Hornpipes and Figure Dancing—Special Medals Will Be Awarded

Handsome Silver Cup Prizes

GAELIC FOOTBALL MATCH, between the Robert Emmet Club, of West Phila., and the **SHAMROCK CLUB**, of North Phila.

EXHIBITION HURLING MATCH, between the **WOLFE TONE CLUB** and the **SARSFIELD CLUB**.

OFFICERS OF GAMES COMMITTEE:

EDWARD McGINTY, Chairman.   HENRY McCARNEY, Vice Chairman.   JAMES DONNELLY, Recording Secretary
MICHAEL McGINN, Financial Secretary.   EDWARD KEARNS, Treasurer.   WILLIAM TOBIN, Master of Games.

Irish and American Dances all day in the Pavilion. Irish Jigs, Reels and Hornpipes danced all day to Irish Music, on four platforms specially erected for that purpose.

Admission to the Park - - 25 Cents

Clan-na-Gael Journal announcement of the Fourth of July Clan na Gael Games in 1914. Source: Digital Library@Villanova University.

communiqués tapped into the demand for an Irish history as ancient achievement pointing out that the feis descended from "the High King of Ireland in
800 B.C.," that his capital was in Tara, the "nucleus of a great parliament." Philadelphia's fall Gaelic language festival of 1912 would be a challenge for many, it
was announced—"all the singing, story-telling and essays will be in Gaelic."[52]

The feis of fall 1912 was followed up a few months later with another Gaelic
fair in the winter of 1913 at the Academy of Music, assisted again by Ireland's
tireless Gaelic League envoy Daniel O'Connor. The format had now become standard featuring "story telling, Gaelic recitation, conversation, essays, rendering
of Gaelic song and the singing of a Gaelic chorus."[53] The feis of 1913 was promoted
in a circulating pamphlet distributed to Irish Philadelphia.[54]

The pamphlet text educated its public on the meaning of feis, "a Gaelic word
meaning parliament, convention or festival"; its ancient heritage in a modern
diaspora setting an event "revived by the Gaelic League in its policy of reviving
the language, literature and customs of Ireland."[55]

1900S PHILADELPHIA: THE CITY OF *FEISEANNA*

The localized branches of the Gaelic League in Ireland were havens of organizing activity; as McMahon observes of preparation efforts in native Ireland, the
committees and feis participants would devote weeks and months on "preparation, planning, rehearsal, memorization, and study that was both personal and
shared."[56] The planning required in committee work, the individual and collective submission to a division of labor, cooperation, persistence and the creation
of novel communicative methods to distribute the word of Gaelic revival all
describe the collaborative efforts of Philadelphia's determined cultural workers
as the Irish feis was introduced to the city.

By the early 1900s, a Philadelphia style had evolved to promote and celebrate
the various Gaelic arts and the Irish language, a public festival, a Gaelic feis
derived from the "great national assembly of ancient Ireland,"[57] set in a vacuous
central city hall exposing audiences to performances and tests of native language
expression, music, dance, essay recitations, poetry, and oratory in Gaelic, often
followed by English translations. The "Great Feis" of 1913 in Philadelphia's Academy of Music featured John McCormack, "the great Irish Tenor," who promised
to "sing in Gaelic and English at the Philadelphia Feis."[58]

Philadelphia was the host of the "Grand Feis and Oireachtas musical festival" in the fall of 1902 at the gilded Academy of Music. Edward P. MacKenna of
the executive committee of the national Gaelic Association was on hand as was
Francis O'Kane, the energetic, perennial president of the Philo-Celtic Society
of Philadelphia; these and other Irish American dignitaries represented "the
most renowned and learned men of the Irish race in this country." MacKenna

DO CHUM GLOIRE DE AGUS ONORA NA HEIREANN

PHILADELPHIA'S

FIRST

ANNUAL

FEIS

WILL BE HELD IN

ACADAMY OF MUSIC

February 11th, 12th and 13th, 1913

At 8 p. m. Doors open at 7:15 p. m.

Tickets at Bernard J. McIlvaine's, 1617 Chestnut St.,
Philadelphia; Academy of Music Booking
Office, and at Feis Office, Room 27,
Parkway Building.

Prices: $3.00, 2.50, 2.00, 1.50, 1.00 and 75c.

Organized by The Gaelic League of Ireland
in conjunction with
The Philadelphia Philo Celtic Society

Circulating handbill of the 1913 Philadelphia Feis. Source: CHRC.

reminded the audience of the mission of the Gaelic League, a movement to retain the "Irish language, the music, literature, folklore, history and antiquities of the Emerald Isle."[59]

The year 1902 was thus a busy one for the city's language preservationists as Irish Philadelphia hosted the National Convention of the Gaelic League in the fall, a three-day event that required substantial preparation. A planning meeting was held in advance at Philadelphia's Industrial Hall, chaired by Francis O'Kane of the Philo-Celtic Society with representatives of Irish American societies, including the Sarsfield Society, the Eugene O'Curry Society, and other associations, resulting in a coalition of Irish civic energy required for the organization and promotion of large Irish gatherings in the early 1900s.[60]

P.C.B. O'Donovan gave a talk at the 1902 National Gaelic Convention in Philadelphia on "Gaelic vs. Anglo-Saxon Civilization," and professors Robinson and J.D.M. Ford of Harvard gave lectures on the Irish language.[61] O'Donovan reminded the audience that "Ireland's sorrow . . . for many years has been that she is prone to listen to honeyed words rather than to honest criticism."[62] The Philo-Celtic Society of Philadelphia asserted its narrower linguistic presence at the national gathering of Irish American Gaelic Leaguers with a show, "Tongue and Motherland"; the evening also included "harp and bagpipe and native dances."[63] The grand three-day caucus ended as most important Irish American events did in the late nineteenth century with a reception at the Irish American Club in Philadelphia.[64]

In August 1902, the Pennsylvania AOH gathered further north, in Wilkes-Barre, Pennsylvania, a coal-mining center 120 miles north of Philadelphia. Patrick Donohue, AOH state president from Philadelphia, spoke at the conference, joined by the voices of representatives of the Knights of St. John and the Catholic Foresters of America. Donohue stated to his AOH brothers, "The feeling is generally that something should be done to further the work of the Gaelic League, both in this country and in Ireland."[65]

In late fall 1910 Rev. Michael O'Flanagan of Summerhill College in Sligo, Ireland, was invited to Philadelphia by Rev. Gerald P. Coglan of Lady of Mercy Catholic Church of Philadelphia. O'Flanagan lectured his Philadelphia audience on the progress of the Gaelic League in Ireland, explaining, "The Gaelic League aims at developing and intensifying the national spirit of Ireland and the Irish people, no matter where located, by fostering all that is best and most characteristic in the Irish race—the national language, literature, art, industry, music and pastimes."[66]

He reported over 7,000 existing branches in Ireland supported by a staff of "130 organizers and traveling teachers." O'Flanagan noted that "the Gaelic League is binding Ireland into a solid national unit" and America was the location of support, so a "national body" of the Gaelic League in America was a necessity for the language movement to progress in Ireland.[67] These messages circulated in Irish Philadelphia, proselytizers from Ireland like O'Flanagan promoting the Gaelic revival.

The Philadelphia feis invited popular contributions from the Irish community, as its promotional pamphlet proclaimed in 1913:

If you can sing an Irish song, tell an Irish story,
Recite an Irish poem or write an Irish essay,
If you can play Irish airs on the violin, piano,
Flute, bag-pipe, war-pipe or Highland pipe,
If you can dance an Irish jig, reel, hornpipe . . .
Write at once to the Gaelic League, 207 Parkway, Philadelphia.[68]

This broad appeal to a wide audience of potential amateur performers of Gaelic popular arts was a strategy of the Gaelic League and its desire to spread a Gaelic revival gospel; the call for all comers in Irish Philadelphia on the piano or hornpipe also distinguishes the language/cultural movement from the more cultivated Yeats Literary revival.

Joseph Clarke's poem, "The Spadesmen of the Gael," was an example of the populist tone in the program for the Philadelphia feis of 1913:

League of the Gael, its praise be sung!
God mark them all to grace,
Who sound in Ireland's ancient tongue
The watchword of our race![69]

Communication of Gaelic League activities across the Atlantic was naturally delayed, but Philadelphia's *Irish American Review and Celtic Literary Advocate*, in its weekly "Gaelic Notes" column, kept the reading public informed, drawing the language movement closer on both sides of the Atlantic; the *Review* was a weekly, like other Irish American newspapers, available Saturday mornings in neighborhood locations for 5¢ a copy. The grand festival of Ireland's Gaelic League, the Dublin *oireachtas*, was a momentous event of interest to Irish Philadelphians. The third annual oireachtas in 1899 was judged to be "more successful than either of its predecessors" with competitions in a wide array of events, song, oratory, recitation, Irish dance, essay writing—it was also noticed that "the public proceedings . . . were most enthusiastic . . . but there was so much English spoken."[70]

The "Gaelic Notes" column also produced its odd critics, including Father Hogan, who spoke up at the Central Branch of the Gaelic League in Dublin, "the Irish in America neglected the old country. The Irish millionaires there had not done a mortal thing to perpetuate and improve the Irish tongue . . . while others intermarried with those of foreign nations."[71]

The Philadelphia Irish in the early 1900s came to mimic the technique and content of the original Gaelic League model, including its adaptive pivot toward popular mass festivals with tests of language dexterity and essay competitions with prizes awarded, as well as Gaelic exhibitions of music, dance, and industrial arts, thus serving as a supplement to the systematic learning through weekly language classes.

In the busy winter calendar of 1913 another festival of the various Gaelic arts took place in Philadelphia's Convention Hall joined by a local church chorus and other choirs displaying tests of proficiency in "language[,] . . . story telling, Gaelic recitation, conversation, essays, rendering of Gaelic song and the singing of a Gaelic chorus."[72] The air in Convention Hall would resonate with Irish music from "selections of airs and dance tunes, flute, Irish pipes, Irish war-pipes, Highland pipers band, Highland pipes and piano solos," accompanied by dancers.[73]

The education of young minds, focusing on exposure to Gaelic icons of a noble past in Ireland juxtaposed with a modernizing present in Philadelphia, was an essential motive in setting the agenda of the Philadelphia Gaelic League celebration. Students in the 1913 Philo-Celtic Society gathering at Convention Hall were asked to submit an essay for a prize on the topic, "the influence of the Irish race in American progress."[74]

In October 1923, Francis O'Kane, the indefatigable past president of the Philo-Celtic Society of Philadelphia, was laid to rest; his funeral was followed by a reception at the Irish American Club of Philadelphia. Philadelphia's Joseph McGarrity, Clan na Gael leader and president of the Irish American Club, spoke, as did Luke Dillon; Joseph McNelis of the Gaelic League of Philadelphia recalled the life and contributions of O'Kane, who had, in addition to so many other projects and promotions of the Gaelic tongue, helped organize Douglas Hyde's tour of Philadelphia in 1905. It was stated that O'Kane, a "noted teacher of Gaelic," combined his devotion to the revival of the Irish language with "Ireland's fight for freedom," a dual allegiance to a broad expression of Irish nationalism shared by many Gaelic activists on both sides of the Atlantic.[75]

Philadelphia Welcomes Douglas Hyde, 1905

Douglas Hyde, founder of the Gaelic League in Ireland and its leading international voice, found his way to Philadelphia during his second tour of the United States in 1905. His visit, which was scheduled at the Academy of Music, came under "the auspices of the Philo-League" of Philadelphia.[76] The planning for Hyde's visit was naturally extensive, and a committee representing a broad swath of Gaelic Philadelphia was organized.

Hyde's exploits in Ireland were well known in Irish Philadelphia; Irish Philadelphians could read in their own ethnic press of Hyde's 1899 visit to Castlebar in the west of Ireland in his talk titled "The Irish Language," in which he stated, "The language of the Gael should be the language of the people of Ireland . . . [and] he hoped that fathers and mothers would instruct their children in Gaelic."[77]

The initial planning session to prepare for the Gaelic League president also elicited donations from financial sources of varying positions on Irish nationalism. Philadelphia's Clan na Gael pledged $1,500 to the event, the Clan's president Joseph McGarrity pitched in $500 of his own money, and AOH Division 36 proudly proclaimed that this one division had also pledged $100.[78] Irish Philadelphia prepared itself to come out in lavish mode for Hyde as his reception would be met by representatives of the "allied Irish societies and a battalion of St. Joseph's cadets" as well as Philadelphia's Archbishop Ryan.[79]

The link between the pugnacious nationalism of Philadelphia's Clan na Gael and the more delicate brand of the Gaelic League might be considered incongruous, but Hyde's reputation and visit induced a binding tolerance across Gaelic groups, as asserted in Ireland's case for nationhood in the 1900s. The Clan na Gael encouraged its membership, "two thousand sons and daughters of Erin," to attend a three-act play at the Academy of Music depicting Robert Emmet's life. In the second act of the play, the Philo-Celtic Society dancing school gave an exhibition by its students who "introduced many old Irish dances."[80]

SOCIAL HIERARCHIES AND GAELIC REVIVAL

Tom Garvin analyzes the class nature of the Nationalist elite in Ireland of the years 1916–1923 and points out that the overlap with cultural revival sympathies and membership in the Gaelic League was significant.[81] Garvin suggests that the revolutionary elite was of the middle classes, reflecting a "petit bourgeois radicalism" found in other strata of the Irish population.[82]

McMahon studied the class makeup of the mature Gaelic League in Ireland and described a varied stratification of language supporters, certainly of the middle stratum, but overall more plebian in nature. Urban Ireland, Dublin, Belfast, and Cork reflected the role of those in the professions, with clergy included as well as managers and employers of businesses. A majority of Gaelic Leaguers were workers of varied occupational backgrounds, including clerks, minor civil servants, teachers, shop assistants, "black-coated workers," skilled artisans.[83]

In Ireland, mutual aid and workers' associations joined forces with the language initiative and adopted resolutions of support setting up Gaelic League branches under the umbrella of the established, central society. In Dublin, the Wellington Quay Workingmen's Club and Inicore Workingman's Club had a Gaelic League branch; in Limerick, the pork butchers society aligned with the Gaelic League, and on remote Achill Island, it was observed that the "the shop assistants, the artisans, the schoolteachers, and the police sat down side by side with the commonest and lowliest of the people" to study Gaelic.[84] Derry recorded shop assistants and those from the "factory hand class" who found time to devote to language classes and the agenda of the Gaelic League.[85]

All over Ireland in the early 1900s associations moved to align their cause and membership with the Gaelic League; in Limerick, voluntary associations of workers, drapers, mechanics, butchers, shop assistants as well as the foresters and odd fellows joined arms with the Gaelic League to support establishing St. Patrick's Day a national holiday.[86] Similarly, in Philadelphia, the Irish-language activists were recruited from the varied layers of an Irish American occupational hierarchy, reflecting the lines of stratification existing in the industrial city of the 1890s; for example, Francis O'Kane was an immigrant from County Kerry.

"BLOCKED AMBITIONS" IN REVIVAL THEORY

John Hutchinson theorizes that entrenched Protestant minorities in the civil service, the state bureaucracy, the professions, and other occupational opportunities blocked rising expectations in Ireland from the Catholic upper-middle and petit bourgeois classes in the late 1800s. This "embittered intelligentsia," which included graduates of Catholic elite schools such as Clongowes and Castlerock, and the new universities at Dublin, Cork, and Galway, funding itself inhibited from favorable career options, pivoted away from an integrative path with established Protestant power to embrace the winds of change, including the Gaelic League and its options for action and expression, language, culture, and, for many, oppositional politics.[87]

However, in Philadelphia, it can be argued that the Irish Americans in the 1890s were not blocked from access to an upward mobility, that segments of the second generation from the Famine years were reaching for acceptance, mimicking patterns associated with established Anglo Philadelphia, constructing institutions of their own, voluntary associations, convivial gatherings, and charity organizations, and cultivating a style suitable for the aspiring, Catholic, urban gentleman. The Catholic clubs of Philadelphia, as represented by the ambitious young men of the Catholic Young Men's Archdiocesan Union, exemplified this new Irish American.

Anti-Catholic prejudice naturally lingered in the waning decades of the nineteenth century, but Irish Philadelphians had achieved a measure of arrival, blunted nativist suspicions, penetrated industrial positions—especially the city's trades—and had been freed by century's end to pursue integrationist options or turn to a preoccupation with identity, with the Gaelic language as a symbol of that search for meaning.

For those in the Gaelic public sphere, the embrace of Irish nationalist expression was partly a voluntary choice. but it was also a reflexive response of decades of exposure to and consumption of an inherited discourse of nationalist ideology, and less a reaction to a static, restrictive social structure with tight boundaries of sectarian opportunity. The persistent monologue of Irish nationalism, passed along as common knowledge, permeated generations of Irish America as a commanding conclusion on the past and a guide to the future. In this respect, E. P. Thompson understands the power of ideas cemented as truths, customs, and concepts, floating forward without opposition, and thus creating "a state of mind in which established structures of authority and even modes of exploitation appear to be in the very course of nature."[88]

The gaze of Irish cultural nationalism during its peak years in the late 1800s and early 1900s was, as Hutchinson reminds us, literate, modern, and forward-looking, and thus serving as a basis for a separate nation with contributions from theater and literature down to folksy exhibitions of native Irish industry.[89] This futuristic hope and vision were backed by visions of a past, Celtic warriors and ancient hurlers, a nostalgia for a departed self-sufficiency in rural Ireland reduced to subsistence by the intrusion of economic markets and social forces more national and international than regional, by native music and dance, and, most importantly, a dying language in the throes of salvation.

Fueling and sustaining Irish cultural and political nationalism was conflict, a communal consensus on the persistence of foes in opposition to the ancestral portrait behind an emerging progress; Hutchinson observes that "conflict is built into the cultural nationalist conception of the nation," with the dismantling of the Irish language portrayed as another victim of British hegemony and the savior a mobilized Irish populace pure in its defense of its national language.[90]

In Ireland, we see the energetic activity of certain status elites, a popular following and an ascending, at times frustrated, Catholic intelligentsia; in this way, a secularism combined with mystic overtones of a spiritual past to produce a cultural nationalism of short-lived influence and resonance. In Philadelphia's Irish community, the turn toward culture in native Ireland did not unfold unnoticed; cultural nationalism also required a vanguard of committed leaders and motivated followers to introduce and spread the ideas and platforms of Irish cultural revival; President O'Kane and his fellow language teachers and board members of the Philo-Celtic Society of Philadelphia were prime examples of the Gaelic initiative.

The initial, substantive message of the Gaelic League—its strategy of preserving the language through evening and weekend educational classes—was followed on both sides of the Atlantic. Conversing in Gaelic outside the classrooms of the Philo-Celtic Society of Philadelphia was problematic for most students; class attendance and an immersion in the language of the Gaels was more an emblem of Irish pride and citizenship in the Gaelic public sphere than a practical act of educational achievement. The singular focus on classroom learning through grammar texts was always backed by a celebration and unearthing of buried, ancient Irish contributions to achievements of the mind; this was a rising ethnic pride based on a retreat, as John Hutchinson states, "into history to claim descent from a once great civilization."[91]

The Literary Diversion to Gaelic Populism

The literary revival was led by W. B. Yeats, a representative and reminder of the Anglo-Irish presence in Ireland; his conception of the Irish cultural revival was of texts created and delivered in English backed by Gaelic emblems and peasant folklore. The aristocratic, scholarly influence of Yeats was reflected in his choice of speaking engagements on his American tour and his stop in Philadelphia in 1903. Although Gaelic League representatives dispatched from Ireland often made their first stop in Philadelphia to Irish American societies, Yeats deviated from this policy and spoke to an audience of students and faculty, a packed house, at the University of Pennsylvania, and his lecture on "the intellectual revival in Ireland" was a more erudite treatment of a tense topic.[92]

A press report on the event stated that Yeats "is not particularly striking . . . rather languid in bearing and typical of the North Irelander." Yeats, confirming the divide between his literary movement and a popular reading of the Irish revival, offered the following parable to his university audience: "An Irish peasant woman in the streets of Dublin once asked, pointing to a passing hearse, 'Whose coffin is in that?' And when she was told it was the body of Thomas Davis she asked 'Who is he?'"[93] Yeats concluded his lecture stating that a national theater in Dublin would elevate the people and bring a "a national unity of the imagination, a folk lore that the people shall all know, and all her poets shall sing."[94]

The attraction of the literary revival had its limits in Irish Catholic Philadelphia, a community not quite prepared to welcome the subtle voice and peasant imagery of the emerging literature of the Irish literary revival. John Millington Synge's play *The Playboy of the Western World* (1907) would test the limits of a Catholic Irish American tolerance within the Gaelic zone of Philadelphia and further widen the expanding divide between the emphasis on Irish language education and populism of the Gaelic League and the literary culture of Yeats, Synge, and Lady Gregory.

Synge's play, which included the creative insertion of Gaelic phrases and evocative images of peasant culture delivered in English text, became a controversial expression of the literary revival. The original production of *The Playboy of the Western World* in 1907 in Dublin's Abbey Theatre resulted in a theater protest and, later, a street riot by those opposed to the play's theme of patricide and its treatment of peasants of the west of Ireland.

Synge's play toured America in 1911 and received a similar reception of Catholic Irish outrage from its production in Philadelphia in January 1912. Joseph McGarrity, the Clan na Gael leader in Philadelphia, led the charge of protest as eleven members of the troupe from Ireland acting in Synge's Philadelphia presentation were arrested on charges of displaying behavior that was "immoral, lascivious and blasphemous."[95] *The Clan-na-Gael Journal* of Philadelphia described Synge's play as pagan travesty; the *Journal* later would, in contrast to

Synge's production, promote the *Irish Rebel* (based on the rebellion of '98) as a "great play."[96]

Adding to the mayhem was the arrest of those Irish Philadelphians protesting and disrupting the production at Philadelphia's Adelphi Theatre, an event described by the press as "a noisy outbreak."[97] Philadelphia Judge William Carr spoke to the arrested Irish American protesters, telling them that "if they wanted to make a noise in the future they had better go to a ball game, and not to the theatre."[98]

McMahon writes, "The Catholic character of the League widened the gulf between those seeking to create a cosmopolitan Irish culture and those seeking to insulate the country through the Irish-Ireland movement."[99] The core of the Gaelic League in Ireland, which was increasingly Catholic after 1910, was expanded by its appeal to Gaelic populism and would eventually collide with the hopes and expectations of the literary revival; Synge's reception in Philadelphia exposed this divide.

Reviving the Past in Gaelic Philadelphia

The Gaelic revival movement in Ireland drifted across the Atlantic to land and influence the diaspora communities of North America. Philadelphia was no exception, and the city came to welcome and replicate in many forms the style and rhetoric of the original model in Ireland, its initial program of basic language education eventually backed by an appeal to a popular message of Gaelic revival and days-long folk festivals of cultural renewal. Irish American activists led the way, with the energetic and determined leaders of the Philo-Celtic Society disseminating the word of Gaelic revival to anyone who would listen in Irish Philadelphia; it was a message of cultural redemption within earshot of the consistent echo of Irish nationalism, both its nineteenth-century past and its pending twentieth-century future.

CHAPTER 3

Irish Philadelphia in and out of the Gaelic Sphere

The Philadelphia Irish had, by the 1890s, created their own subsociety within the larger community of Irish Americans, a Gaelic public sphere devoted to the exploration of ancient roots and preservation of its language, a cultural nationalism that also embodied political aspirations for an Irish free state. This hypostatized Gaelic zone of cultural revival existed within the larger population of Irish Americans settled in 1890 Philadelphia, an ethnic mass also conditioned by a separatist mentality but normative in its orientations, certainly Catholic, a people defined by the necessity of work and loyalties to family, neighborhood and to the local Catholic parish.

The Irish Americans of both realms bound their multiple life worlds through an imaginative and adaptive deployment of the communicative media of the day, Irish American newspapers, pamphlets, parish calendars, reprints of lectures and speeches, commercial advertisements, all circulated in an immediate network of neighborhood sociability and in the more formal setting of associational gatherings. By 1900, two zones of Irish American content emerged, one a "counterpublic" of a sizable but minority population ideologically bound and moved to action by the rising tide of late nineteenth-century cultural nationalism, and a brother community, a majority of Irish Philadelphians finding security and meaning in belonging to a nexus of neighborhood contacts, including parish— one public seeking Irishness, another bumping into the late nineteenth-century Irish narrative in the normal course of living.

The normative zone of Irish Catholic life and interaction with neighborhood, family, work and church often overlapped with the Gaelic sphere committed to cultural revival, both ethnic domains influenced by the not so distant memory of Philadelphia's nativist past. One of the consequences of the mid-nineteenth-century anti-Catholic, nativist violence—the 1844 Philadelphia street riots—was

1844 street riot in Philadelphia. Source: Digital Library@Villanova University.

a defensive bonding of Irish Catholic opinion into a more determined ethnic block of separatist protection. Kathleen Gavigan reminds us that the Irish American motto in Philadelphia after 1844 was, "we will be better off by ourselves."[1]

Educational separatism, as practiced through the parochial school movement, flourished in the aftermath of the mid-century riots, as the city's Irish, who were spatially diffused across neighborhood boundaries, developed methods and strategies for building institutions of their own making. A self-imposed Irish isolationism born of the need for sectarian shelter in Philadelphia was transformed into a lasting mentality, with the parochial school system attached to neighborhood churches and parishes an example of this defensive, adaptive posture. In 1898 the Archdiocese of Philadelphia recorded 115 parish elementary schools, a minor core of whose graduates moved on to Roman Catholic High School.[2] Úna Ní Bhroiméil comments on the separatist instinct in Irish America, saying, "The Irish, humiliated, resentful and exiled, remained isolated from the dominant group of Anglo-Saxon culture of America."[3]

THE GAELIC SPHERE BY THE NUMBERS

The United States census of 1890 lists the population of Philadelphia as 1,046,964, with foreign-born representing 27.74 percent. The Irish contribution was naturally significant as it extended over multiple generations.[4] Counting Irish Philadelphians with both parents Irish-born and adding in the sizable population with one parent born in Ireland, Philadelphia residents of Irish descent recorded in the 1890 census were 165,128, or 15.8 percent of the general population, representing 61.4 percent of the city's "foreign" born.

The number of Irish Americans in the late-nineteenth-century Gaelic sphere in Philadelphia can be estimated from multiple sources, including society minute books, newspaper reports, circulating pamphlets, parish publications, and an assortment of historical records, which, when combined, produce a numerical description of a vibrant Irish ethnic spirit of the times. Culling numbers from members of the Philadelphia Clan na Gael—with fifty-one camps in 1903—the ninety-eight divisions of the Ancient Order of Hibernians (AOH), thirty divisions of the women's auxiliary AOH, the Philo-Celtic Society, the Irish National League and its multiple branches, the 1,000 members of the Gaelic League of Philadelphia, neighborhood Gaelic language societies, Irish county associations, the Gaelic Athletic Association and Hibernian rifle clubs, and other Irish American societies and clubs that were active in the 1890s and early 1900s, we arrive at an understanding of the breadth of the Gaelic public.[5] Thus, a figure of 25,125, or 15 percent of Irish Philadelphia, provides a quantifiable context for understanding the extent of the Gaelic public sphere.

The quantitative assessment of Irish American engagement provides an imperfect portrait of the scope of action in Philadelphia's Irish communities, as it is an estimate derived from multiple, diverse sources available to the historical researcher. The Gaelic public sphere, however, exercised a voice larger than its numerical footprint, keeping alive, through its ceaseless energy and innovative practices, the spirit of cultural reinvention and language survival in a hardworking city of Irish followers. Parish and neighborhood existence, however, defined the existence of many in the Irish community, providing meaning and security and acting as a touchstone of the familiar.

Familial Bonding in Irish Catholic Philadelphia

St. Anne's Parish in Kensington, two blocks from the Delaware River, was an Irish parish in the 1890s covering extensive urban territory, a series of neighborhoods supporting small-scale industries, especially textiles, supplemented by work at the Delaware River docks, such as shipbuilding and stevedore labor; whole blocks of affordable brick row homes for its working class were imbedded in the leftover spaces between the warehouses and industrial enterprises of the Kensington area.

St. Anne's Parish, from its beginnings in 1845, assumed an Irish identity, with the "pioneer pastor" Reverend Hugh McLaughlin (born in Urney, Donegal), arriving in 1846. McLaughlin would lead the expansion of St. Anne's until 1864, overseeing the building of the church structure, the school, and an adjoining rectory. Father Thomas Kiernan (of Armagh, Ireland) followed McLaughlin and served until 1884, when he was succeeded by Thomas F. Mullen (born in Galway but raised nearby in Wilmington, Delaware).[6]

In nineteenth-century Philadelphia, labor followed work and the positioning of railroad lines delivering coal to Philadelphia river ports created immediate industrial outposts and a demand for Philadelphia's mobile working class. Port Richmond and Kensington emerged as a rival to the Schuylkill River ports, which had long been receiving coal from Reading and other upstate locations, when the Pennsylvania and Reading Railroad extended its service directly to the Delaware River in 1842. Irish laborers flocked to the new location and initially settled in makeshift housing nearby, "in patches [and] swampy stretches" of land near the river.[7]

Eventually occupying real homes as owners and renters, consisting of blocks of solid brick row homes, a labor force of Irish workers followed opportunity, creating and supplying the demand for a Catholic Church. The church raised funds from its new population—workers often earned $25 a week as handloom weavers—resulting in a pattern of giving that would become a regular expectation and a status marker of neighborhood parish life, a system of monthly obligation binding the individual to the nearby Catholic Church and its community.[8]

Giving to Irish causes and its attendant value as a public gesture was a valued pattern in nationalist circles; in June of 1916, just after the Easter Rising, the Clan na Gael solicited funds from its followers to be sent to Ireland, while cautioning that "the man who will hold his purse strings tight at this time when distress is abroad at home should be despised by the Irish race."[9]

And in 1914 Philadelphia's Clan na Gael helped sponsor a massive fundraiser to support Ireland's burgeoning Irish Volunteers tapping a broad section of the Gaelic sphere, twelve divisions of the city's AOH, the Mayo and Cork societies, the Vinegar Hill Society, Shamrock Football and Emmet Hurling clubs, and over 1,900 Irish American donors who made pledges of from 5¢ to $50. The public record of donation, the opportunity to be counted among the commune of Irish national backers in a public document, counted; Clan na Gael president Joseph McGarrity gave $1,000.[10]

The church at the corner of Lehigh and Memphis Streets attracted a sizable population, with its impressive pink stone edifice an architectural monument to Irish American Catholic initiative and its funding derived from the industrial wages of its Irish American members, who squeezed what they could from tight family budgets. The "Christmas Collection" for 1902 alone counted 820 church member donors offering an average of $1; in 1902 it was estimated that St. Anne's was home to 10,000 Catholics in its parish boundaries.[11]

St. Anne's sponsored multiple societies, including a branch of the Total Abstinence Benevolent Society of Philadelphia (1873), which required a pledge to abstain from alcohol; the insecure and, at times, hazardous nature of work in industrial settings was the primary message of St. Anne's abstinence society,

Academy of Music

Tuesday Evening, April 24, 1917

8 o'clock Sharp

ONE NIGHT ONLY

Ireland's Easter Week Rebellion

A great play in three acts, written and staged by Bert Gael who were friends and associates of Pearse and McDonough, two of the principal leaders of the Irish Rebellion.

Act I—Scene 1. St. Enda's School, near Dublin. Established and presided over by Patrick Pearse

Scene II—Count Plunkett's Home. Joseph pursued by the military.

Act II—Scene I—O'Connell Street, Dublin. The General Post Office.

Scene II—Interior of Post Office. Defence by the Patriot Forces.

Act III—Scene I—Richmond Barracks. Courtmartial of Pearse, McDonough, Plunkett and De Valera.

Scene II—Marriage of Joseph Plunkett. His execution.

Scene III—One Year later, Count Plunkett's home. Result of Roscommon Election.

TICKETS 25, 50, 75 and $1.00.

For Sale at Irish-American Club, 726 Spruce Street

Phone Keystone 6872 Main

1917 newspaper advertisement for a Clan na Gael–sponsored drama on the Easter Rising of 1916. Source: CHRC.

which was "organized for the purpose of protecting workingmen from the Immoral and Social evils resulting from a life of arduous and precarious labor."[12] The church was home to the "Workingman's Association" (1870), the Rev. Hugh McLaughlin Beneficial Society (1867), and its own "Literary Society," which was given to organizing social gatherings.[13]

THE WAGES OF CATHOLIC SOLIDARITY IN IRISH PHILADELPHIA

The monthly "block collections" organized by St. Anne's to raise funds for various church projects were blueprints of organizational design and efficiency, whole neighborhoods of row homes divided into districts with collectors assigned to each district. These were women mainly, with individuals named Nellie McCarthy, Mary Daly, Maggie Feeny, and Alice McSorley active in 1902 as parish accumulators of 25¢ or 65¢ donations. In the end, just over 2,140 St. Anne's church members contributed to the February fund in 1902.[14]

Giving to church funds was a duty that satisfied fealty to multiple icons of meaning for the Irish, naturally, with the church's insatiable demand for building donations, family, neighborhood solidarity, and the pride of working-class Irish Catholics contributing to the construction of their own community; reward for the donation was the recognition derived from the very public accounting of the various church campaigns printed in the monthly parish calendars. To be counted among the Church's published collective, finding the means to give and then be recognized, became a symbolic measure of citizenship in the parish community.

Eighteen years later, in 1920, St. Anne's launched a campaign to raise $75,000 from the church members of this river district, employing an identical strategy of assigning specific church members as agents to canvass neighborhood blocks. Tables 3.1 to 3.4 provide insights into the social composition of a sample of the parish giving population, with data on ethnic roots, nationality, and the occupational structure of St. Anne's donors contributing to the church's fundraising campaign in 1920.

DEFINING PARISH HONOR IN WORKING-CLASS PHILADELPHIA

Irish American giving to the church campaigns was an expression of familial loyalty and pride, with many outsized donations in the memory of a departed family member, a symbol of close family bonds; these were honorific testaments of ordinary people made public in the monthly accounting of campaign donations published in a parish calendar. Mary Rockford, a widow of Irish descent, donated $50 to the St. Anne's church fund in honor of her departed husband. John Keane, a clerk in a corner grocery store, whose parents emigrated from

TABLE 3.1

OCCUPATIONAL STRUCTURE OF HIGH-END
($50–$100) DONORS TO ST. ANNE'S PARISH

Occupation Category	Share
Professional	8%
Business	0%
White collar[a]	27%
Skilled labor[b]	58%
Unskilled labor[c]	8%

Sources: "The Handsome Hand-Sum," 1920, PA43,
CHRC; U.S. Census Bureau, 1920.

Note: The percentages in this table and others that
follow may not exactly sum to 100 due to rounding.

N = 98.

[a] Includes clerks, salesmen, stenographers, and real
estate salesmen.

[b] Includes machinists, electricians, and carpenters.

[c] Includes manual laborers.

TABLE 3.2

OCCUPATIONAL STRUCTURE OF LOW-END
($25–$50) DONORS TO ST. ANNE'S PARISH

Occupation Category	Share
Professional	0%
Business	0%
White collar[a]	11%
Skilled labor[b]	76%
Unskilled labor[c]	14%

Sources: "The Handsome Hand-Sum," 1920,
PA43, CHRC; U.S. Census Bureau, 1920.

N = 87.

[a] Includes clerks, salesmen, stenographers, and
real estate salesmen.

[b] Includes machinists, electricians, and
carpenters.

[c] Includes manual laborers.

TABLE 3.3

ETHNIC DESCENT OF HIGH-END ($50–$100) DONORS
TO ST. ANNE'S PARISH

Ethnic Background	Share
Irish (parents born in Ireland)	75%
American (parents born in United States)	25%
German (parents born in Germany)	1%

Source: "The Handsome Hand-Sum," 1920, PA43, CHRC;
U.S. Census Bureau, 1920.
N = 98.

TABLE 3.4

ETHNIC DESCENT OF LOW-END ($25–$50) DONORS
TO ST. ANNE'S PARISH

Ethnic Background	Share
Irish (parents born in Ireland)	93%
American (parents born in USA)	7%
German (parents born in Germany)	2%

Sources: "The Handsome Hand-Sum," 1920, PA43,
CHRC; U.S. Census Bureau, 1920.
N = 87.

Ireland, found the means to donate $50 in his parents' name. William McClos-
key, second-generation Irish American, twenty-seven years old, a brakeman on
the Pennsylvania Railroad, living at home in a large household, gave $50 in the
memory of his departed brother.[15]

Tables 3.1 to 3.4 describe a cohort of St. Anne's church members of Irish ancestry working in skilled industrial positions. This Irish proletariat of the river
wards also expressed the dignity of their class through giving, stretching
working-class wages to exercise one of the few options available for public
recognition.

Women donors were prominent in the record of church givers, with women
often holding down family and home, including many widows of the industrial
workers of the district; in this way a single family member took responsibility
for the community presentation of the family name. Mary Bradley, whose parents

born in Ireland, donated $100 in 1902 in honor of her deceased husband, John, a wholesale merchant, while Ann Larkin, also second-generation Irish, donated $50 for her departed son, Michael.[16] Mary Coleman, a widow, working as a "soaper" in a nearby hosiery mill, donated a symbolic $1 to the church fund in honor of her thirteen-year-old son Thomas, a token gesture for her young son reaffirming a communal lesson on family and the generational connections and expectations of Irish Catholics in the industrial city.

At the Church of the Ascension, also in Kensington, a textile area further west of St. Anne's but also within walking distance of the Delaware River and its northern docks, a matrix of small and medium-sized warehouses surrounded by block after block of red brick row homes catered to an Irish American working class. Proximity to labor opportunities mattered, and the many small and medium-sized industrial works at the docks on the Delaware were within walking distance.

The members of this neighborhood Catholic Church were an urban collection of workers, many Irish, living their lives in the shadow of an urban architecture designed for small-scale industrial production, where the church's importance was cemented by weekly giving. Patrick Leary attended one of the two Sunday masses and paid the weekly assignment of 65¢ in 1910 for church maintenance and other building needs of the Irish-dominated Archdiocese of Philadelphia. Leary, who was of Irish descent, worked nearby as a pipe fitter, owned his row home, and lived there with his wife and two children and a boarder. The Building Fund Society of Ascension Parish suggested in 1910 that every church member contribute 5¢ a week.[17]

Much of the life of neighborhood in the industrial city was of the church, attended by men and women who were self-recruited to the factory districts devoted to textiles, brick making, and a myriad of other small industrial works. Parish and neighborhood defined a normative Irish Catholic public in the 1890s, a spatial focal point for interaction, education, discussion; the only requirement for membership was Catholic identity or heritage, and its actors created a community. The church was a central point of information and communication as local commercial concerns advertised in parish publications, with stores and outlets within walking distance adding another plank to the support of neighborhood and parish meaning.

At the turn of the nineteenth century in Philadelphia there existed compound forces of cohesive influence on Irish Americans living in neighborhoods within an industrial matrix. The Irish American working class was responsive to labor opportunities and changing markets, influenced by the ups and downs of personal life chances in the 1890s, which made it a mobile population but also created a community support system in the dispersed parishes of the Catholic Church, whose many programs traversed the grounds of education, leisure, and Irish Catholic identity. Parish life had its own set of attractions and rewards and

a tenuous and at times fractious relationship with the legacy of Irish nationalism, but it also provided a secure platform in Irish Philadelphia that, in the crev-
ices of Catholic identity, overlapped with a surging cultural nationalism.

Neighborhood existence for the Irish was made less arduous and tedious
through the dynamism of parish life surrounding Catholic churches in the 1890s.
St. Agatha's in West Philadelphia sponsored a "Grand Concert of Sacred Music"
on a February Wednesday evening in 1892, charging 50¢ for admission. Perform-
ing on stage that evening were Lizzie MacCartney, Caroline McCaffrey, tenor
Joseph Cottringer, and baritone Thomas Kane.[18]

IRISH CATHOLIC COMMITMENT TO A CIVIC CULTURE

Voluntary associations were everywhere in the late 1800s and early 1900s and
Philadelphia was one of the epicenters of this communal system of self-support,
with an Irish American contribution that was truly abundant in this age of civic
action. The rules and codes of behavior in meetings were often identical across
association types, encoded in pocket-size handbooks distributed to members,
in constitutions and bylaws, a mobile language of sodality borrowed from multiple sources and employed across political affiliations.

Societies abounded in parish locations. These were church-sponsored organizations devoted to secular goals, education, sport, saving funds, temperance,
all elements of an achievement and self-improvement agenda associated with the
Church. Temperance societies were also mutual aid associations requiring dues.
In 1909 the League of the Sacred Thirst in 1909 asked for 5¢ a week and a pledge
against drink; the Men's Beneficial Temperance Society of Ascension Parish was
a mutual aid society, parish members paid 50¢ a week in dues and committed to
abstaining from alcohol and received a reciprocal commitment for sick benefits
of $5 a week and a death benefit of $75.[19]

PARISH NATIONALISM IN PHILADELPHIA

Parish life provided a context for all sorts of interpretive messages of Irish content and identity. Irish nationalism was constantly circulating in late-nineteenth-
century Irish Philadelphia and simply carrying an identity of Irish descent
required some acknowledgment of the symbolism and rites of Irish history and
ongoing influence.

The Philo-Celtic Society of Philadelphia was singularly committed to the
teaching of the Irish language to all comers, yet its message of cultural regeneration was couched in an English language communiqué that appealed to a generalized Irish public, one that understood the separatism of Irish Catholicism
in Philadelphia. As Úna Ní Bhroiméil notes, "The Irish language became a
building block of ethnic pride and separateness."[20] A 1901 open letter from the

Philo-Celtic Society to the Irish of Philadelphia blamed the British for the loss of its national language—"to enlarge the English and extinguish the Irish has been the steady and consistent aim of the English government for centuries."[21]

Questions on ethnicity and religion, and specifically the Catholic place in a Protestant America, were topics of interest in the city's church salons of the 1890s. On one Sunday evening in 1891, parishioners of Our Lady of Mercy were invited to a lecture by their pastor, Rev. J. L. O'Neill. The title was "the philosophy of Irish history," a topic promising members knowledge of the "present serious crisis in Irish affairs."[22]

Irish nationalism inserted itself in the collectives of ordinary Irish Catholics as it did in 1868, when the members of the St. Charles Catholic Beneficial Society in West Philadelphia were contacted by the city's Fenians: "a communication was received from the Fenian Brotherhood. It was read and accepted and the committee of arrangements was ordered after a motion to support the Fenian event."[23]

LABOR AND LIFE IN INDUSTRIAL PHILADELPHIA:
IRISH CATHOLIC DEFENSES

The Irish Catholic Benevolent Union (ICBU) was a national mutual aid society for Irish Catholics that sponsored branch associations across Irish America. It was founded in 1869 in Dayton, Ohio, "to create and foster a feeling of fraternity and fellowship among the various Irish Catholic Beneficial Societies . . . [and] aid in alleviating the suffering of said members."[24] The guidelines of St. Agatha's parish branch in Philadelphia spoke for the ICBU when it formed its society in 1891 stipulating the following guideline for membership: "only practical Catholics not over 45 years can become members."[25]

There were fifty ICBU branches in Philadelphia in the 1890s, many located and operating within parish churches, with twenty-two branches added in 1891 alone and three branches for women "organized for domestics and other working women."[26] An ICBU Ladies Branch was located in South Philadelphia's Temperance Hall; it proclaimed in 1890, "All Catholic ladies between 18 and 45 are invited to become members."[27] The unifying message of the St. Joseph's ICBU branch focused, as did many parish mutual aid societies, on the specter of industrial labor, proclaiming in 1891 that "beneficial Societies have become an acknowledged necessity to the man depending on weekly wages, as sickness comes to all of us."[28]

Philadelphia ICBU president Edward Murphy sent a series of letters in 1890 and 1891 to the city's branch societies; Murphy, in his communication to Irish Catholic Philadelphia, writes, "It is to be hoped that the various societies will take a more active interest in the Labor movement." Murphy followed this com-

Irish Catholic Benevolent Union concert announcement, 1891. Source: CHRC.

munication the following year with an appeal for "the creation of a Labor Bureau, formed for assisting members in obtaining employment."[29]

The hard facts of labor in a northeastern American city, especially its potential toll on the spirit and body of Irish Americans, was a real issue in the late 1800s, and Irish Catholic working-class associations responded to this threat. Mutual aid in the industrial city was often the only option of protection, providing modest health and death benefits commensurate with working-class wages.

Societies also protected themselves from runs on their meager financial resources, including their pool of disposable funds from dues and fines reserved for sick and death benefits. The actuary table for the Father Mark Crane Beneficial Society of Philadelphia had specific age requirements—no members over forty years—and a sliding scale of fees that favored youth.[30] In Kensington, a textile center of the city, the maximum age for membership was thirty years at the Kensington Catholic Benevolent Society.[31]

The language of a peoples' associationalism, which had long been encoded in documents, rule books demanding sobriety and decorum for public gatherings, and primers on the presentation of the self in front of others when engaged in formal discussions, constituted a code of solidarity for fellow members, including carpenters, painters, machinists, and women working in textile mills. The format and setting for Irish Catholic associationalism was established early in the 1800s in Philadelphia, with the St. Augustine Beneficial Society first welcoming Irish Philadelphians in 1828. Expectations surrounding workingmen's funerals in Philadelphia's Irish community were identical to those of native Ireland, with St. Augustine's of Philadelphia prescribing the various roles of the officers, stewards, and members required "to join in the ceremonies" of the church burial.[32]

Stewards were called on to perform duties that kept the society solvent and functioning, the assignment and rituals of funerals, and the administration of health benefits. For the Bishop Hughes Beneficial Society of Philadelphia, once a member sought benefits, a steward was asked to visit the home—with a visitation limit of three miles—within twenty-four hours and then check in twice a week after the initial visit. The roaming steward was an extension of the society's discipline imposing a communal vigilance on the member claiming benefits in case he was working on the side.[33]

The Catholic Mutual Benefit Association (CMBA), a citywide association, promoted its services to a parish population in the early 1900s. A working man of age twenty-one could pay 50¢ a month to receive benefits, which constituted a limited form of workers' insurance against sickness or injury; the CMBA was promoted in Irish Philadelphia as "Catholic—hence filled with high-minded, God-fearing men and future modernists, saving for those you leave after you."[34]

The network of Catholic mutual aid associations advertised through the normal channels of parish communication, printing circulars that made the rounds of church and neighborhood. The Cardinal Gibbons Benevolent Society promised in 1888 "for the nominal fee of 60¢" to give membership to "healthy Catholic men under 45 years of age," a form of parish-centered mutual aid for its working-class members.[35]

The Sphere of Philadelphia's Catholic Irish American Women

Irish American women organized societies of protection against the pitfalls of work and life in Philadelphia in the late 1800s and early 1900s, adding to the city's robust record of civic action. Women in Philadelphia formed mutual aid societies for the support of working women, for self-education, and for abstinence from alcohol, with some women's societies positioning men as officers and others operated exclusively by women.

Women's societies in Philadelphia were often associated with a parish or a neighborhood identity. While the formal rules of membership, codes of behavior, and structure of dues and health benefits were often identical to men's societies, women's Irish American associations also addressed women's concerns: there were special benefits for managing childbirth written into the member's contract.

The Rev. M. Filan Catholic Male and Female Beneficial Society articulated an ethic of care and support for its members, carefully crafting words acknowledging the need for financial assistance in the world of work. The men and women of this mutual aid organization required its members to be "Roman Catholics," and to come together "for the mutual assistance of ourselves and families in case of sickness, accident or death."[36] Filan and other societies of mutual aid were open to men and women, including Irish women in the workforce; the Filan Catholic Male and Female Beneficial Society offered its members a minimal safety net "to mitigate the severity of misfortune and distress" of labor and life encountered in their midst.[37]

St. Regina's Beneficial Association of Philadelphia (1870) was a women's mutual aid organization; it allowed male members but stipulated that "no more than ten male members can belong."[38] Our Lady of Lourdes Catholic Beneficial Society, established in 1877, as well as St. Catherine's Beneficial Society of Philadelphia, begun in 1869, were parish mutual aid societies for women.[39] Another such society was St. Veronica's Female Beneficial Society of Philadelphia; in 1899, St. Veronica's rules did not permit new members older than thirty-five years of age.[40]

Saint Vincent's Beneficial Society in the industrial Frankford section of Philadelphia was a mutual aid society for men and women. It allowed for childbirth benefits for its working women members after a five-week waiting period after birth: "no female member shall receive benefits for parturition, until five weeks after the event."[41] St. Veronica's Female Beneficial Society of Philadelphia had similar childbirth support in 1871 through the late 1800s, with benefits allowed after a four-week wait after birth for its female members.[42]

Women's associations required discipline and congruity with the expectations of public order in public gatherings, but the proscription and warnings against alcohol were missing from the requirements of conduct. Ladies Catholic Union No. 1 of Philadelphia fined members $1 for "disorderly conduct," as personal control was assumed in the self-definition of a "ladies'" society.[43]

In the Frankford warehouse district of Philadelphia, the St. Agnes Ladies Benevolent and Social Association catered to Irish women workers in this mill town of textile factories and shops.[44] St. Agnes stipulated in 1869 that the "society shall be composed of twenty-one male members . . . [and] an unlimited number of females." All the officers were men, and a John McBride was president, while the stewards and society messenger were women.[45]

St. Agnes would have attracted a membership from Ascension Parish, such as Annie Gill, a second-generation Irish American and a weaver in one of the neighborhood textile shops; Mary Dunn, also a second-generation Irish American and widowed, who was sharing a row home in the Kensington district with Elizabeth and Abbie Johnson, sisters in their early twenties, who were knitters in a hosiery business; Annie Tighe, an oyster dealer in Kensington; and Anna O'Hara, a yarn wincher, all of whom were of Irish descent.[46]

It has been noted that Irish American mutual aid societies were organized for working Irish American women, many of whom worked as "domestics."[47] However, a closer inspection of the occupational backgrounds of many Irish American women who belonged to mutual aid associations found women at home managing family and household. Many were married or widowed, but the focus of women's mutual aid in the 1890s covered the varied work and home patterns of women moving in and out of the workforce; in addition, the meetings and interactions generated in women's associations, opportunities for conversation outside the home, were, like men's societies, powerful drawing forces for Irish American women to embrace communal practices.

In Kensington's AOH Ladies Division 9, Mary Maloney assumed the responsibility of financial secretary; she was married to a metal worker from the Delaware River shipyards and managed a home that included her own family, a sister-in-law, and a niece. The society's vice president, Alice Toman, who was born in Ireland, was the sister of a coal peddler. while treasurer Mary McFadden had a full household of six and her husband, a stone cutter.

Five miles south along the river, in AOH Ladies Division 11, members Mary Taggart, a seamstress born in Northern Ireland, and Martha Neallis, keeping house in a family of five, were counted among the Irish American women of this branch beneficial society.[48] The benefits of mutual aid societies for working women were attractive in themselves, but the opportunity to follow leads of a husband or brother and assemble in the community of women of Irish background was part of the pull of women's associationalism in the Irish community of Philadelphia.

In South Philadelphia, Our Lady of Lourdes Female Beneficial Society, originating in 1877, distributed its annual financial report in 1891. This was a sizable Catholic women's association, which divided membership into first- and second-class types; that year there were 271 women listed in first class, 304 in second class, for a total of 575 dues-paying members. It was a mutual aid society with a business ethic, investing savings accrued from dues and fines in local savings and loan associations. In 1891, Our Lady of Lourdes Female Beneficial Society collected $3,418 in dues and fines and paid out $2,425 in sick benefits and $420 death and funeral benefits, ending the year with $4,523 in savings.[49]

The Archdiocesan Catholic Reading Circles Union in Philadelphia was another Irish Catholic women's society, modeled after the Chautauqua movement of self-education started in Plattsburgh, New York. Most of these reading societies met at parish churches; the Champlain Reading Circle of Philadelphia gathered every other Friday in 1893, with host locations moving "from house to house of members."[50] There were twenty-one circles recorded in Philadelphia in 1895, which gathered "all intelligent and interested students of the leading topics of the day in every intellectual field."[51]

WHITENESS IN CIVIC PHILADELPHIA

Southwark was a neighborhood adjacent to the original, colonial hub of the port of Philadelphia, near the old colony's central point of origin on the Delaware, just south of the stately Georgian homes lining Penn's outline of squared streets in the old city. Southwark in the nineteenth century was a maze of row homes and side alleys supplemented by backyard structures housing a mobile set of diverse peoples who found work and housing where they could, including Irish, English, Germans, and Americans of African heritage.

Noel Ignatiev notes a special tension between African Americans and Irish Catholics in nineteenth-century Philadelphia, a conflict based in the competition between the two groups for scarce labor opportunities on the docks of the city's two river ports. Ignatiev's premier work poses a fundamental question, asking "how the Catholic Irish, an oppressed race in Ireland, became part of an oppressing race in America."[52] Irish Catholic associationalism responded to the nineteenth-century racial divide in the city with its own rules of exclusion.

The Southwark Beneficial Society catered to a Catholic Irish clientele, its doors open only to "white" Catholics, a racial restriction in 1870 remnant of the region's racialized street violence of previous decades.[53] The Premium Loan Association, the Irish American equivalent of a dividing society whose primary function was to offer building loans to Irish Americans, also required its members in 1855 to "be white citizens of the United States," as did the St. Charles Catholic Beneficial Society of Philadelphia.[54] By the 1890s, the "whiteness" clause for admission to Irish American associations in Philadelphia had disappeared from its rule-books, a subtle formal acknowledgement that failed to mask perpetual conflict along racial lines.

As Ignatiev notes in his work *How the Irish Became White*, the mid-1850s were stressful for emigrating Irish Catholics to Philadelphia; it was a time of high nativist tension that pressured the Irish, who were at the bottom of a working-class hierarchy, to fall back on "whiteness" as a status marker of differentiation.[55] Frederick Douglass summarized the contentious dynamic of the city's working classes, writing in 1862, "There is not perhaps anywhere to be found a city in which prejudice against color is more rampant than in Philadelphia."[56]

SECRET SOCIETIES AND PARISH ASSOCIATIONS

The Catholic Church did, however, extend its aversion of Irish "secret societies" into the ordering of Irish Philadelphia's associational consciousness and its language of inclusion, a reminder of the Philadelphia Archbishop Wood's 1864 denunciation of the Fenians. The standard nineteenth-century question posed to prospective members of Catholic mutual aid societies in Philadelphia was "Are you a member of any secret or sworn society condemned by the Catholic Church?"[57] The St. Monica Male and Female Catholic Beneficial Association of Philadelphia followed the protocol of the times and imposed a loyalty oath against secret societies in 1880.[58]

In 1889, the Robert Emmet Beneficial Society of Germantown expected its members to renounce secret societies banned by the Catholic Church, an awkward requirement for an association named after one of Ireland's most admired martyred rebels. And St. Anne's Total Abstinence Society of Philadelphia asked its parish applicants for membership in 1873 whether they belonged "to any sworn or secret society condemned by the Church."[59] This stricture was eased by the 1890s, as the Church, which influenced civic culture, relaxed control.

As noted, the Irish Catholic Benevolent Union (ICBU) branches also reflected the nexus of industrial work and nationalist memory and influence that was alive in Irish working men and women in all corners of the city, and as expressed through associations such as Workingmen's Society, the Kensington Society, and the Celtic Society.[60] The ICBU scrutinized its members, carefully stipulating that "the societies are barred from admitting other than practical Catholics, and must forbid the election of members of condemned secret societies."[61]

A code of conduct swept across associational Irish Philadelphia, with the words altered slightly but the underlying motivation of control and discipline clear. Discipline, both personal and collective, was prominently featured and written into the rules of associational booklets on both sides of the Atlantic well before the revival years of the 1890s, in not so gentle reminders to Irish Americans who had inherited an undisciplined reputation. In industrial Kensington the rules were overtly strict and reminiscent of the hard edge of working-class Dublin: "Any member while receiving benefits from the Society be detected in gambling, intoxication or frequenting tippling houses or taverns [shall] be expelled."[62]

Confronting the Specter of Alcohol

The Catholic Total Abstinence Union societies, a descendant of Father Theobald Mathew's movement in Ireland, were products of the broad missionizing agenda of the Catholic Church in Philadelphia. The titles of branch societies revealed the connection between church and people: "Holy Family," "Nativity," or those associated with established parishes in Philadelphia, "St. James," "St. Anne's" and a host of other Irish Catholic churches.[63] In Philadelphia, an "Emigration Committee" of the Abstinence Union was organized in 1875 to assist Irish emigrants with settlement and applications for American citizenship.[64]

The Abstinence Union of the Archdiocese of Philadelphia was established in 1872 and recorded 150 branch societies in the city within a few years, many as mutual aid associations. By the 1890s, it was estimated that Philadelphia had 16,000 members taking the pledge of abstinence.[65] The Abstinence Union promoted a firm message to its people, a reminder of ethnic content, heritage, and responsibility, and it was written into its codes, a contract of personal and collective renewal—a notice distributed in 1874 read: "The great object of the Union is to regenerate and elevate the Irish Race in America."[66] Temperance in the late 1800s in Irish Philadelphia required a strict code of adherence to the pledge, "abstinence from all intoxicating drinks for three years," and a code of "self-denial" administered formally to be interned in its individual followers; branch societies doubled as beneficial associations.[67]

Seemingly all societies of Irish American content in the late 1800s in Philadelphia were vigilant about a past Irish essentialism that defined drink and the potential toxic effects of alcohol upstaging serious gatherings of the Irish—for the Workingmen's Beneficial Society of Philadelphia, the first associational rule fined any member $3 for entering the "club in a state of intoxication."[68] The Loyola Club walked out of a general meeting of the Catholic Young Men's Archdiocesan Union of Philadelphia (CYMU) in 1901 because the board failed to deny the use of liquor at club meetings.[69] It was recorded that a new club of the Catholic Union, the Philopatrians, had set up "a sideboard and dispensing liquor in their new clubhouse," sparking the Loyola protest against alcohol.[70]

Meetings of abstinence societies in Philadelphia were not necessarily dull affairs. For example, the Assumption Total Abstinence society held a gathering at their hall at 11th and Spring Garden in fall 1899, and the "entertainment committee [had] worked industriously in making up the program." With James Craig on the piano, a series of songs filled the meeting followed by recitations, a violin solo, a "clog dance," and finally, "refreshments and cigars were served."[71]

And yet saloons, taprooms on many a corner of working-class neighborhoods were part of a neighborhood social amicability in the 1890s, an unavoidable pillar of identity and expression in the ethnic subworld. The Clan na Gael of Philadelphia's "Irish Patriot Martyrs Anniversary Magazine" of 1917 celebrated the heroes of Easter 1916, advertisements of Irish American commerce filling the pages of its polished pamphlet. In the sixteen pages of Clan na Gael's text and pictures appeared twenty-five promotions for saloons and liquor shops, including Kensington's Son of Erin saloon and James Reilly's in South Philadelphia, which advertised the "best rye in the field," typical of the appeal to Irish Philadelphia. Ostendorff's German Restaurant and Café also found a comfortable audience among Clan na Gael followers in celebrating the Easter Rising in Ireland in April 1917, the month America entered World War I on the side of the Allies.[72]

CROSS-FERTILIZATION OF GAELIC CONTENT IN CIVIC PHILADELPHIA

Parnell's National League had established itself by the 1880s, with forty-five branches reporting in Pennsylvania in 1882 in support of Parnell's more moderate campaign of parliamentary action.[73] The Philadelphia Municipal Council of the Irish Land League of America was the umbrella organization for the thirty-five branch societies in Philadelphia in 1885, which was organized for "the development and encouragement of the labor and industrial interests of Ireland." In 1885, $1,390 was collected from donations of the city's branches for the "parliamentary Fund."[74]

ANTI-EVICTION.

A LITERARY, DRAMATIC & MUSICAL ENTERTAINMENT

IN AID OF THE ANTI-EVICTION FUND,

Will be given under the Auspices of the

Hugh Lane Branch, Irish National League

IN THE SCHOOL HALL, BROAD & CATHARINE STS.

Thursday Evening, January 6th, 1887.

Tickets, 25 Cts.   Reserved Seats, 35 Cts.

1887 announcement for an Irish National League fundraiser for evicted tenant farmers in Ireland. Source: CHRC.

There was much sharing of causes in late-nineteenth-century Irish Philadelphia, church societies and organizations getting behind a more moderate interpretation of the nation-building mission of Ireland. Delegates from the city's branch societies of the National League, the Robert Emmet Branch of West Philadelphia, the Wolfe Tone, Free Soil and Tyrone Clubs, and various AOH divisions, boarded a train to Chicago for the national convention in summer 1886. It was reported that "five hundred Irish compatriots" saw the train off at the Broad Street station.[75]

The Philadelphia Council of the Irish National Federation held a meeting in 1894 at Philopatrian Hall for the purpose of "raising money to sustain the Irish National party."[76] The Cathedral Total Abstinence Beneficial Society pitched in to solicit donations from its members to support the parliamentary movement in Ireland, funds forwarded to the Philadelphia Council of the Irish National Federation. The Philadelphia Council had ten branches in Philadelphia in the 1890s supporting the Home Rule movement in Ireland; it found space in its mission to support the language initiative, "to acquire a knowledge of the Celtic tongue as a means of securing Irish liberty."[77]

In addition, eight divisions of the AOH, the Star Literary Club of Germantown, and six branches of the Irish Catholic Benevolent Union—the Pius X and St. Elizabeth's Clubs—contributed to the Parnell fund. The branch societies of the Philadelphia National League symbolized an Irish hope for Ireland in their selection of titles: the Celtic Sons, Michael Davitt, Thomas Davis, Robert Emmet, John Mitchel, and Wolfe Tone branches, alongside the "General Andrew Jackson" branch, communicating a content that united American national symbolism with Irish separatism in the early 1880s.[78]

The interests, motivations, political and cultural orientations for identity and action overlapped in the network of communication in Irish Philadelphia. Irish American societies advertised in the same ethnic newspapers, distributed handbills to every Irish point of contact, published notices in nationalist newspapers and church calendars, and shared the same meeting spaces. For example, the Father Mathew Club of Philadelphia met at the Sheare's Club at 8th and Walnut, home to so many meetings of Irish Philadelphians with nationalist leanings.[79]

The Philadelphia weekly, the *Freeman and Irish American Review*, which described itself as "devoted to the interests of the Irish race," advertised in Catholic parish newspapers. Its message promoted various nationalist causes, the Irish National League, the AOH as well as "church news and items of interest for women."[80] The president of AOH Division 21 in Port Richmond spoke to his members in 1899: "President Leverty arose and also spoke of the *Irish American Review* and recommended it to all members of his division."[81] The *Catholic Total Abstinence News* also advertised in neighborhood parish calendars, a newspaper naturally offering news on temperance, but one that "aims to be a general vehicle for the dissemination of Catholic intelligence."[82]

In addition to the more intensely ethnic—Irish—character of organizations like the Clan na Gael, the AOH and the cultural emphasis of the Philo-Celtic Society of Philadelphia, a multitude of Catholic Irish societies that were decidedly less ideological existed side by side, occupying the same urban space, marginally separated. These were beneficial societies associated with a parish, such as the St. Patrick's Beneficial Society of Manayunk. St. Patrick's of Manayunk rejected membership to any individual "detected in habitual intemperance, vice or immorality to the prejudice of his health," principles carrying religious weight but also a protective, conservative purity designed to temper the Irish American personality.[83]

The civic world of Philadelphia's vast network of neighborhood parishes was unified by a protocol of restraint, the denial of emotional expression in public settings, a code of personal control, and a deference for rules; it was also animated by a benign parish nationalism that penetrated the life and mentality of ordinary Irish Catholics in late nineteenth-century Philadelphia.

A Gentlemen's Elite: Irish Catholic Clubs in Philadelphia

The Catholic Young Men's Archdiocesan Union, with its many branch clubs dispersed throughout the city's extended network of neighborhood parishes, emerged in the 1890s and early 1900s as an active expression and symbol of civic vitality, an elite representation of Irish Catholic assimilation, and the youthful aspirations of upward mobility. The Catholic clubs recruited a certain type from the Irish Catholic parishes, ambitious young Irish Americans of the second generation of the Famine era, freed, by the 1890s, from the rigors of physical labor, a status implication that marked the existence of their immigrant, Irish-born parents. The young Irish men of the Catholic clubs, working behind desks and leading a gentleman's lifestyle in leisure, represent an aristocracy of Irish Catholic Philadelphia at the turn of the century, a minority cohort of Irish descent searching for a normative acceptance within a working-class population.

Irish Catholic athleticism, a masculine culture elevating sport, and the moving, physical body as within the requirements of a gentleman's honor formed an essential component of this new, urban, ascending Irish American personality. CYMAU societies portrayed themselves as "devoted to the social and artistic rather than to the . . . sociological features of church work," gathering young Catholic men, predominantly Irish, of the city to recline to "entertainments in comfortable and refined quarters, where meet all the best and most attractive features of the gymnasium, the library and the clubhouse."[84] The original model, the Young Men's National Union, offered the following guide in its constitution: "The objects of the Catholic Young Men's National Union are the cultivation of mutual acquaintance, fraternal, unity and intellectual and physical training among Catholic youth."[85]

In 1895 the CYMAU of Philadelphia counted thirty-five branch societies within its union, with club titles more scholarly than athletic, the Catholic Philopatrian Literary Institute south of Center City, St. Mary's Literary Institute in old city, and St. Malachy's Literary Institute in industrial Kensington.[86] Elocution contests among the young men's Irish Catholic clubs were constant in the 1890s and early 1900s, formal, scripted evening events of serious and, at times, comic order. The 1901 contest of the CYMAU opened with a piano recital, later followed by a song sung by a tenor, a short speech, and a "comic duet by the Cullen brothers of Xavier Catholic Club." After the panel of judges delivered their decision on the five contestants, the evening closed with a piano finale.[87]

The CYMAU of Philadelphia had a yearly full schedule of events designed to keep its young men on the go. Elocution contests in the spring and winter months were devoted to debates among Catholic clubs and drama productions by branch clubs. In 1891, a production of Shakespeare's *Julius Caesar* was presented in 1891 by CYMAU members at the Academy of Music.[88] Indoor winter sports and games included bowling, pool, checkers, pinochle, and shuffleboard. Late June was the highlight of the year's calendar, featuring the athletic sports of the track and field day; these sports, games, and contests had a secondary purpose, to serve as a brake on the temptations of the street, as noted in a Catholic Union statement: "Competition when properly controlled serves to stimulate the interest and arouse . . . loyalty."[89]

TABLE 3.5

OCCUPATIONAL ANALYSIS OF THE
LEADERSHIP OF THE CATHOLIC YOUNG MEN'S
ARCHDIOCESAN UNION OF PHILADELPHIA,
1900–1903

Occupation Category	Share
Business[a]	6%
White collar[b]	57%
Skilled labor[c]	34%
Unskilled labor[d]	4%

Source: "List of Elected Delegates of the Catholic
Young Men's Archdiocesan Union of Philadelphia, 1900," 1895–1910, MB80b, CHRC.

N = 82.

[a] Includes small business owners.

[b] Includes clerks, salesmen, stenographers, and
real estate salesmen.

[c] Includes machinists, electricians, and
carpenters.

[d] Includes manual laborers.

Tables 3.5 and 3.6 describe characteristics, personal and social, of the leadership of the CYMAU of Philadelphia at the height of the club's ascension in Irish
Philadelphia, from 1900 to 1903. The club leadership reflected in these tables consisted of the elected top officers of the club in addition to five members selected
as delegates to attend the city's annual meeting of the union.

Tables 3.5 and 3.6 define a portrait of Irish Catholic male youth, a modest elite
whose parents were born in Ireland and immigrated to Philadelphia to work in
manual or working-class occupations; the second generation eschewed the narrow occupational paths dealt their parents, opting for work that was less physical, less dangerous, and more often in offices as clerks, stenographers, telephone
workers, real estate or insurance agents, and salesmen.

The young leaders of the Catholic Union also worked with their hands, as
skilled workers, machinists, foremen, and electricians, but manual labor, which
so was often identified with the Irish American experience, did not define this
leading group of Irish Philadelphians. The requirements of inclusion in this male
subsociety of Irish Catholics were having skills in interaction and calculation,
being literate, being backed by a leisure curriculum schooled in debate, and being

TABLE 3.6

AGE DISTRIBUTION AND ETHNIC ORIGIN OF THE LEADERSHIP
OF THE CATHOLIC YOUNG MEN'S ARCHDIOCESAN UNION
OF PHILADELPHIA, 1900–1903

Average age	*26 years*
Members with one or both parents born in Ireland	87%
Members with both parents born in America	12%

Source: "List of Elected Delegates of the Catholic Young Men's Archdiocesan Union of Philadelphia, 1900," 1895–1910, MB80b, CHRC.
N = 82.

adept at making toasts. This was an aspiring group most often still living at home
with siblings and boarders and working-class parents from native Ireland.

The members of the CYMAU of Philadelphia were not representative of the
"counterpublic" of the Gaelic sphere, which was bound to the reconstruction of
the memory of a sacred island, a living of its nationalist history in thought, song,
and, at times, action, supplemented by an ongoing reinvention of Irish language
and ancient culture. The young men of the Catholic Union were exposed to, but
did not intern the unavoidable discourse of Irish national history; it was a cohort
intent on upward mobility, infused with modernist tendencies yet also, by birth,
committed to a version of Irish identity associated with religion.

Table 3.7 connects the occupational patterns of the first generation born in Ireland, having emigrated and settled in Philadelphia, with the occupational opportunities of the second generation of the Irish Catholic leadership of the CYMAU.
It describes a strategy of integration central to the American myth of ethnic
achievement, a pattern of initial settlement, a subsistence struggle, followed by an
American-born generation establishing itself as a deserving meritocracy.

The young men of the Catholic clubs were the second generation of parents
departing Ireland in the aftermath of the Famine, parents who might have coun-
seled attention to the social markers of upward mobility and security becoming
available in late-century Irish Catholic Philadelphia. This second generation born
of Famine expatriates, a numerically small, select group, was conditioned by a
parish education as it followed opaque visions of a pluralistic America.

In 1899 AOH Division 68 in South Philadelphia debated the tensions surrounding generational differences and life choices confronting the Irish in the
industrial city as it accepted the gift of a John Landy, a youthful member who
had stitched an emerald flag for the society: "Mr. Landy never saw 'the green
fields of Erin,' but the patriotic spirit infused into his young heart by his Tip-
perary father took root." In contrast, the meeting recorded, "You can find men

TABLE 3.7

COMPARATIVE OCCUPATIONAL ANALYSIS ACROSS GENERATIONS
OF THE LEADERSHIP OF THE CATHOLIC YOUNG MEN'S ARCHDIOCESAN
UNION OF PHILADELPHIA, 1900–1903

Occupation Category	First-Generation Parents	Second-Generation Sons
Business[a]	0%	6%
White collar[b]	8%	58%
Skilled labor[c]	48%	32%
Unskilled labor[d]	44%	4%

Source: "List of Elected Delegates of the Catholic Young Men's Archdiocesan Union of Philadelphia, 1900," 1895–1910, MB80b, CHRC.

N = 82.

[a] Includes small business owners.

[b] Includes clerks, salesmen, stenographers, and real estate salesmen.

[c] Includes machinists, electricians, and carpenters.

[d] Includes manual laborers.

in this country born of Irish parents who say 'I'm not Irish,' at the same time exhibiting the utmost indifference as to the fate of the land for which their forefathers fought and nobly died."[90]

The dual spheres of Irish Philadelphia moved together in the streets, meeting halls and concert halls, neighborhood shops and taverns, and churches of the city, loosely tied by common bonds of ethnic and national origin, and distinguished in type by varying degrees of intensity in their commitment to Irish nationalism and, in the 1890s, Gaelic purity. Most of Irish American Catholic Philadelphia shared urban space with Gaelic activism but was defined by the normative requirements of living, the necessity of labor; the comforts of kinship, friends, and local community; the church with its many neighborhood attractions offering support and meaning. For the normative sphere of Irish Philadelphians, the emotional tug of Irish cultural nationalism was only the background, a movement to attend to and drop in on when possible, but not a life sustaining force of Irish meaning.

The leadership corps of the CYMAU was only the avant-garde of an aspiring, middle-class outcome to Irish American settlement in Philadelphia; the normative corpus of Irish Catholic Philadelphia was still of the laboring classes. The Gaelic public sphere would overlap with the normative, numerically greater population of Irish Philadelphia, with both groups defined by common facts of socialization and cultural heritage, thinly separated by an intense commitment to Gaelic revival exercised by a group of Irish American activists.

IRISH CATHOLIC ATHLETICISM IN THE "QUAKER" CITY

The 1901 meeting of the National CYMAU was held in Philadelphia. The published welcome to the national convention in Philadelphia of the CYMAU stated, "We might say Philadelphia, the Catholic City . . . the title 'Quaker City' is now a misnomer."[91] In concert and contrast, the Clan na Gael of Philadelphia joined the city's youth club movement sponsoring their version, the Irish American Athletic Club, offering "boxing, wrestle, bag-punching, military drill" as well as Irish football and hurling.[92]

Sport, with its disciplinary code and its secondary mission of redirecting male youth from the rough side of street life in Philadelphia, became, by the close of the nineteenth century, a consuming enterprise for a youthful Irish Catholic male elite. One rule defined the games of the CYMAU: "No person shall be eligible to compete who is not a Roman Catholic."[93]

The premier athletic event of the CYMAU, the annual field day, was held on Labor Day each year. It was an example of Irish American organizational skill and advanced planning, a mass sporting event that netted a modest profit without charging admission fees to the sizable crowd that turned up annually. Lawrence McCrossin, president of the CYMAU, estimated crowds at the athletic games in the early 1900s as "3,000 to 5,000 of both sexes—three-fourths of whom can be called young."[94] The games were funded through the sale of advertising for the games program, a campaign begun six months before the actual event.

The 1904 Field Day sports were held in West Philadelphia on the Pennsylvania Railroad Grounds with eighteen events in track and field. The premier events were the 100-yard dash, the 440-yard run, and the Relay Race of 4.5 miles; and there was the 65-yard sack race, an all-inclusive form of athletic comic relief. There were 2,500 people in attendance for over four hours, and the Xavier Catholic Club captured many of the events.[95]

In 1899, the Clan na Gael Games of Philadelphia were hosted at Washington Park along the Delaware River, just north of the city, attracting "over 15,000 natives of the Emerald Isle." The Clan na Gael Games proceeded with a nationalist complexion, with its participants lauded as ideal specimens of a Celtic race—"broad shouldered and stately sons of Erin glowing with the flush of health"—taking part in many of the same events sponsored by Catholic sport, with long jump, half-mile and 220-yard races, throwing a sixteen-pound ball, a sack race, and bicycle events included. The CYMAU Games were fiercely contested track and field events, with the winning Catholic club exercising citywide bragging rights for the year; the Clan na Gael Games also featured competitions in the jig and Irish dancing and a hurling exhibition.[96]

A formal banquet with an elaborate menu naturally followed the sporting games of young men's clubs in the 1890s and early 1900s, and the Catholic men's clubs did not falter in this gentleman's tradition. The 1899 CYMAU banquet in Philadelphia's Horticultural Hall was a tightly scripted affair, in which representatives of the over thirty-five clubs were recruited and assigned as event ushers, wearing red bow ties, and with club officers sporting bow ties reflective of their societal status and event responsibilities: a white bow for event manager Gallagher, blue for Flaherty, yellow for treasurer Sunderland, and lavender for secretary Shea.

Music was reflective of American tastes rather than native Irish, with "Rag Melodies," "The Winner," and "Topsy's in Town" favorite choices of young men clubbers on the town; the jigs and reels of a rural Irish village heritage were eschewed for waltzes, polkas, and "two-steps" reflective of an urbane Irish Catholic aristocracy.[97] It was reported that the "dancing was indulged in until the late hour."[98]

The 1905 CYMAU banquet was held at Boothby's, with the second floor taken up by the event; the program featured photographs of the society's officers, Fitzgerald, McCrossin, Redmond, and Dougherty, which show young men in wool suits and bow ties, in their mid- to late twenties, sporting sartorial poses representative of a comfortable, athletic, confident Irish America. The event's menu was impressive, with a first course of Rockaway oysters, followed by "baked bluefish Italiene" and "ice cream fancy cakes," and topped off by coffee and cigars.[99]

Archbishop John Hughes of New York in 1905 weighed in on the contribution the Catholic clubs were making to the Irish American community, arguing that the "boys clubs and societies have been organized and maintained with more or less success." But Hughes lamented the overemphasis on athletic sports and the enthusiasm for winning contests, cautioning against the secular drift of sport: "no religion in the schools, no religion in the homes, no religion in the clubs," with the result an athletic "paganism."[100]

But sport's appeal in the 1890s was infectious as a social marker of a rising ethnic group; the Catholic clubs invented hearty songs of support for their heroic athletes, Aquinas among the more colorful with "Our Racers":

Our Irish racers never need pacers
In any race that's run,
Just look at Furey no sporting jury
Could ever connect that Son.
That's the Aquinas the rest are behind us
For can't you easily see,
We are winning Trophies by the score
All for old Aquinas.[101]

Aquinas in 1909 claimed and announced that "when it comes to the manly sports," its club was on top of Irish Catholic Philadelphia.[102]

THE CONFLUENCE OF PARISH NATIONALISM
AND GAELIC CULTURAL REVIVAL

It has been proposed that the Gaelic public sphere was a "counterpublic," a sizable minority of Irish Philadelphia not only pledging a rhetorical allegiance to the Irish/Ireland movement but also supporting, through initiatives and actions of their own, a position on the reintroduction of Irish symbols of the past. This turn to cultural nationalism in its peak years of influence represented, not only a loyalty to the long-serving narrative of Irish nationalism, but also a choice on ethnic separatism in a city of pluralistic possibilities.

The larger community of Irish Americans was naturally focused on the primary supports of life in Philadelphia—family, work, neighborhood, and citizenship in a voluntary association—drawn closer together by the many programs of parish sponsorship touching those of the Catholic Church. The neighborhood Catholic parish produced a religious message coupled with an ingrained expectation among its working-class constituency to support church projects; in return, Irish Americans were welcomed into a neighborhood nexus of church-sponsored activities, educational, youth-oriented, cultural, or leisurely in nature, with mutual aid societies of church origin offering real-life support for a working class.

It has been noted that the altruistic act of giving to church projects, the individual's voluntary submission to the systematic, highly organized machine of Catholic Church fundraising, was also an honorific gesture of solidarity to family honor, Irish identity, and the neighborhood parish community. To be counted as a donor in the register of the monthly parish calendar reflected the reciprocal pull of church and identity, a reward and a signature statement for an ethnic working class on Irish American citizenship. The parish, thus, was an assembly site for secular lessons on communal commitments, civic education, and interaction with localized commerce and neighbors of similar social conditions existing in close proximity. It has been observed that the lessons and comforts derived from neighborhood parish existence often overlapped with the perpetual aspirations of Irish American nation building in the late 1800s, early 1900s.

Two zones of Irish American meaning and existence surfaced in the 1890s in Philadelphia, one driven by the persistent nationalist hopes and a recent revival of cultural icons expressed in the language movement, a Gaelic public sphere buttressed by a reading of history as unavoidable victimhood combined with a willingness to redress that legacy of injustice. The active Gaelic sphere was supplemented by a second zone, comprising the mass of Irish Americans living in an industrial megalopolis defined by work, family, neighborhood, and, for so many, church.

The two realms were distinguishable but not entirely separate as crossover between a normative Irish Catholic consciousness and the Gaelic sphere was unavoidable if you were Irish in Philadelphia in the 1890s and early 1900s. In fall 1891 Philadelphia's Clan na Gael sponsored a "grand Musical Celebration" to commemorate, once again, the Manchester martyrs, who were tried and hung by the British in 1867 after their attempt to rescue Fenian prisoners ended in the death of a policeman. The Clan na Gael event was held at Musical Hall, 8th and Locust, and it was a celebration that brought together supporters of physical force nationalism and others less committed to the direct intervention and support of the cause of Irish liberation; admission was priced for those of modest means, 25¢, and Irish Philadelphia responded.

The musical program for the Manchester martyrs opened with the "Star-Spangled Banner" sung by the De Sales Quartet of the De Sales Catholic Club. The De Sales Institute of Philadelphia was a society for "Catholic gentlemen," who came together to relate faith with "moral and intellectual culture," as well as giving to the charities of the city, an association attracting Irish American Catholics as well as Catholics of other ethnic backgrounds.[103]

Most of the songs at the Clan na Gael event had a nationalist tinge, "America's Irish will Set Ireland Free," "The Green Old Flag," "Farewell to Ireland," and a recitation on "Allen, Larkin and O'Brien." But others invoked a cultural memory, however, such as "The Blackbird" and banjo solos. The evening naturally ended with "God Save Ireland," a fighting song of revolutionary Ireland and the Manchester martyrs, which includes the lines:

High upon the gallows tree,
Swung the noble-hearted three
By the vengeful tyrant stricken in their bloom,
But they meet him face-to-face,
With the spirit of their race,
And they went with souls undaunted to their doom,
God save Ireland! said the heroes[104]

The Philadelphia Clan na Gael retrospective of the Manchester martyrs in 1891, twenty-four years after the event, was all part of a program of diaspora Irish remembrance of a victimized past, a memory of failed risings and fallen warriors. The musical program identified the enemy: "The democracy of John Bull is but skin deep—scratch him, and you find a Tartar: that is, a savage."[105]

The fluid nature of Irish Philadelphia in the years of cultural revival brought together men and women of Irish descent in urban spaces erected for industrial production, which were inverted for mutually agreeable and, at times, conflicting moral messages. Irish nationalism was a separatist discourse that defined the Gaelic resurgence but also penetrated the consciousness of ordinary Irish Americans, who were not bound to serious ideological commitments but exposed, by heritage, to expressive remnants of the nationalist cause. Similarly, concerted devotion to nationalism in its multiple forms—an inherited sacred text on history, an organizational plan for action, cultural remembrance, and active resurrection of a language—required Gaelic activists to be aware of local conditions and tolerant of their less committed brothers and sisters, an approach that united elements of Irish Philadelphia at the turn of the nineteenth century.

CHAPTER 4

Transatlantic Origins of Irish American Voluntary Associations

IRELAND'S MOBILE PEOPLE

Mobility for the Irish was a long-established pattern of subsistence survival, a finding that militates against the image of static existence in tradition-bound villages in native Ireland. Before the mid-nineteenth-century Famine and beyond, seasonal migration sustained large sections of rural Ireland, whether the farmer of Mayo making his way to England's Midlands in the early 1800s or a small holder in West Donegal sojourning to Scotland during down times in the farming cycle.[1]

The pre-Famine record of Irish seasonal migration, to Dublin for construction work, to its surrounding counties of Wicklow and Meath for agricultural labor, and further afield, to England or Scotland, was a sustaining, hidden movement of rural Ireland that presaged the mass exodus of the 1850s. The construction industry in Dublin in the 1800s required laborers to work alongside the skilled, bringing rural migrants into contact with the ways of working-class Dublin. Ruth-Ann Harris, in her study of pre-Famine Irish migration, writes that "short-term migration has often functioned as the prelude to permanent emigration."[2]

The mid-nineteenth-century agrarian crisis accelerated an existing pattern of mobility to escape the declining life chances for survival on the home island, creating multiple overseas diasporas. Ireland's depopulation in the wake of the Famine was simply massive: 7 million between 1846 and 1914.[3] The Irish Memorial in Philadelphia is a reminder of the legacy of the Famine and emigration in Philadelphia; it was created and placed in a prominent position for all to observe along Philadelphia's Delaware River port in 2002; a segment of its inscription reads: "when more than one million Irish were starved to death and another million forced to emigrate. We celebrate the indefatigable spirit of the Irish that enabled them to triumph over tragedy."

Philadelphia's Irish community was formed through emigration, at first slow-moving waves of diverse populations and occupational niches beginning in the eighteenth century, and then a movement that accelerated from 1815 to 1845, only to spike further with the Famine exodus.[4]

Early trade patterns established the Delaware River as a deep-water channel for trade and for Irish emigration. The ports of Derry and Newry assembled the emigrating Irish from the surrounding counties of Donegal, Tyrone, Derry, Antrim. and Fermanagh and sent them across the Atlantic directly to Philadelphia or just south, to Newcastle, Delaware, leaving a short journey to Philadelphia. Dublin was also a principal port of departure in the eighteenth century for ships docking in Philadelphia, and the *Dublin Packet* a regular visitor.[5]

Philadelphia thus became an early receiving port for all peoples of Ireland, including artisans, farmers, shopkeepers, and indentured servants. The *Pennsylvania Gazette* reported in 1730 that "forty-five hundred persons, chiefly from Ireland," had arrived in Philadelphia in the past two years while "swarms of Irish . . . were being driven over into America," because of rack-rents.[6] Landing in Philadelphia from the brig *Patty* in the 1770s were the unskilled of Ireland but also groups of skilled workers, as the ship log recorded: "smiths, nail-makers, shoe-makers, tailors, skinners [and] carpenters."[7]

In the late 1840s and early 1850s the short and often dangerous trip across the Irish Sea from Dublin to Liverpool was a first stop on the journey to Philadelphia for those Irish of lesser means; the Dublin shipping firm of H. & A. Cope Company, which had five ships in 1848, departed Liverpool to Philadelphia on the twelfth of every month. J. Matthew Gallman, in his study of Famine immigration to Philadelphia, notes the mid-century exodus of an almost wholly Catholic rural proletariat: between 1840 and 1855 over 150,000 Irish migrants made it to Philadelphia, 9,000 via the route from Liverpool in the first half of 1849 alone.[8]

Donegal and Philadelphia have historic ties that bind the remote, wind-swept region of Ireland's northwest with the industrial city; Donegal and Philadelphia were bound by immigration serviced by the McCorkell Steamship and other transatlantic carriers in the nineteenth century. The McCorkell archives of that shipping firm contain records of 5,278 Irish bound for Philadelphia in 1864–1871, tickets booked through a single Philadelphia agent. It is worth noting that when occupations were listed by the McCorkell Line, those with artisan skill, mainly in textiles, were underrepresented as the emigration of skilled workers was forbidden; this constraint was avoided by listing one's occupation as farmer, which was not wholly untrue as some textile work also went along with agricultural work in this part of Ireland in the mid-nineteenth century.[9] It was also noted that industrial workers tended not to emigrate but textile workers did, thus representing a stratum of labor that hid its artisan status as they headed out of Ireland.[10]

People from Donegal were also given to long-established patterns of internal migration within the British Isles contributing to the pre-Famine practice of seasonal migration east across the Irish Sea.[11] The pre-Famine migration scattered the Irish to fields and industrial sites in England, a yearly cycle that began in the spring after crops were planted in Irish ground and was completed when this part-time, wandering rural proletariat reached Irish soil for their own harvest in late November. Patterns of mutual aid associations were carried wherever the mobile Irish roamed; for example, in Manchester, in the decades before 1850, a group of 150 Irish bricklayers started a mutual aid society; their employer noted that the bricklayers had started a "club . . . meant to be a sick club and for the protection of their wages."[12]

Finally, Irish overseas emigration was not wholly confined to the rural population in the mid-1800s, the dwindling rural proletariat of farm workers and small cottiers, but also included those "from the more modern element of the home society where they had worked as artisans, merchants and professionals."[13]

TRANSPLANTED CULTURAL KNOWLEDGE

The transplanted, mid-nineteenth-century Irish Americans in Philadelphia wasted little time in forming their own associations in industrial Philadelphia. It is improbable that this cohort of now-Catholic, mid-century Irish immigrants had been exposed directly to the American model of local, small-town democracy or had been able to learn associational practices from more established American societies, many of which were Protestant in content and spirit; even the Hibernian Society of Philadelphia, which was established in 1790 and populated by an established, commercial Irish American elite, was out of the reach of Irish newcomers of the Famine generation.[14] As James Barrett notes, because they were "excluded from much of the city's public life, the Irish immigrants fell back upon their own communities and institutions."[15]

However, it has been noted that American democracy was in the air in the nineteenth century, a practice and value commitment that covered all forms of institutional life. As Alexis de Tocqueville observed, small-town American democracy had a way of seeping into the pores of civic life, including those of the Irish; he wrote of the "ceaseless agitation" of democratic life in America that "influences all social intercourse."[16]

There were other models available to the Irish in the 1800s of Philadelphia, but the Irish preferred to cultivate a separatism, an oppositional stance to Anglo influence and institutions, in their late-nineteenth-century civic life; the memory of the 1844 Philadelphia anti-Catholic, anti-Irish street riots instilled a linger-ing legacy of self-reliance. Mary Ryan also comments on the social isolation of the New York Irish, saying, "the ethnic partitions of cities such as New York were constructed in the space between an Old World culture and New World discrimination."[17]

Even existing within the realm and reach of American associational practices, it is likely that the Irish in Philadelphia relied as much on the cultural knowl-edge of voluntary associations in their native Ireland, adapting earlier models and experiences to American conditions, forming Irish American versions of transplanted prototypes, with the workers' mutual aid model just one example of a popular choice of the Irish on both sides of the Atlantic. As an example, Pat-rick O'Neill rose to become president in 1893 of all of Philadelphia's Ancient Order of Hibernians (AOH) branches, having emigrated from County Mayo in 1871; his rapid ascendancy within the matrix of Irish American associations in Philadelphia illustrates the general pattern of quick adaptation to local condi-tions that helped make the Gaelic public sphere.

Mary Clawson studied fraternal societies in England, Scotland, Ireland, the continent, and early America in the 1700s and 1800s, and her work observes an identical pattern of model sharing and a reliance of a stock of accumulated cul-tural knowledge in the rapid, spontaneous spread of fraternal associations. She writes, "It is not necessary to draw precise organizational links in order to iden-tify continuities of theme and style" to explain the spread and influence of asso-ciational practices in Western society.[18]

As suggested in the pages that follow, by the 1890s, the Irish of Philadelphia had established their own type of societal organization, a combination of working-class mutual aid that simulated established associational practices in Ireland and a society in Philadelphia that was more open in terms of discussion and debate, with attention to the humanitarian concerns of its members and the Irish community as well as increasing the financial stability of the society.

Cultural learning, involving the internalization of norms and practices, is an invisible process of encoding modes of action that penetrate the consciousness of the individual, influences of lasting impact that transcend national borders and even vast oceans. The immigrating Irish men and women, having been exposed in their homeland to methods of group organization in small societies, whether a rural cooperative, a Gaelic sports club, a city or town tontine, or a rural friendly society, carried with them an appreciation and understanding of formal rules and order in small groups; these parliamentary practices were eas-ily acquired in diaspora settings through participation in a meeting where the rules of order applied and constitutional matters were taken seriously.

In Philadelphia, the associations, which were endowed with the surplus derived from the wages of working-class and petty bourgeois occupations, expanded the limits of the association model in an age of civic engagement. One example was the Irish Co-Operative Society, formed in Philadelphia by working men and women in 1885, a revenue-sharing, consumers' co-op which opened eight co-operative stores in working-class neighborhoods of Philadelphia; however, the Irish cooperative movement in Philadelphia was short-lived and eventually dissolved after five years.[19]

The Irish Industrial Development Company of Philadelphia promoted itself in 1913 as "an Irish-American Co-operative society." It promised to "co-opt all its customers as members and partners in the business. The purchase of a suit of Irish tweed, serge or homespun [equaled] one share of interest in the company." This Irish Philadelphia workers' cooperative promised to handle "none other than Irish manufactured goods," a stricture following the lead of Horace Plunkett's cooperative movement of rural Ireland.[20]

The vast network of Irish associations in Philadelphia were formed primarily as mutual aid societies providing workers' insurance, a subsistence-level social net to support ethnic laborers in the case of sickness or injury, a replica of the Irish friendly society and many other models of associational support. Philadelphia was also the early home of Irish American associations recruited from an elite of earlier nineteenth-century emigration, which promoted charity rather than mutual aid; the Sons of St. Patrick (1868), the Hibernian Society (1790) or the De Sales Institute (1872), and even the Emerald Society (1880) were organizations initiated by established Irish Americans, often of mixed sectarian backgrounds, that extended aid to less fortunate Irish immigrants as they struggled with the hard facts of emigration and settlement in Philadelphia. Unlike the Irish mutual aid society, the established Irish American societies did not welcome the fresh immigrants into their meeting rooms, and it is unlikely that ordinary immigrant workers would have been inspired to start their own beneficial organization based on their subaltern, superficial contact with the higher-status Friendly Sons of St. Patrick of Philadelphia.[21]

This work states that the Diaspora Irish of Philadelphia of the 1890s, in their public institutions, were able to move beyond a previous concern over subsistence and survival in a hard, industrial city to create through communicative mechanisms a vast civic culture of communal support and Gaelic meaning. The original inspiration for this late-nineteenth-century achievement existed across the Atlantic, in previous models of associational customs, and in the winds emanating from the Irish cultural revival. But, as this chapter will reveal in its transatlantic comparative analysis, it was only the Philadelphia Irish, endowed with certain favorable conditions and high motivation, who were able to expand their vision to create ethnic supportive institutions of their own; in native Ireland the restrictive agents of church and state, combined with the declining life chances of economy and society, compelled a vision based on subsistence and survival.

Announcement of a Philadelphia society banquet on St. Patrick's Day, 1910.
Source: CHRC.

ASSOCIATIONALISM, MUTUAL AID, AND FRIENDLY SOCIETIES
IN IRELAND

What follows is an attempt to establish the comparative basis for an understanding of the structure of Irish American associationalism in Philadelphia. This study concludes that the inspirational universe for a civic Irish Philadelphia was first established in Ireland, interned as social learning in the emigrating Irish, and was reconstituted in Irish Philadelphia. Comparative instances of meaning will be offered to provide historical and social context for an understanding of the public sphere in Philadelphia.

Irish friendly societies had been established in Ireland from the late eighteenth century. British Parliament's Friendly Society Act of 1855 strove to save, sanction and control a specific type of voluntary association, the democratic, member-administered society governed by elected officers, subject to regular membership meetings, written records and a visible mechanism of financial control that disclosed the society's record of expenditures.[22]

The British state in Ireland required the printed rules and bylaws of the association to be sent forward to the register for friendly societies in Ireland as well as the submission of the standard form that defined the purpose of the society.

Irish friendly societies were mutual aid organizations offering sick and work-related injury benefits, local organizations identified with a particular place populated by the lower levels of a rural, town, or urban working class as well as skilled artisans; each society constructed its own set of rules and was responsible for the drafting of its own constitution, yet, when it came to the writing of the society constitution, there was much borrowing of previous examples and precedents in the production of regulations.

The Dublin tontine became "the ordinary friendly society" of the capital city, a true member-driven organization similar to the early British friendly societies, a local association with a small membership of laborers associated with a trade or urban place.[23] Trade societies had a long history in Dublin dating from the early 1700s combining charity toward trade members with convivial largess.

In the countryside, tontine-style societies were established in the 1750s; Cork City counted four by 1758. Cork's societies would eventually split over sectarian differences and reconstituted themselves as either Catholic or Protestant; by the 1860s, there were six tontines in Cork, three Protestant and three Catholic. Outside Dublin and Cork, by the late 1700s, friendly annuity societies also appeared in Limerick, such as the Limerick Annuity Society and, later, the Annuity Society of the City of Limerick, a society reserved for Catholics. Tontines were also organized in the late 1800s in Waterford and Cork City.[24]

The Dublin tontine in the nineteenth century operated as a beneficial society supplying sick and death benefits but also developed its own Irish tradition of the Christmas "division," the dividing of a pool of the association's surplus funds out to members as a form of disposable cash to be used at Christmastime. The societies in nineteenth-century Ireland were generally of modest size, which allowed for an ease of administration below the gaze of authority; members all knew each other, which also militated against potential fraud in sick benefit claims. The secretary of Dublin's St. Peter and Paul's Tontine stated in 1870, "We are limited to 80 members. Big societies are bad. In a society the size of ours the yearly claims for sickness and burial money are so few that every member can see for himself that they are set down right in the accounts."[25]

The preference for small associations in Ireland was also a protection against the practice of member abandonment after the cash reward at the traditional Christmas divide. The Emerald Society stated in its 1889 constitution that "this society shall not be dissolved so long as nine members may wish to continue it," a commitment that served to soothe the fears of those, especially older members, who had long invested in the association, that the society was prepared to last.[26] The Irish friendly society or the Dublin tontine was primarily an urban institution; in 1911, Dublin registered 167 associations while County Cavan had 3 and County Donegal 2.

Francis O'Burne of St. John's Tontine said of his nineteenth-century Dublin association, "I don't believe in any society so big that the members can't serve in turn. . . . We have 40 members . . . and if anything goes wrong, we can get most all the members to meet and lay it before them."[27] Another Dublin society, St. Paul's, had seventy-two people in 1912—thirty skilled workers, twenty unskilled laborers, and a few clerks, solicitor's assistants and other white-collar members. Its Christmas divide ranged from 18 shillings to £1. The dividend was calculated by subtracting expenses from income and retaining between £8 and £10, "one member's death benefit," a popular practice in labor-poor Dublin that led societies to skimp on the sick and injury benefits during the year to increase the pot at Christmas time.

The True Sons of St. Kevin was a tontine in Dublin that catered to "working men"; there were sixty members in 1870,[28] while the Emerald Society of Dublin in the 1880s restricted its size to one hundred members.[29] Hence, a type was evolving in nineteenth-century Ireland, an association given to working men's support under the close watch of benefits whose primary financial aim was the payout at the end of the year, which amounted to a mutual aid ethic that often lost sight of its primary mission of material support for sickness and accidents, and was a model that the Philadelphia Irish altered.

Members assumed the duties and responsibilities of the running of an Irish society under a voluntary system backed by a set of punitive sanctions, as a check on the moral commitment to the group, a reflection of the conditions facing working men in nineteenth-century Ireland. The typical Dublin tontine required its members to share in the responsibilities of running the association; the most time-consuming yet vital function was accounting for sick benefits, which involved personally checking up on those who claimed to be ill and deserving of weekly support from the society's stretched resources.

Typically, several association members in Ireland were selected as stewards to monitor those claiming sick leave, and any found working while receiving benefits were subject to expulsion; failure to serve in this rotating policing role was also subject to a fine. The steward's role was vital to the financial solvency of the association and the assigned member would "have to see the sick member once a day, and this may be done during the hour allowed for dinner, or after the day's work is over."[30]

PUNITIVE SELF-GOVERNANCE

The Dublin system had fines for just about everything—the secretary was required to keep an updated "check-fine book" to record the weekly fines members incurred. The secretary was subject to a fine for incorrect keeping of the fine book: "for each mistake he may make, he shall be fined sixpence."[31] Members were fined for not attending the general meeting of the society "at least one half hour after the appointed time," for failing to serve as chairman or steward, for failing to repay a loan or any debt to the society and for breaking codes of behavior in public places such as drunkenness.[32] If you hosted a monthly society meeting in Dublin in the 1890s you were obliged to keep an accurate clock—if the home owner's clock in the Emerald Society was "found to differ five minutes earlier or later than the city time, he shall be fined 1s."[33]

Fines were long-established practices ubiquitous for associations, a way of controlling behavior and augmenting dues and fundraisers as a source of society income. For example, in the 1770s Philadelphia's Friendly Sons of St. Patrick imposed fines of five shillings on its membership for missing meetings.[34]

So focused was the mutual aid society in Ireland on savings funds and the possibility of fraud in sick benefits that it often refused to admit tailors or shoemakers who could work at home on their trade and escape detection from association checkers. A Mr. M. Rooke was secretary of the St. Peter's and Paul's Tontine in Dublin in 1874, and he stated: "We don't admit tailors and shoemakers because we don't feel sure that they won't work when sick, and it is hard to find out. Slaters are also excluded on account of the danger of going on roofs."[35] The Emerald Society of Dublin allowed men of all trades "unless such trade be unlawful or dangerous, work-related injury a drain on the group's resources."[36]

The Emerald Society even required that its "chairman ... accompany a proposed member to the doctor for examination."[37] The society did its best to uncover any preexisting medical conditions that would require substantial health benefits; it questioned prospective members—"can you safely declare that you (and your wife) are at this time free from any infirmity (either in constitution or limbs) ... and are not afflicted or likely to become a burden to this society?"[38]

Governed by suspicion when it came to health benefits, the Irish neverthe-
less viewed their friendly societies as outposts of worker democracy and member control, a savings club and a form of health insurance. They were described
as voluntary associations whose "main object is relief in sickness" supported by
"contributions generally brought by members to a center."[39] These were local
organizations in which "members . . . [are] acquainted with one another," and
local governance the preferred method as "officials [are] generally appointed by
intelligent consent of the members."[40]

The friendly society in Dublin catered to the subsistence life of what constituted the working class of Dublin's late nineteenth century—a minimal regard
to benefits, a consuming focus on the cash surplus at Christmas—and, yet, the
society also allowed for a small loan during personal hard times. Underemploy-
ment in Dublin made for an ultracompetitive labor market—in the 1880s unem-
ployment hit building laborers and, as Mary Daly relates in her history of Dublin's
late-nineteenth-century economy, "former craftsmen" were chronically out of
work in late-century Dublin.[41] One Dublin association's rules stated that the society can "lend any sum not exceeding 1£ to each member (in actual distress)," and,
as noted in the practices of Dublin's Emerald Society, members were charged
interest and fined if the loan was not paid back in time.[42] The Dublin Friendly
Society was a mix of cultural support and constraint, supplying a limited supportive hand for hard times yet requiring sober, consistent habits of life, organizational purity, and control consistent with the emerging bourgeois norms of
modernity in the nineteenth century.

EXCLUSION AND CLOSURE: DUBLIN'S RELIGIOUS DIVIDE

Dublin was the center of the British state in Ireland and the heart of Protestant
influence, and the popularity of friendly societies in the nineteenth century led
the Anglo-Irish to form their own friendly and mutual aid associations. Protestant
influence in Dublin's public life waned in the nineteenth century as this group
relocated to the suburbs, in an "exodus, both from the city and from municipal life
[that] undoubtedly reduced the quality of municipal life."[43] The silk industry dried
up in the nineteenth century; it had employed Protestant skilled workers, a stratum of the Protestant working class that then simply disappeared.[44]

The structure of voluntary associations in nineteenth-century Ireland followed the religious divide that permeated all aspects of life in Ireland from
politics to sport.[45] It was observed that in the 1870s "the Protestant societies [did]
not admit any but Protestant members," and while the far more numerous Catholic societies that catered to the Catholic working class did not pose formal
religious barriers, Catholic customs and Catholic society tended to seal their
association borders around religion as well.[46]

Sunday society meetings were often the only time the Catholic working class could find time to get together, but it was a day most Protestants refused for any type of business or leisure. Catholic associations also had rules that all members, subject to fines, must be in attendance at funerals in Catholic churches and Catholic burial grounds, a prospect not very enticing to potential Protestant members.[47] Still, the spirit of association could bridge the tensions between Protestants and Catholics, as Andrew Pearce, secretary of the Protestant St. George's Friendly Brothers Tontine, described of his society: "We don't keep out any man on account of his creed or occupation. I often hear of societies refusing men on account of tailoring being their trade, but there's more talk in it than anything else."[48]

In contrast, the Amicable Society identified itself as "Protestant, and consequently Christian, [and its] character deserves attention, because, in proportion as the generous and God-like principles of Protestantism are cultivated, the minds of their recipients will become enlightened and elevated."[49] The men of the Amicable Society met at a Methodist Church in Dublin every Tuesday evening, 8–10 P.M., and this friendly society operated in much the same way as the Catholic organizations.[50]

The Protestant associations also strove to create a moral framework for their members in and outside the society meeting, denying benefits and eventually membership for "drunkenness, or unjustifiable quarreling and fighting"; members were admonished not to "lead an irregular life."[51] The Amicable Society required a high level of personal responsibility from its members that did not extend to religious tolerance; it excluded Irish Catholics, and the following question appeared on the member's questionnaire used for admission to the society: "Of what community of Protestants are you a member?"[52] The Protestant Friendly Benefit Society of Dublin (1843), the Protestant Pembroke Society of Tradesmen (1833), and the Wesleyan Methodist Benevolent Union Society (1832) all refused to betray the Anglo-Irish ascendancy and maintained Protestant exclusionary practices.[53]

DISCIPLINE IN PUBLIC

It is suggested in this study that in their associations, the Irish Americans deliberately pursued a course of communal discipline and strict adherence to protocol, amounting to an adaptive restraint that militated against the stock image of the Catholic Irish immigrant as a hard-drinking, boisterous, combative *enfant* incapable of managing his own private life, to say nothing of the more complex life of a public institution. In 1847 during the height of the Famine the *London Times* described the Irish as subject to "inveterate indolence, improvidence, disorder, and constant destitution," a people further defined by "inertness, dependence on others."[54] The social discipline and personal control, the deferred rewards of savings and planning, were qualities that surfaced immediately for the Irish in Philadelphia and other diaspora locations.

Discipline and a care to avoid politics and sectarian conflict were part of Irish Catholic associational tradition. As an example, the Friendly Brothers of St. Patrick, a society dating from the 1750s into the 1840s with multiple "knots" distributed around Ireland, stipulated against "any religious, political, national or party debates."[55] It is also conceivable that the transatlantic Irish American code of discipline and suspicion of the influence of alcohol had its roots in the unsavory reputation of the Dublin tontines, a good number of whom met in public houses which did little to improve the stereotype. The image of the Dublin Friendly Society was synonymous with drink as the "meetings of many societies took place in public houses, leading to the practice of 'treating'" (i.e., buying rounds).[56] Michael Rorke, secretary of the St. Peter's and Paul's Tontine, asserted that "meeting in public houses is ruinous to a poor man . . . the rent of the meeting room ought to be paid equally by all the members, which it is not when the landlord is paid through liberal drink."[57]

Dublin and Philadelphia: Comparative Financial Strategies and the Care of Identity

The congruence between the practices, shapes, and styles of the Irish friendly society and the Irish American associations in Philadelphia later established by the Diaspora Irish is evident in certain areas of overlap. The mutual emphasis on health support in an unforgiving society; the democratic nature of governance and control through weekly and monthly meetings of members with voting rights, supported by a system of member-staffed committees that did the practical work of the organization; the formal constitutions and bylaws that were adopted by the society, to be scripted in small books or pamphlets and passed out to each member; all were shared characteristics of the working men's associations on both sides of the Atlantic. The Irish friendly society and the Irish American beneficial association both laid a foundation, through the many formal, written rules and regulations devoted to disciplined and controlled behavior in public places, and enforced their codes by punitive sanctions such as fines to create a moral order both in and out of the association.

The ability to construct one's own constitution and set of bylaws, a process that appeared to involve much borrowing of previous works and models and adapting of the content and wording, was an emblem of ethnic pride for the Irish on both sides of the Atlantic. Given the debates over the interpretation of bylaws and the deference and care that members in Philadelphia associations employed in constitutional discussions and the application of rules, the books of rules were both symbols of ceremonial achievement that ordinary Irishmen could point to as well as practical, working documents. We need only to witness the long discussion that the Donegal Association put its members through in 1915 over the simple reworking of the bylaws to accommodate what was a necessary demand of its hard-pressed stewards: a stipend to help with the cost of travel in the city to visit sick members.[58]

There was a congruence between Dublin and Philadelphia that linked the style, structure, and tone of the Irish in their public realm. The following letter was sent to the Donegal Association of Philadelphia in 1915 by a Reverend McGlynn at the Parochial House in Shaurter, County Donegal, thanking the association for sending its book of the constitution and bylaws: "I am proud of that little book, it is so perfect in all its details and so admirably drawn up. Its authors were wise, thoughtful and farseeing. It is a bulwark of strength to your admirable association."[59]

The Irish American association in Philadelphia, as a type, was similar to the beneficial structure of the Irish friendly society, but in time it deviated from the parent model. The differences in associational structure between the Irish and its diaspora representatives in America also determined the way these two peoples defined themselves. The Dublin tontine was an association intent on material support and rewards, charging members' fees to support the outlay of sick and death benefits and the much anticipated "surplus" at the end of the year that was to be divided: judging from the amounts of various Dublin tontines, there was a sizable pot at Christmastime.

There was a censorship in force on the open inquiry and public debate in the tense political setting of late-nineteenth-century Dublin, with rules to guard against political or even religious discussion, which was a necessary precaution in gatherings of Irish men to prevent attracting the stigma of a "secret society," or perceived threat to the state. The legacy of secret societies in Ireland carried much weight; in the Loughera district of Donegal, in 1882, in the wake of Land League agitation, six murders were recorded in six months, "three cases of firing into houses, thirteen assaults, twenty-two midnight attacks, one hundred twenty threatening notices, and twenty-one threatening letters," all attributed to the work of "secret societies" operating in the area.[60]

American Irish associations had little to fear from an inquiring state suspicious of any gathering of Irish Catholics in their midst, and while many associations printed the disclaimer of not being a secret society, there was none of the desperation of avoiding that label in Philadelphia in the 1890s. As we can see from the content and debates of the Irish in their Philadelphia associations, the discursive life of the society was more of an open forum and freedom of expression remained intact.

This study exposes links to the social learning of native Ireland, with its urban and rural traditions of voluntary associations of many types and varieties, as well as the lessons learned from a mobile people. It also refutes the claim that the Irish Americans were trapped in time, traumatized exiles incapable of adapting to urban America, prisoners of a village culture of stagnant ambitions. Migrant rural laborers in England and Scotland were subject to all types of pressures and limited opportunities, but they also found space to form mutual aid societies. As an example, in the 1850s, a family member reported that a harvest worker from County Longford in Ireland had joined the local circle of the Fenians while sojourning in England; he reported that "if he didn't he wouldn't be let work."[61]

The recently arrived Irish of the Famine era to America were also adaptive and quick to apply sophisticated approaches to work settings as reported by Cormac Ó Gráda's study of the banking habits of Irish immigrants in the notorious Five Points district of New York City. The study notes that "the poorest immigrants, including those who had recently arrived from the remotest corners of Ireland, were keen to save and often able to save substantial sums."[62] Also, social learning through the proximity of neighborhood sharing of information is supported in these findings as neighbors in the Five Points region mimicked each other in their saving patterns, following established networks in native Ireland whether it was a kin relationship or people from the same parish.[63]

The Irish Americans had more in concert with the original British friendly societies when it came to self-education, creating an atmosphere of inquiry and ethnic meaning that went well beyond the more mundane responsibility of the society to maintain its members' health and provide some extra cash at Christmas. And yet, the Irish Americans exhibited a reluctance to allow challenges of the inherited, sanctioned canon of Irish history, with its shared agreement on nationalism and English culpability for Ireland's malaise, and rarely produced individual voices of independent thought within the public sphere; instead, the Philadelphia Irish demonstrated what Foster describes as a character trait: "the tendency to defer to established authority and the low tolerance for individual deviation."[64]

A Tale of Two Cities: Civic Engagement in Dublin and Philadelphia

Tables 4.1 and 4.2 compare the spending strategies of the typical Irish friendly association and a large Irish American society in Philadelphia. The Donegal Beneficial, Social and Patriotic Association of Philadelphia was initiated in 1888, a society that opened its doors to Irish immigrants and descendants in Philadelphia from County Donegal in the far northwest of Ireland. It was a mutual aid society whose primary mission was to provide a working men's health insurance to its membership, and it was in many ways similar to a Dublin tontine.

The Donegal association, however, differed in its approach to finances and its value commitments to real health support, spending profusely on member sick benefits yet also finding resources to support other projects connected with

TABLE 4.1

SPENDING PATTERNS OF A SAMPLE OF IRISH
FRIENDLY ASSOCIATIONS IN THE LATE
NINETEENTH CENTURY

Shares Spent or Invested[a]

Sick benefits	12.0%
Death benefits	11.0%
Christmas divide	67.0%
Invested	5.5%
Miscellaneous items	4.5%

Source: Appendix to "Report by E. Lynch
Daniell, Esq., on Friendly Societies in Ireland,"
1874, in *British Parliamentary Papers* 5, 112.
N = 14.

[a] The mean average share was £81.

TABLE 4.2

SPENDING PATTERNS OF THE DONEGAL BENEFICIAL, SOCIAL AND PATRIOTIC
ASSOCIATION, 1909–1910 AND 1912–1915

	1909	1910	1912	1913	1914	1915
Total annual dues	$4,730	$4,682	$5,057	$5,411	$5,377	$5,358
Share spent on sick and death benefits	86%	91%	74%	76%	81%	80%
Share invested	4%	9%	20%	10%	4%	9%
Total assets	$8,291	$8,189	$10,084	$10,654	$11,375	$12,654
Year-over-year change in assets		−1%	23%	6%	7%	11%

Source: "Minute Book of the Donegal Beneficial, Social and Patriotic Association of
Philadelphia, 1905–1925," Irish Center of Philadelphia.

Note: 1911 figures are not available in the minute book of the association.

Donegal or the Catholic Church as well as for Irish independence; after meeting these obligations of Irish American duty each year, the Donegal Association managed to squeeze surplus dollars into long-term investments.

The figures in Tables 4.1 and 4.2 describe two similar types of associations of the late 1800s that came to emphasize different value codes: the Dublin Irish spent 11 percent of their annual operating funds from dues and fines on sick benefits compared to over 80 percent for the Irish Americans of the Donegal Association.[65] The Irish did, however, allocate 66 percent of their operating funds on the Christmas bonus—Irish American associations had no Christmas payout and looked to invest in long-term securities or a property to house their association in contrast to their brothers on the other side of the Atlantic.

In the late nineteenth century Dublin "experienced a considerable degree of economic stagnation," and its working class was overwhelmingly Catholic and underemployed.[66] Manufacturing in the city declined throughout the nineteenth century, revealing a portrait of opportunity "concentrated in the unskilled casual sectors rather than in skilled manufacturing industry."[67] The Darwinian struggle for labor opportunities was intense during the nineteenth century as rural migrants competed with native Dubliners for what work was available; Guinness Brewery, the city's largest employer, preferred rural migrants for their more robust health, stature, and discipline compared to working-class Dubliners.[68]

In Dublin's work-impoverished economy, men worked through all kinds of deprived health to stay on the job and therefore were not eligible, by tontine rules, for sick benefits.[69] Claiming society benefits was a serious matter in work-poor Dublin and the cause of tension among members in friendly societies, who looked forward to the surplus at the end of the year; the Emerald Society found reason to even fine the man who "upbraids another of receiving benefit."[70] The stagnant nature of the Dublin economy in the nineteenth century produced a working environment that did not allow the Dublin laborer the luxury of being sick; the chance for a wage was much higher than any sick benefit derived from membership in a friendly association, and laborers simply stayed on the job.[71] Regulations against a man "working at his trade or at any other business or if he shall buy or sell wares or commodities" while receiving sick benefit were standard practices of Irish societies in the late nineteenth century.[72]

On the other hand, the opportunity for getting money at the end of the year was worth the paucity of sick benefits allowed (the exceptions were burial rites and death benefits, as there was a high cultural commitment in Catholic Ireland for working men to receive a decent ceremonial burial). Dublin friendly societies invested little of the association's resources in permanent assets: less than 5 percent, compared to well over 60 percent of the treasury devoted to the Christmas divide at the end of the year.

THE PHILADELPHIA MODEL: MUTUAL SUPPORT, SOCIAL DISCIPLINE

While the Irish Americans copied much from the early Irish example, they deviated substantially in their more sophisticated financial approach in organizing themselves for longevity. Discipline was vital to the Irish American image, from the scrupulous running of monthly meetings with strict agendas and timeframes, control extended to the account of finances and the implementation of long-range financial planning. Restraint, sobriety, thrift, and responsibility became goals for the Irish in Philadelphia; these values and practices were not always adhered to but were a purposeful attempt to counter the insult of past representations of an ethnic type.

By the 1890s, the Philadelphia-styled Irish association had evolved in different ways from the tontines and friendly societies of Ireland. Dublin's Samaritan Good Tontine Society (established in 1853) had 120 members in 1871, which made it one of the larger voluntary associations in that city. In 1871, it spent only 3 percent of its members' fees on sick benefits and death benefits, handed out £125, or 56 percent of its yearly fees, for the Christmas divide, and allocating £4, or 2 percent, of its money in savings.

A DECENT BURIAL FOR A HARD LIFE

As the preamble of the St. Thomas Burial Society states, Irish burial societies were devoted to providing for "the decent and Christian-like interment of its members."[73] Meetings were generally held once a week at a time when working men were free to get together; for example, the Milltown Burial Society held its meetings every Sunday from 3 to 4 P.M., in the Milltown Schoolhouse.[74] Members were admitted up to age fifty and children above the age of three could also be included in the spectrum of benefits. The simple premise of the burial society—"the aspiration to respectability . . . in the desire to avoid a pauper's funeral"—accounted for its popularity among the working classes of Dublin and Ireland in the late 1800s and early 1900s.[75]

Burial societies were administered by officers and stewards whose duties included managing the death benefit and putting on the ceremony of the burial. The stewards were responsible for keeping the burial equipment in good order, "the sheets, well washed and mangled, and candlesticks, properly cleaned."[76] Burial societies catered to the working class as evidenced by the rules of St. Bridget's Burial Society which forbade "any member . . . dying at the poor house."[77] St. Paul's Tontine and Burial Society in 1868 had in its material possession "six sheets, two napkins, six candlesticks, snuffers and a snuff dish." Members could use these and return them after four days.[78]

The Emerald Society membership met at the home of the deceased for the viewing and could either join the procession of the coffin through the streets to the burial ground or make their way to the grave site on their own. No member was obliged to attend a funeral beyond two miles walking distance, but he had to show respect by a clean-shaven appearance—and the member turning up for a funeral with his "beard on, hands or linen dirty, or indecent" was fined.[79]

Like other Irish societies, the burial societies' year-end surplus was divided as a Christmas "bonus" that families looked forward to and wives guarded with intense scrutiny: "at Christmas she [member's wife] will often accompany him to the meeting room, and either receive the money herself or return home after it is paid."[80] The St. Bridget's Burial Society of Dublin defined the purposes and potential uses of its annual Christmas divide—"such dividend shall be applied . . . in the purpose of food, firing, clothes, or other necessaries, the tools, implements, education of his or her kindred or children."[81] Such were the real fears of Dublin working men wasting their precious Christmas funds at the pub.

The pattern of a complete spend-down of wealth, with very little emphasis on saving or investment, suggests that the associational life of late-nineteenth-century Ireland was a communal expression of individual interests, a personal investment in a men's gathering that offered some protection against sickness and a moment for modest leisure, a guarantee of a decent burial and a savings club that bore fruit at Christmas. By definition the association could not engage in political debate or discussion against the Crown; instead, the Irish burial society was another model of the voluntary association, its methods and practices reflective of the realities of the working class in nineteenth-century Ireland.

CONGRUITY OF RULES AND BYLAWS BETWEEN DUBLIN SOCIETIES AND PHILADELPHIA'S IRISH ASSOCIATIONS

If the rules and regulations of a Dublin friendly society, the Inchicore society of railroad workers west of Dublin, and the normative regulations of Philadelphia's Irish associations are set side by side, the congruity between the style and structure of rules of this Irish society and later Philadelphia Irish American associations becomes apparent.

The Inchicore Friendly Society of Dublin had sixty-three members in the 1870s and a constitution that specified just about every contingency this association could face. Inchicore was an industrial center west of Dublin, the home of the Great Southern and Western Railway Company, which employed 625 workers at its plant in the 1870s.[82] It professed a commitment to a wide set of communal values starting from its initial premises, that it brought men together "for the purpose of mutual relief in case of sickness and for the burial of the members, their wives or children."[83] Meetings were held twice a month on Friday evenings at the Dublin home of a member; members were fined for missing the quarterly meeting and for not serving on the stewards' committee of six when called.

The restrictions on behavior in Dublin were specific and describe a blueprint for bourgeois respectability, a longing for respect due workingmen who adhered to a code of restraint. Meetings were expected to be orderly, members required to speak and act in "a cool, dispassionate manner" and stay on topic. Fines were stipulated for the disruption of a meeting, "for striking a brother in the society or elsewhere . . . for speaking in a degrading or distracting manner to a brother . . . for coming to society intoxicated . . . for cursing or swearing."[84]

This Dublin society invested its funds in the James's Street Savings' Bank, but it is hard to imagine that it had much to lay away in the bank after a Christmas divide. Rule 26 stated: "On the 23rd of December in each year, if it should appear to the society that there is a surplus of stock and funds . . . such surplus shall be divided equally in just proportions amongst the members."[85]

The Friendly Brothers of the Harp and Shamrock Tontine Society (1856) listed forty-five rules in its constitution which was handed out to its members for a small fee. The society supported communal aims, "the mutual relief and maintenance of its members in sickness, and their decent interment after death," a gathering of Dublin working men who prided themselves on admitting all "with no objection . . . on account of . . . trade, calling or religion."[86] The Harp and Shamrocks was administered by a committee of twelve members who rotated service every three months and restricted age to men under forty-five years. Meetings were held every Sunday from noon to 2:00 P.M., at a private residence in Dublin.

The Harp and Shamrocks also had strict codes of behavior for its members in public places. Sick benefits would be suspended if caused by "abuse of drinking, quarrelling . . . or by an unlawful act." The Harp and Shamrocks was not, in the tradition of Philadelphia's Clan na Gael and AOH divisions, a gathering for political debate, public discussion, or educational advancement, for Rule 33 stated that "no religious or political discussions will be allowed to take place in the society during the hours of business."[87]

We can extract from the great number of rules and the detailed description of unacceptable behavior the degree to which the Irish associations struggled to construct a moral code for its members to follow in and out of the beneficial society. The Harp Society imposed sanctions for infractions of the code outside the society, for being "engaged in any riot or quarrel" or being arrested and, inside the meetings of the group, for "challenging to fight, or offering to make wagers, or coming to society intoxicated [or for] . . . cursing and swearing."[88]

As the Irish Americans reveled in the discourse of opposition and revolt within the sanctuary of their associations, constructing whole societies such as the Clan na Gael on the premise of active support for an Irish revolution, the Irish in Dublin imposed a self-censorship on its members to protect against state surveillance. Dublin's St. Lawrence Tontine, on its entrance questionnaire, asked prospective members if they belonged to "any disloyal, unlawful, or seditious association, or any secret society or unlawful combination." The "unlawful combination" was interpreted as "a man who combines with others against the Government . . . an avowed Fenian," which was a code term for the coalescing of men and political forces intent on overcoming British rule in that island colony.[89]

The moral code of the Dublin associations could also extend to a complete ban on alcohol. The St. Lawrence Tontine Society was founded in Dublin and required members to take "the total abstinence pledge from every species of intoxicating liquors," and faced expulsion and loss of all invested funds should that pledge be broken.[90] The St. Luke's Friendly Society forbade men on sick leave to "make use of spirituous liquors which are improper for his disorder."[91] The St. Lawrence Society also forbade members from "resorting to a dancing house" or "cordial drinking," offenses that led to immediate expulsion.[92] In 1889, the Catholic Total Abstinence Union of Philadelphia recorded 18,089 members in 150 associations dispersed throughout the city, in branches that governed their own local societies.[93]

Mutual Aid at the Site of Work

Mutual aid or beneficial societies were also organized at the site of work in Ireland. For example, employees of the Dublin, Wicklow and Wexford Railway established a mutual aid society for railway workers and in Belfast the Letterpress Printers Society was established by 1871. The Midland Great Western Railway Benefit Society was another work-related beneficial society with a large membership in Ireland in the 1870s.[94]

These societies took in funds and kept them secure for the payout of sick and death benefits; the Dublin Railway Beneficial Society had sufficient surpluses from time to time that tempted them to offer seasonal payouts to its members, which was a subject of debate within the association. Also in Dublin, the Literary Teachers Society was funded in the late 1700s for "literary teachers, and persons engaged in education" and operated through the nineteenth century as a beneficial society for that specific set of Dublin workers. In Belfast, the Belfast House-Painters Society had seventy-five members in 1871.[95]

In Dublin, the Dublin General Post Office Letters Carriers' Friendly Beneficial Society was established in 1860 and claimed fifty-four members in 1871; the society was small and rule 21 of its constitution stipulated that it could only be dissolved if its numbers fell below eleven members.[96] This was a society that provided sick and death benefits and, like most Irish associations, engaged in the divide of its yearly "surplus" at Christmas; its 1860 constitution states, "The objects of this Society are, decent interment of its Members, to afford assistance during illness, and divide the Surplus Funds, if any."[97] The society administered itself by electing two trustees, a treasurer, and a "committee of management" that consisted of six members.

The Dublin Letter Carriers also opened their association to those who were not letter carriers, but they were extremely wary of a potential run on sick benefits and therefore restricted membership from workers who would be difficult to monitor because they worked at home or had mobile jobs. Thus, Rule 5 states, "No person can be proposed as a candidate whose trade . . . is a baker, cook, confectioner, boot or shoe maker, tailor, bookbinder, painter, decorator, or paper." The letter carriers took their aid seriously, requiring members claiming sick benefits to be practically quarantined at home: "any sick member wishing to walk out for the benefit of the air must first obtain a written order from the doctor" stating the hours of the day that the patient was allowed outside. If a member was found out of his home during nondesignated hours, he was removed from sick call and could not receive sick benefits for another three months.[98] Such was the level of associational trust in the Letter Carriers' Society, which was bent on minimizing its spending on members' health and ferreting out any fraud.

The standard society in Ireland was one that offered sick and death benefits and in Cork, the leading city of Ireland's southwest, the Cork Mechanics' Provident Society was a classic example of this type. It was founded in 1823 in southwestern Ireland's leading city and catered to the skilled working class of Cork; its operating understanding was "to allow weekly money in sickness, and money after death."[99]

The Cork Society had only fifty-two members in 1871, a reflection of its restrictive entrance requirements that allowed membership to only the aristocracy of labor. Following a debate over the choice of society physician in 1869, a group of members broke away in favor of their own doctor and formed a competing society, the City of Cork Society, which was less restrictive and allowed clerks and mechanics' assistants to hold memberships.[100] Cork Mechanics' members dropped in weekly to pay money into the general pool; the Cork Society did not allow membership to any worker over thirty-six years of age and had a sliding scale of initiation payments for the young.

The Cork Mechanics Society had the dreaded run on its yearly funds in 1849, a Famine year, when cholera swept the city, and the society was forced to defer death benefit payouts to a future time when it had restored its pool of funds. This was a society that elevated the value of supporting the sick over member dividends; Cork reported that "in some years we have nothing to spare" and the scrutiny and care of sick benefits was an early associational habit easily transferred to the New World.[101]

The Cork Mechanics also had strict rules about drunkenness and would refuse benefits to anyone whose malady was caused by excessive alcohol consumptions.[102] Bourgeois respectability was a value nineteenth-century artisans took seriously and used as a way to separate themselves from lower orders. The Cork Mechanics preferred to present itself as an apolitical association and an association of limited social interaction and leisure: it followed the "rule that no political or religious subject shall be discussed."[103] Meetings were held at a private home and the association was proud that it did not meet at a public house.

The Cork Mechanics even had a fund for emigration available to its artisan members: "a member of two years' standing may obtain ... emigration money; but the sending home of money for this purpose by those who have emigrated, not only to near relatives but even distant ones, and even to mere friends, is so common amongst the ... peasantry of Ireland, that a fund for emigration has never been found necessary in societies."[104]

The Darwinian calculus on men's life expectancy, the censure imposed on potentially divisive topics, and the singular focus on cash reward strangled the growth of a public sphere of the working class in nineteenth-century Ireland; in contrast, the Irish American association engaged in a lively discourse on local issues, embraced Irish culture, supported Irish national causes and ran the monthly meeting as a session in parliamentary procedure.

Temperance societies and working men's societies existed in Cork from the early 1800s, but it was reported that "the greater proportion of them failed in the time of the Famine."[105] Exceptions were the Mechanics' Provident Society of Cork, and new mutual aid societies starting in the 1870s around certain trades such as tobacco sellers, seamen and "victuallers."[106]

The age restriction was a means of guarding against a run on the pool of funds available for sick benefits. Advanced age was a real liability when it came to beneficial associations in Ireland; it was calculated that a man of twenty had four sick days per year on average while a man of forty-five years averaged eight days.[107] The division at Christmas was perceived as a way of balancing age; instead of keeping the money inside the mutual aid society as a guarantee against a future run on sick benefits, it was distributed regardless of age.

The rules and regulations that the Philadelphia's Irish Americans adopted to govern their mutual aid associations were congruous with the original models of old Ireland with a few important exceptions. In Philadelphia, stewards were elected and paid a small salary to check on members who claimed sick benefits; the home visits seemed to be more of a humanitarian gesture than a surveillance tactic. The Irish in Philadelphia required a doctor's report of good health as a requirement of membership, codes that enforced propriety in public places, courtesy to fellow members, restrictions against fighting and drunkenness, and written requirements on how to address the group during the formal proceedings of meetings.

IRISH BUILDING SOCIETIES

Irish Building Societies were both investment clubs and mutual aid societies; members borrowed against funds invested for the construction of their homes.[108] The Cork and South of Ireland Permanent Building Society was begun in 1853 and was one of the largest in the southwest of Ireland. The form and structure of these associations were familiar, with a slate of officers and a board of directors and the recording secretary doing much of the society's work including record keeping. Members were assigned rule books similar to beneficial associations, and instead of dues, they paid in "shares" as an investment into the association.[109]

The Cork Building Society allowed members to tap into their investments based on the number of shares they had on record. Cork recorded ninety members in the late 1800s. It recruited its membership from the "middle classes," the skilled artisans, who made up the upper stratum of the working class and were given to status aspirations and bourgeois habits. In Cork's struggling nineteenth-century economy, this building society strived to maintain its numbers, "chiefly owing to our not having the same number of well-paid mechanics as in England, the particular class for whom building societies have the greatest interest."[110]

THE IRISH AMERICAN MODEL; MUTUAL WORKERS AID

The Irish American mutual aid associations of Philadelphia in the late nineteenth and early twentieth centuries followed many of the forms and practices of workers' societies in old Ireland; however, once established in Philadelphia, the Irish altered the value structure of communal commitments to mutual aid. The Irish Americans eschewed the legacy of the Christmas divide and were disciplined in their approach to long-term financial planning, making investments in banks, savings and loans, and even stocks. At the same time, the Irish Americans were steadfast in their support of members down on their luck and time after time when it came to a vote they would award sick or death benefits to a member who was unemployed, sick but who had allowed his dues to lapse.

Brother Gallagher of Philadelphia's Donegal Association was unable to work during summer 1906 and could not pay his dues for a few months; after a committee of the association investigated, it decided that "the Society [would] pay up his dues until July."[111] The humanitarian largess and financial planning of the Philadelphia Irish societies was made possible by a more vibrant industrial economy that provided a measure of social surplus to the working class Irish of the city; in contrast, in Dublin and Cork and all over the island, Ireland's deindustrialization in the nineteenth century made for more desperate conditions that restricted the vision and breadth of its working-class societies.

Older members in Philadelphia were revered for their service and wisdom, as was President Michael Brady who had led the Cavan Catholic, Social, and Beneficial Society of Philadelphia as president for twelve straight years and at age fifty-six was still a member and attending meetings; the society eventually established a "vacant chair" in his honor.[112] In similar fashion, financial secretary Daniel Dever of the Donegal Association was given a banquet in his honor in 1910 for his eighteen years of service as financial secretary.[113]

The Irish Roots of American Hibernian
Associationalism Reviewed

It has been suggested that there was a connective thread between early Irish associationalism and the surge and form of Irish American civic institutions in the
late 1800s and early 1900s in Philadelphia. When we route the map of historical
cultural connection of the late-nineteenth-century Irish American Philadelphia
through Ireland and consider the influence on the American-bound Irish derived
from Irish friendly societies and the diverse, broad heritage of beneficial societies, fraternal orders, building and burial societies, agricultural cooperatives,
Gaelic sport clubs, and working-class communal savings associations, a persuasive line of connection emerges.

Symmetry exists in the style and structure of these associations, which were
essentially working-class communes designed to support a vulnerable strata of
the population through the hard times of living and coping with certain social
facts, declining life chances for work in Ireland of the nineteenth century and
rampant and, at times volatile, industrialization in Philadelphia. The Irish Americans of Philadelphia cloaked their communicative message in the rhetoric of
nationalist resurgence, motivated by their own reading of Irish history and its
companion mission in Irish America, in a sincere reach among ordinary men
to understand their past, govern themselves, and create a separate sphere of public action and meaning.

Those men and women in late-nineteenth-century Philadelphia who had only
common means and limited social capital went on to establish their societies
with scrupulous attention to parliamentary procedure and financial responsibility, receiving their training on the job, influenced by direct or indirect cultural connection to the Irish tradition of small group democracy, and bound by
the contents of the associational rule books, which acted as instant primers on
disciplined social action in public settings.

This chapter's transatlantic comparative analysis suggests that the Irish of the
Diaspora, bestowed with certain advantages as well as the structural impedi-
ments of the industrial city, were able to use Irish proto-models of civic action
to create a public sphere of Gaelic content and meaning in the waning decades
of the nineteenth century. Old Ireland had its public institutions, its voluntary
associations, but the controls of church and state, combined with the withering
nature of the nineteenth-century economy in Ireland, narrowed the possibilities for associational expression in the native land.

CHAPTER 5

A Microanalysis of Irish American Civic Life

IRELAND'S DONEGAL AND CAVAN EMERGE IN PHILADELPHIA

Rudolph Vecoli writes that ethnicity is "a subjective sense of peoplehood based in common memories, and manifested in symbols which evoke those memories. . . . [It is] 'shared history and culture.'"[1] In the late nineteenth and early twentieth centuries, Irish Americans in Philadelphia established associations based on cultural memories derived from place and descent, organizations that attracted large memberships. These were primarily "county" societies and even though the home parish was the local store of shared memory in Ireland, in Philadelphia, the Irish chose the county as the boundary for their new associations and thus formed the Cork, Galway, Wexford, Tyrone, Derry, Cavan, and Donegal Associations. The Connaught and Mayo associations of Philadelphia were based on Irish provinces, in this case the most western regions, which had been subject to devastation and emigration during the mid-nineteenth-century great Famine of Ireland.

Two Irish American associations, the Cavan Catholic, Social, and Beneficial Society of Philadelphia (1907) and the Donegal Beneficial, Social and Patriotic Association (1888), form the basis in this chapter for a case study, a more detailed insight of Irish American construction of an ethnic association of cultural identity in the late 1800s and early 1900s. These associations were beneficial societies for the working class and an Irish neighborhood petty bourgeoisie, shop owners and clerks who constituted membership in these beneficial associations, many of whom were recent immigrants from Donegal and Cavan. David Brundage recognizes a similar trend in his study of Irish American nationalism; the surge in the early years of the 1900s was due to "unskilled recent Irish immigrants" of the period, "peasants or recently proletarianized agricultural laborers from the west of the country."[2]

John Ridge, in his study of county associations in New York City, discovered trends similar to those evident in Philadelphia county associations, finding societies populated by a surge of Irish immigration in the 1880s due to tensions over Land League disturbances and the threat of a renewed famine. The county associations were devoted to a nostalgic rendition of native lands, subject to high rates of member abandonment due to the high mobility of working-class existence, and populated by both American- and Irish-born, with the latter designation dominant. As in Philadelphia, a society of the working class positioned men of status and achievement out front, as elected officers; Ridge notices that "every society seemed to have its doctors, lawyers, and successful contractors serving as officers."[3]

This chapter will also analyze the pre-emigration, native Irish sources of civic engagement in the rural zones of Donegal and Cavan and suggest linkages between early cultural contact and patterns of socialization with the norms of communal associations in rural Ireland and their influence on the later record of a more sophisticated enactment of communal action in Philadelphia.

The Organization of Memory: The Donegal Beneficial, Social, and Patriotic Association of Philadelphia

The presence of Donegal immigrants and second-generation Irish from that far northwestern county in Ireland had achieved a critical mass in Philadelphia by the 1880s; the early organization of Donegal descendants in Philadelphia was confined to spontaneous, isolated initiatives to assist poor farmers experiencing continual rural crisis in Donegal. Due to the efforts of Hugh O'Donnell, sufficient momentum was established for a citywide collection of the Donegal Irish that led to an all-Donegal association in Philadelphia in the late 1880s.[4]

The first meeting of the Donegal Association was held September 18, 1888, at Lewars Hall at 9th and Spring Garden Streets, near Center City Philadelphia; only those born in Donegal were eligible for membership, a rule that was later amended in 1896 to allow for broader membership and included Irish descendants from Donegal. James Dolan was the first president and Hugh O'Donnell was secretary, joined by magistrate Maurice Wilhere and Philadelphia postmaster William Harrity as association officers.[5] The association was primarily for that county's new urban dwellers in America, but there was constant interaction and communication with the towns and villages of Donegal: as just one example, in 1905 a priest from Killybegs dropped in on a fall meeting to visit with "old friends."[6]

Meeting locations moved around in the city, and in 1897 the association held its monthly gathering at Fairmount Hall, 2100 Callowhill Street, a location just north of Center City in the warehouse district of Philadelphia. Eventually,

Donegal Association

Meets this and the Third Sunday of
every month at 2.30 P. M., at

Philopatrian Hall,

211 S. Twelfth Street, third-story front,

AND IS NOW A FLOURISHING SOCIETY.

Sick Benefits per week, - -	$ 5.00
Death Benefits, - - -	60.00
Funeral appropriation on death of	
member's wife, - -	30.00

Men in Good Health, practical Catholics,

Natives of Donegal or their Descendants,

from 18 to 45 years of age only,
are eligible for membership.

Initiation Fee, - - -	$1.00
Dues per month, - -	50

Having the necessary qualifications, come
and you will receive a cordial welcome.

D. J. Gallagher & Co., Prs., 420 Library St., Phila.

1888 advertisement to join the Donegal Association.
Source: Digital Library@Villanova University.

Industrial Hall at 314 North Broad Street, just above Vine Street, became the longtime home of the association.[7] Donegal men and women were spread out all over the city, and this location was hardly within walking distance of most members.

The Donegal Association was primarily a beneficial society providing subsistence-level financial support in the form of sick and death benefits. The association also established the Donegal Building & Loan in its early years, which provided investment income for the association and loans to members who could not qualify for home mortgages due to an uneven employment record.[8]

In 1905 the association accepted a fifty-year purchase of bonds for the Philadelphia Rapid Transit Company, an investment in the "Market Street Elevated Railroad Company" that was thought of as a safe bet and a stake in Philadelphia's transportation future. The association's investment in the subway and the "El"—"the lines of the Company, consisting of a subway on Market Street . . . from the Delaware to the Schuylkill; the new bridge crossing the Schuylkill, and the elevated Railway extending to the City Line"—was a modernist approach to urban transport, and also a way for the Irish to escape the confines of neighborhood and travel to the centers of the Irish cultural movement.[9]

The Demographics of Irish Civic Expression

The occupational analysis of the Donegal Association in Table 5.1 demonstrates that the Irish who joined this ethnic association in the late 1890s and early 1900s were predominantly working class, occupying positions as skilled workers in the industrial matrix of Philadelphia. Many Donegal men worked in the Baldwin Locomotive Works, and others worked as bricklayers, plumbers, and ironworkers. Donegal men were also established in white-collar positions, including many saloon owners and owner-operators of neighborhood grocery stores, occasionally self-employed building contractors or boarding house owners, and, increasingly, clerks.[10] Two of Donegal's presidents were lawyers—James Friel (1906–1909) and Francis A. McCarron (1909–1912), representing an impulse to position respectability and status front and center in an organization of working men and many recent immigrants.

If we look in microcosm of a sample of Donegal men at the turn of the century, we find Peter J. McGee, who was twenty-five when he joined the Donegal Association in 1909. He had a wife and a small family of two sons and a daughter living in a home he owned. John J. Murray was thirty-five when he joined the Donegal Association in 1909. He lived in a rented home on 18th Street with his wife and his sister-in-law; he was a plumber who ran his own shop.[11] John McGlinn was a dyer who lived as a lodger on North Third Street; he was forty-two years old when he joined the association.[12]

TABLE 5.1

OCCUPATIONAL STRUCTURE OF
PHILADELPHIA'S DONEGAL ASSOCIATION,
1905–1910

Occupation Category	Share
Professional[a]	6%
White collar[b]	39%
Skilled labor[c]	45%
Unskilled labor[d]	11%

Source: "Minute Book of the Donegal Beneficial, Social and Patriotic Association of Philadelphia, 1905–1925," Irish Center of Philadelphia.

N = 113.

[a] Includes attorneys and physicians.

[b] Includes shopkeepers, grocers, and saloon keepers.

[c] Includes machinists, textile workers, and railroad men.

[d] Includes manual laborers.

DEMOCRATIC LEANINGS

The Donegal Association would eventually have a large membership, but the monthly meetings attracted only a fraction of the total. Judging from voting patterns on debates and meetings in which the elections of officers took place, a good turnout would represent a third of the membership. For the election of officers and stewards and association physician in a membership of 713 in 1907, 216 were in attendance and voted; in 1910, 223 voted in a society of 686.[13]

Table 5.2 demonstrates the steady growth of the Donegal Association, which became a large and relatively affluent association in a city already crowded with Irish American societies. High membership meant security and influence, and in years when membership waned or growth was slow, members were assigned to make home visits to brothers who had allowed their dues to slip. During the drop in membership in 1909–1910, the association voted to put $100 into the contingency fund to allow officers to "assist any delinquent member who desires to continue his membership, the amount to be advanced as a loan."[14]

The careful financial planning of the Donegal Association, which was based on the income from dues and fines balanced against the demand for sick benefits,

TABLE 5.2

MEMBERSHIP COUNT OF THE DONEGAL ASSOCIATION, 1895–1925

Year	Number of Members	Year	Number of Members
1895	251	1911	736
1897	282	1912	752
1898	329	1913	780
1901	407	1914	788
1902	440	1915	781
1904	462	1916	757
1907	713	1917	809
1908	825	1922	741
1909	698	1923	789
1910	686	1925	885

Source: Donegal Association Minute Book.

Note: Data not available for all years.

left the association with financial options, which it exercised through its "contingent" fund. This fund was used for donations to all kinds of causes, including requests from Philadelphia and Donegal churches, from individual brothers in special need, and for contributions to Irish independence.

The sizable population of the Donegal Association and the dispersion of its members throughout the city exacted a toll on the association's four stewards who were charged with the responsibility of visiting members at their home and doling out sick benefits. The stewards stood for election each year and received a salary, but the task of visiting each member who requested sick benefits was formidable. In 1907, Donegal Steward Gallagher handed out $855 in sick benefits. Steward Murray made even more home visits in 1907, 175 for the year; in 1908, Steward Murray made 242 home visits, handing out $1,210.[15] The stewards were also responsible for getting the society's "flags and banners" ready for the St. Patrick's parade.

The association membership acknowledged the "hard circumstances" that faced a widow named Boyce in 1905 and voted her an additional $25 above the death benefit.[16] And, after the wife of a member named McDermitt died, it was decided after a close vote—thirty-four to thirty-one—to pay $30 in death benefits even though the member had not paid his dues for several months.[17] The Donegal Association also looked after its members in hard circumstances: as an example, in 1913 it was reported to the association that member Pat McLaughlin "was confined in the insane dept. of the Phila. Hospital and that he was apparently sound in mind and body, that he had been visited by Dr. McDermott and Dr. O'Donnell about two months after being detained in the hospital."[18] The Donegal Association, by managing its assets carefully and following its own set of mutual aid values, spent extensively on the welfare of its members through a yearly outlay of sick payments and, through the Contingent Fund replenished each year by annual winter ball proceeds, extended a humanitarian hand where needed and took stands on public issues of meaning to its members such as Irish nationalism.

The Donegal Association meetings were also moments for leisure and cultural revival. For St. Patrick's Day 1910, "cigars were passed around, and an hour was given by several members contributing to the entertainment by singing Irish songs."[19] Sunday afternoons were also times for Gaelic sport and Donegal joined other Irish American teams in Philadelphia with names such as Young Ireland, Mayo, Tyrone, and Kevin Barry. These traditional Irish sporting events were a prelude to a Sunday afternoon picnic or an evening dance accompanied by Irish music.[20]

THE DONEGAL DEBATE IN ITS PUBLIC SPACE

The association's contingent fund, which was replenished each year through profits from the annual Donegal ball, provided the financial source for the association's values. The association reached into the fund to support the Gaelic League's Irish-language movement, sending $50 to the Philadelphia branch in 1906.[21] In 1920 the Donegal Association voted to buy bonds for the Irish Republic to support Ireland's fledgling independent state; later, $300 was dispatched to the Friends of Irish Freedom in Philadelphia, an action committee intent on pushing the American government to recognize Ireland's new independence.[22] In 1906, the association received a letter appealing for financial support from the Irish United League and dispatched $250 to Ireland for the "Irish Parliamentary Fund."[23]

Donegal's monthly meetings set aside time for "patriotic sessions" in which public issues were discussed, motions raised and voted on. This structured space was the members' zone for expressions, the association's public sphere; its serious agenda outside the mundane management of the association's financial matters allowed for a construction of Irish identity, and while the men of Donegal were never long-winded or overly expressive, they were consistent in their views, siding with the emerging cultural and political nationalism of the late nineteenth and early twentieth centuries, with the Gaelic League, and naturally with the movement for Irish independence and the Irish-Anglo War of 1919–1920.

In 1906 "the Irish language question was introduced and quite a discussion followed—those who desired to join an Irish school for the purpose of studying the language should give in their names and they would be called together sometime later."[24]

The association voted to "co-operate with the Philadelphia Celtic society to receive Dr. Douglas Hyde, the great promoter of the Irish language, when he comes to this city" when he toured Philadelphia in fall 1905. Donegal meetings were often ended in sentimentality, in remembrance of a past brother or in song, as an August meeting in 1905 in which the "meeting adjourned with a song by Mr. McElwee."[25]

Donegal was a region of Gaelic speakers and so it is not surprising that Donegal men and women in Philadelphia would support the revival of the Gaelic language. The language movement in Gaelic Philadelphia in the early 1900s signaled something larger than its communicative potential. As Seamus Deane writes, "The abandonment of the language involved the abandonment of so much else in traditional customs, practices and ways of thought that the security of any group identity or of what the 19th century called 'national character' was seriously weakened, if it survived at all."[26]

In contrast to the Irish friendly societies and the Dublin tontine, which were forced to censure potentially explosive debate on politics, the Irish Americans carved out a more expansive public forum. As an example, in 1914, on July 19, Philadelphia's Donegal Association sent $25 to the "Irish Volunteers, more if wanted," as the Irish Army of Independence was forming from its civilian volunteers during the years leading up to 1916.[27]

DONEGAL'S CLUBS AND SOCIETIES, 1880–1912

The County of Donegal is a windswept coastal region of farmers and sheep herders, and the towns of Letterkenny and Donegal are commercial outposts for the rural and town economy. In 1890, Donegal town had thirteen boot makers, seventeen bakers, seven butchers, eight blacksmiths, fifteen carpenter shops, and one bank.[28] Donegal was also a center for the production of linen from the cultivation of flax in the nineteenth century.

If rural Donegal in the late 1800s and early 1900s did not have a base of beneficial friendly societies to act as incubators of civic learning, it did possess a diverse set of clubs and associations that operated under the principles of local democracy and ordered financial accounting. The Ballyshannon Protestant Young Men's Christian Association (YMCA) was prominent in the 1880s in Donegal, when it was led by the Reverend S. G. Cochrane, who strove to run the society along democratic lines. It boasted a reading room and weekly meetings; on a winter's evening in 1880, Reverend Cochrane entertained his young members with a reading of Oliver Goldsmith's poetry.[29]

The Ballina YMCA (1882) followed the example of Ballyshannon and recorded thirty-four members in 1883. It held weekly meetings, elected its officers, and its fundraiser for the year was "for purchasing new books for the library."[30] Derry also had a branch of this Protestant club for youth established by the mid-1880s.[31] And Strabane, southwest of Londonderry on the border of County Donegal, was home to the Strabane Young Men's Mutual Improvement Society in 1885. The Protestant youth clubs of Donegal and Derry, with their focus on reading and self-improvement, might not have had a direct impact on the cohort of Catholic rural farm workers or the sons of small farmers who were given to emigration and arrival at Philadelphia's Donegal Association, but the spread of proper civic form and constitutional order was horizontal, and Catholic associations such as Gaelic sport clubs easily borrowed the forms of respectability when it came to legitimizing their associations.

Temperance societies were also part of the associational landscape in nineteenth-century Donegal. The St. Eugene's Temperance Society of Strabane put on a day of sports to promote its association in the spring of 1885. The two-mile walking race was a popular event that attracted a large number of participants and spectators.[32] Omagh in County Tyrone also had an active St. Eugene's Temperance Society in 1890, and the town of Drumquin and the parishes of Upper Badoney and Banagher had their own societies.[33] Banagher held a winter ball in January 1890 that attracted "not less than 300 people" and featured exhibitions of "jig-dancing" and singing that lasted through the evening.[34] The Limavady Catholic Temperance Society met in a winter meeting to distribute silver medals to members who had achieved temperance and contributed to the society; the evening ended with a series of songs with "Miss Mullan presiding at the piano with her usual pleasing renditions."[35]

GAELIC SPORT AS SOCIAL LEARNING

The Erne Football Club of Ballyshannon, a Gaelic football team associated with the Gaelic Athletic Association (GAA) of Ireland, emerged in the early 1900s along with many other small sporting clubs in Donegal. GAA sport teams had their focus primarily on football and hurling, but each club was run as a formal association with its own written constitution and rulebook, elected executives, monthly member meetings and financial records following the model of other voluntary associations in Ireland. Knowledge of associational practices and norms in one society was easily transferred to others; in Kerry, Gaelic Athletic clubs used "the National League as a blueprint for their clubs."[36]

The GAA in Donegal supplied a form of rural popular culture and filled a void in local society that had been in decline since the Great Famine. On a January evening in 1906, Ballyshannon came out to support their Erne Football Club with a fundraising concert: "Bandmaster Eldon gave two banjo solos with piano accompaniment" while the singing of Richard Deacon "brought down the house."[37]

In sparsely populated Donegal, a dominant Catholic region with a sizable Protestant minority population, the sectarian divide was of necessity ignored when it came to filling out a roster for sport including the clubs of the GAA. In the late 1880s and early 1890s, the Burt Hibernians were 46 percent Protestant, the Moville Harps were 22 percent Protestant, and when the Killea Hibernians hit the football field, their club had a majority of Protestant members (63 percent).[38] In Donegal, GAA clubs celebrated Gaelic nationalism in the naming of their clubs, with the Sinn Feins of Bundoran, the Young Irelanders of Doorin, the Buncrana Emmets, and the Kevin Barrys of Burnfoot.[39]

Gaelic sporting clubs devoted to Irish football and hurling substituted for schools on small group democracy, with the rural population of growing sportsmen exposed to the formal rules of voluntary associations and informal norms of action in public settings. Thus Donegal's mixed sectarian population in a remote corner of the country allowed for a crossing of the religious divide in its associationalism.

DONEGAL LAND LEAGUES

The agricultural crisis of 1879–1880 in Donegal was fuel for the growth of the Irish National Land League and branches sprouted in the region. The acrimonious debate over the power of landlords to evict and control rents escalated during these years of hardship made poignant by the memory of the mid-century Great Famine. The "tenant-farmers" of Claremorris in County Mayo met in 1880 to form a branch and were addressed by the parish Catholic priest who told them, "The goal . . . is the riddance, root and branch, of the odious system of landlords."[40]

Inver and Ballyshannon had Land League branches that opposed "the unwise and blundering policy of coercion and arrests" in response to the tenant movement in Donegal.[41] Land League branches in Donegal were also run like local associations, with elected officers, regular meetings, and public financial records all legitimized by the ubiquitous constitution and book of regulations available to members.[42]

Donegal and northwestern Ireland also produced branches of the Irish National League, in Gweedore, Inishkeel, Strabane, and East Urney. Weekly meetings were held, and the associations were administered by a slate of officers and a small committee.[43] The rhetoric of these rural associations was heated as it supported Irish Home Rule. For example, a resolution of the Inishkeel branch read, "We demand the restoration to Ireland of her native Parliament, and declare that there can never be peace or posterity in this country as long as the Irish are ruled by English-made laws."[44]

GREAT ANTI-EVICTION MEETING!

A Demonstration of the Citizens of Philadelphia,
UNDER THE AUSPICES OF THE

Municipal Council of the Irish National League,
WILL BE HELD AT

HORTICULTURAL HALL,
Broad, above Spruce Street,

ON FRIDAY EVENING, DECEMBER 17th, 1886,
AT 8 O'CLOCK.

To denounce the eviction and coercion, and to express sympathy with
the Irish people in their struggle for self government.

COMPLIMENTARY—ADMIT ONE.

JOHN F. MURPHY, PR. 227 S. FIFTH ST.—BELOW WALNUT.

Notice of an Irish National League public demonstration against the ongoing evictions
in Ireland. Source: CHRC.

Donegal Agricultural Cooperatives

Killybegs, a fishing center and regional town center along the northwest coast
of Ireland in County Donegal, established an agricultural cooperative in 1895.
It legitimized its presence with a president, a treasurer, a secretary, and a "committee of management" that acted as a board of counsel and oversight. Like all
rural cooperatives in Ireland in the early 1900s, it was governed by a lengthy set
of printed rules distributed to each of its members, who were its shareholders;
this was a set of standard regulations adopted by the Irish Agricultural Organization Society to govern rural co-ops in Ireland.[45]

From the Rules of the Killybegs Cooperative, it is possible to outline the traces
of a formidable parliamentary structure that governed the meetings and business methods of these societies of small farmers in the late 1800s and early 1900s
in Ireland. Loans could be made to members for a one-year period with a £100
limit; individual loans to farmers were made for high-cost agricultural items
such as the purchase of livestock.[46]

The cooperative aimed to lower prices of material needed for agricultural production, to regulate prices it charged for the cooperative's products and at the
same time earn something for the association and its members. Any money left
over at the end of the year—but no more than 10 percent of the total profits—
was plowed back into a savings or could be used to promote the general agricultural cooperative movement in Ireland. The Managing Committee had discretion
on the use of profits over the 10 percent range. However, cooperatives did not
allow the Christmas divide and no surplus could "be divided by way of bonus,
dividend, or otherwise amongst the members."[47]

Like the Irish friendly associations, rural cooperatives strove to sidestep the image of communal associations as potential agencies of opposition and revolt, and co-ops therefore stipulated that "no political or sectarian discussion" was allowed in any of its meetings. Like the friendly societies, members were also held to a high moral standard and faced expulsion if arraigned for a crime or for breaches of acceptable behavior in public places.[48]

Donegal's Letterkenny Cooperative Flax Society was established in 1905 for "flax scutching" in the area, a process of refinement that helped produce linen from flax. In 1914 the society had fifty-one members who paid an average of £3 for shares that year.[49] The Donegal Cooperative Agricultural and Dairy Society was another Irish co-op that operated in the northwest of Ireland in the early 1900s; it serviced the region surrounding the town of Donegal.[50]

The Irish cooperative movement of the late 1800s and early 1900s in rural Ireland was part of the expanding awakening of Irish cultural and political nationalism, a form of rural "home rule" that sought to empower small farmers through a communal taking back of local agricultural markets. In essence, the cooperatives were voluntary associations with an explicit commercial goal buttressed by an ideology of opposition to the emerging national and international markets, resisting products produced and imported from outside the local circle.

In Donegal, in its societies of multiple visions and practical applications, proto-models of associational behavior were part of the social landscape of existence in this rural outpost given to so much emigration to Philadelphia. The rule books, the forms and the norms that defined decorum and control in the small democracies of the required association meetings, the expected duties of membership, and even the political and cultural divisions and allegiances were all part of a Donegal transportable ethic of civic action.

A Transportable Associational Spirit

The Cavan Catholic, Social, and Beneficial Society of Philadelphia was established in 1907 for Irish Americans who were either born in Ireland's County Cavan or could establish "Cavan descent."[51] Max Weber writes that ethnic groups are bound by "the vague connotation that whatever is felt to be distinctively common must derive from common descent."[52] The simple principle of common descent established the boundaries of closure for an insular ethnic identity devoted to Cavan awareness in Irish American Philadelphia and, as it did for the Donegal Association of Philadelphia, it defined the organization's purpose for existence in the early decades of the twentieth century.

County Cavan is in North-Central Ireland, bordering Ulster, a rural barrier between the Republic and Northern Ireland. It is one of the few counties that was originally part of Ulster but located within the Republic of Ireland. Its northern location and its population mix of Protestant and Catholic have required its people to reach across the religious divide. A resolution from the Catholic-dominated Crosserlough branch of the Irish National League in 1903 proudly announced its donation of £90 to the Tenants Defense Fund, noting "there were amongst the contributors a large number of our Protestant neighbors."[53] Cavan was an agricultural area hard hit by the Famine ravages that swept the counties to the west, and it was thus a zone of emigration, with its own set of harsh conditions that sent many from its small villages and parishes to Philadelphia in the late 1800s and early 1900s.

While the Clan na Gael of Philadelphia and, to a lesser extent, the Ancient Order of Hibernians (AOH) extolled a nationalist mission with a more militant approach and interpretation of Irish national memory, the Cavan Society of Philadelphia was content to construct its version of ethnic awareness around the singular premise of common location and religion in Ireland and the set of rural memories and traditions associated with country life.

The first Cavan meeting was held on a Tuesday evening in February 1907 at 8:00 P.M. at 1534 Ridge Avenue, several blocks north of Philadelphia's city hall, which would be the home location for the Cavan Society for many years. Thirty-two members attended that first meeting of the Cavan Society on a winter's evening, paying the $1 initiation fee and an additional 10¢ for a copy of the association's constitution. Elections for officers were immediately held and the following leaders selected: president, L. J. Clarke; vice president, John Fox; financial secretary, James Kelly; recording secretary, Joseph Smith; treasurer, Pat Higgins; and sergeant at arms, Bernard Keenan. The newly elected officers "thanked the brothers for the Honor and trust they placed in them" and settled into running the newest Irish society to enter an already overcrowded establishment of ethnic associations in Philadelphia.[54]

To gain membership in the Cavan Society, in addition to the modest initiation fee, new members had to be sponsored by two current members and were then subject to an "investigation" of their reputation. The age limit for full initiation was posted to be eighteen years of age, but so compelling was the spirit of Cavan that communal norms were relaxed, which allowed for those underage Irish eager to join the society. In 1922, the meeting acknowledged "the initiation of Andrew Sexton who just became eligible to membership through having reached his 18th year and who has missed very few meetings for the past 3 or 4 years."[55] Meetings were held on Sunday afternoons at 2:30, on a day free from labor and at a time that allowed some rest after attending morning mass.

The Cavan spirit in Philadelphia had found its public expression in Philadelphia, and membership rose rapidly as word of this new ethnic society spread. At the next meeting in March 1907, 21 new members were initiated for membership, followed by 6 more in April and 7 in May, 2 in June, 14 in July, and 12 in August, producing a healthy society of 94 in the rush of membership initiation of the first six months.[56]

TABLE 5.3

OCCUPATIONAL STRUCTURE BY PLACE OF BIRTH
OF THE CAVAN SOCIETY, 1907–1926

Occupation Category	Share	Born in Ireland	Born in the United States
Professional[a]	03%	0%	100.00%
White collar[b]	12.50%	93.80%	6.30%
Skilled labor[c]	60.00%	85.50%	14.50%
Unskilled labor[d]	24.50%	100.00%	0%

Source: "Minute Book of the Cavan Catholic, Social, and Beneficial Society of Philadelphia, 1907–1926," Cavan Society of Philadelphia.

N = 334.

[a] The Cavan Society initiated one lawyer from Chestnut Hill during these years.

[b] Includes shopkeepers, grocers, and saloon keepers.

[c] Includes machinists, textile workers, and railroad men.

[d] Includes manual laborers.

OCCUPATIONAL ANALYSIS OF THE CAVAN SOCIETY

This Irish county association reached out to anyone in Philadelphia with Cavan roots, but its membership rolls were filled with men drawn from specific occupation niches, modest locations within the class and status hierarchy available to the established Cavan colony in Philadelphia and its sizable cohort of recent immigrants. Table 5.3 presents an occupational profile of Philadelphia Cavan men for the period 1907–1926.

The occupational structure of the Cavan Society favored the skilled worker: 60 percent of the members had learned an industrial skill and were employed as either machinists, ironworkers, or firemen in Philadelphia by the early 1900s; many Cavan men found employment in the Baldwin Locomotive Works.[57] In addition, shopkeepers and men of small property joined the association as saloon owners or neighborhood grocers, and this cohort was also an overwhelmingly immigrant cohort of Cavan, with 94 percent born in Ireland.

The Irish unskilled rural or town laborer continued to emigrate well into the early decades of the twentieth century, and this type of worker, who was at the bottom of the labor hierarchy, is reflected in the demographics of the Cavan Society. Unskilled laborers, all Irish-born, comprised 25 percent of the Cavan membership; this was an occupational group that must have often stretched its meager financial resources to find the means to pay the dues and refreshment fees and the cost of urban transport to meetings and Cavan Society events. The Cavan Society was staffed by men born in Ireland, many coming from the parishes of Killeshandra and Drumreilly/Corlough and thus in the early 1900s the society was continuously fed by a steady supply of rural and town workers born in Cavan.

Rural farm workers in County Cavan in the late nineteenth and early twentieth centuries were a disappearing cohort of the Irish labor force. As William Redmond addressed a crowd of over 400 in a field in 1903 in Cavan's Bailieboro parish, his speech extolling the prospects of the pending Land Bill was interrupted by a shout from the large crowd, "What about the labourers?" Redmond responded, "Men of Cavan . . . little or nothing has been done for the labourers this year I admit," and he promised attention to this downtrodden strata of rural labor and urged farmers to hire agricultural workers to help run the farms and stem the tide of emigration.[58]

The time, distance, and expense required to participate in an ethnic voluntary association was itself an index of ethnic meaning and identity in Philadelphia in the late 1800s and early 1900s. The many branches of the AOH were established as neighborhood outposts of the parent organization, but many members lived outside the normal walking zone, and the monthly meetings attracted brother "guests" from all over the city who opted to pay the cost of a trolley ride or two.

The Cavan Catholic, Social, and Beneficial Society of Philadelphia held its meetings at 15th and Ridge, close to Center City, and this "headquarters," while central in location, was not convenient to the mass of members dispersed throughout Philadelphia. Cavan birth or descent, not neighborhood or walking distance to the association, defined the boundaries of ethnic awareness, and the basis for social inclusion was the pool of Cavan men and women scattered throughout the city. Cavan, like all ethnic associations in these years, struggled from time to time with attendance at meetings and functions as well as periods of declining membership rolls, but this was a vibrant and lively association that members willingly paid the cost of travel to join. Table 5.4 displays the travel distance to headquarters of the members of the Cavan Society in the period 1907–1926.

Walter Licht writes on finding work in nineteenth-century industrial Philadelphia, "Young entrants to the labor market, the unskilled, new immigrants, and people laboring alongside kin tended to have the most unstable employment histories."[59] The occupational analysis of the Cavan Society would suggest that a membership in which 25 percent were unskilled and recent new citizens to Philadelphia would destabilize in response to the demographic burden. The society reflected the mixed-class basis of the Irish American association in the

TABLE 5.4

TRAVEL TO MEETINGS: SPATIAL SEPARATION FROM HOME AND
ASSOCIATION IN THE CAVAN SOCIETY, 1907–1926

Distance between Cavan Members' Homes and Cavan Society Headquarters	Share
Less than 1 mile	12%
1–5 miles	22%
Greater than 5 miles	66%

Source: "Minute Book of the Cavan Catholic, Social, and Beneficial
Society of Philadelphia, 1907–1926," Cavan Society of Philadelphia.

Note: The distance to the meeting was derived from the home
addresses of Cavan Society members as indicated in the Society
Minute Book.

N = 334.

late nineteenth and early twentieth centuries, which was overwhelmingly working class in nature and dominated by skilled workers, with a small strata of
shop owners and clerks contributing to the association's profile, backed by a
sizable minority of the unskilled. Instead, Cavan remained remarkably stable
for a mobile urban population of workers, as the society constantly replenished
its ranks with newcomers; to join an association with its disciplinary codes and
emotional ties to the overseas homeland provided a sense of stability that coun-
tered the trend of urban mobility among the working class.

Cavan members such as Andrew W. Quinn, a cigar manufacturer who was
fifty-one years old, born in Pottstown, Pennsylvania and living in the Chestnut
Hill section of Philadelphia and Michael Brady, who was president in 1913 when
he convened meetings in a second-story room on Ridge Avenue, altered the
working-class profile of the society. Brady was Irish-born, from Cavan's Killinkere parish, but he was a saloon keeper from the Delaware River district of
Kensington, dubbed "Fishtown," and at age forty, older than most members. He
was committed to the association and rarely absent as president, donating additional time and energy to the work on the society's committees; he received one
of two prizes awarded in August 1915, for his services to the all-important ball
committee, which raised vital funds to support the organization.[60] His tenure
as president lasted until 1918, when Terence Smith took over. And so was created Cavan, a haven of traditional ethnic meaning for new entrants to the working class of Philadelphia, a location of relaxed sociability, and a primer on
constitutional methods and civic responsibility.

IRISH AMERICAN DISCIPLINE: SOCIAL LEARNING TRANSPORTED FROM CAVAN TO PHILADELPHIA

It has been suggested that the strict adherence to group codes of behavior and discipline found in the Irish American association was a compensatory response to a stereotype of Irish American disorder, the perceived failure of Catholic Irish working men to be able to govern themselves. E. P. Thompson evokes such an ethnic comparison when he describes the difference between the English industrial worker and the Irish immigrant laborer: "the heavy manual occupations at the base of the industrial society required a spendthrift expense of sheer physical energy—an alternation of intensive labour and boisterous relaxation which belongs to pre-industrial labour-rhythms, and for which the English artisan or weaver was unsuited."[61]

It was against this intractable legacy of the Irish as capable laboring beasts, unable to adapt to the rhythms and discipline consistent with an industrial economy, that the Diaspora Irish in Philadelphia worked in small ways as they formed their ethnic societies. Once assembled in their own ethnic associations, they imposed a discipline on the formalities of civic democracy expected in small groups.

Cavan was also sensitive to this well-worn public image of the Irish and used its own ethnic organization to combat the "Paddy" legacy in Philadelphia. President Brady reminded the brothers that "all matters profaning against Catholic endeavors should be brought before the meeting" and that people in the "work shops and places of employment" should report offensive remarks against Philadelphia's Irish.[62] And so it was in Philadelphia's Cavan Society in the early decades of the twentieth century, a gathering of members of the Catholic ethnic working class who were sensitive to the insults of their social and historical group, having been disciplined in the application of inherited norms and rulebooks of past associational life that framed their present.

A TRANSPORTABLE ETHIC: CAVAN COUNTY ROOTS OF IRISH AMERICAN ASSOCIATIONAL SPIRIT

It has been noted that the Philadelphia Irish applied a social discipline derived from proto-models of behavior in public institutions to insulate their associations from outside criticism and unwelcome depictions as an ungovernable mass; it is argued that the immigrants of Cavan also borrowed civic lessons that were part of the cultural experience of life in the small parishes of this Irish county.

Like the ethnic associations of late-nineteenth-century Philadelphia, the friendly societies in Ireland in the nineteenth century operated as mutual aid societies that secured sick and death benefits. By the late nineteenth century, there were fewer friendly societies operating in the rural sections of the country, as many had succumbed to the devolution of the early nineteenth-century, pre-Famine communal norms and traditions in the wake of "Black 47."

Yet there were multiple forms of communal association other than formal friendly societies alive in the late nineteenth century in County Cavan that would have sustained Irish patterns of social learning on the forms, methods, and spirit of democratic voluntary associations. The AOH was established in the small parishes of County Cavan and, unlike the Dublin tontine's imposed silence on political stances, the Hibernians of Cavan were openly partisan in their support of an Irish republic and stridently anti-British in their rhetoric of opposition. The Fermanagh branch declared their support of Irish Parliamentary Party agitators in the early 1900s, celebrating the release from prison of M.O. John O'Donnell, who had "been condemned by the hirelings of the tyrannical British government for his love of Ireland." The Greenans Cross branch of Killevan Parish and the Newbliss Hibernians, both of nearby County Monaghan, also endorsed the Irish National Party in public statements.[63]

The meetings of these rural outposts of the AOH followed the standard parliamentary format normal to Irish voluntary associations with the election of officers, the distribution of the AOH constitution and book of regulations, the reading of minutes, the presentation of quarterly financial status, and with debate and discussion at members' meetings proceeding in an orderly manner. The president of AOH Newbliss, County Cavan, "exhorted [the brothers] to have the rules and constitution of the Order strictly adhered to."[64]

The United Irish League also surfaced in County Cavan with branch societies that operated as voluntary associations devoted to the promotion and support of constitutional reform and support for Irish independence through the Irish party's initiatives in the British Parliament. The United Irish League was a political movement designed to return grazing lands in the western agricultural zones of Ireland back into small farms; its methods were persuasion and political organization, but its message invoked a radical reordering of rural Ireland's land use.[65] Branches of the League emerged in Aghabog, Kingscourt, and Larah Parishes in Cavan, and these local branches also elected officers, held Sunday afternoon meetings, established and administered their own finances, and voted on resolutions during meetings.[66] The Larah branch declared in 1903 that, "after centuries of unparalleled sufferings and misery" there seemed to be progress made to "reconcile the bitter racial and political enmities" that had governed agricultural life in their parish and in Cavan.[67]

Agricultural societies and cooperatives appeared in Cavan by the early 1900s. The Cavan County Agricultural Society was just such a cooperative, having been established in 1901 to "promote horse and cattle breeding and home industries."[68] The society registered seventy-two members in 1912.[69]

The Cavan Cooperative Creameries Co. was another co-op, a countywide enterprise with a central creamery and fifteen "auxiliary" creameries operating in 1902.[70] The co-op was administered through a central committee, with regular meetings that included members from surrounding towns, from Belturbet, Tullyvin, Drumurcher, Redhills, Urney, and Nahilla.[71] Cavan Creameries appealed to Horace Plunkett's local enterprise movement as advertised in the Cavan press: "Why send your money to foreign countries for inferior food and beast when you can produce it cheaper and better at home?"[72]

Like the Donegal scutchers who put together their own co-op, scutchers in Cavan formed their own co-op as well, the Bailieborough Scutchers Union, which charged members co-op-level fees for flax raw materials to make their products.[73] Scutchers refined their flax by beating it and eliminating rough fibers from the product they would eventually weave into linen.

Cavan men and women were active in the Cavan branch of the Leaseholders' Enfranchisement Association, a movement of renters that began in England and established branches in Ireland. The Cavan branch in 1892 was an association of advocates for the rights of renters, which acted for a "long suffering and ground down class."[74] The spirit and practice of running associations were part of the fabric of life in post-Famine County Cavan, a region hit hard by the Famine, which caused the devolution of its traditional rural economy and emigration. While Plunkett's rural cooperatives took aim at the trend of the consolidation of small farms into larger holdings, the modernization of the countryside continued as the expanding numbers of recently arrived members to Philadelphia's Cavan Society indicated.

THE IRISH NATIONAL LEAGUE IN CAVAN

The Irish National League was founded in 1892 as a political association for the purpose of supporting independence for Ireland through constitutional reform in the British Parliament. Branch associations were established all over Ireland and sprouted in County Cavan, in Cootehill, Denn, Virginia, and Ballinagh, and in Killeshandra, which named its association "The Insuppressible Wm. O'Briens" after the United Irish League organizer. Officers and committee members were elected; the Denn branch of the Irish National League held its meetings every month on the first Monday evening.[75] Each branch had a slate of elected officers and an elected committee of twelve who were responsible for doing the work of the association and were required to attend meetings.[76]

By 1903, National League branches were more deeply dispersed across Cavan, in parishes and small towns such as Bailieborough, Lavey, Belturbet, Knockbride, Kingscourt, Killeevan, Castlerahan, Aughnamullen, and Drumgoon, each with its own local association governing itself.[77] The Killeshandra Insuppressible Wm. O'Briens were indeed insuppressible as this branch had a "vigilance committee," which kept an eye on area landlords and "landgrabbers" who took advantage of tenants and small farmers; the vigilance committee reported in 1903 on "traders" in Killeshandra who did business with those identified as commercial pariahs to the community.[78] The Ballinagh branch also reported to their membership during their twice-monthly meeting that "goods had been supplied to a noted grabber and his assistant by a trader"; town merchants were expected to boycott the identified public enemies of cooperative Ireland in the early 1900s.[79]

The branches of the National League in County Cavan saw themselves as advocates for the dispossessed classes of this rural area, the expanding under-class of agricultural workers with few prospects for work. For example, the Cros-serlough Branch passed the following resolution condemning "the action of Mr. Renold Kilnateck in going before the Cavan Board to object to a labourer's cottage built on his holding."[80] Likewise, the Killinkere branch sent a public warning in 1890 to a Mr. O'Hara, who was a "shareholder in the Smith-Barry Eviction Company," putting him and others on notice when it came to evictions of poor farmers and laborers in the region.[81]

ALCOHOL, ABSTINENCE, AND CIVIC DISCIPLINE

The Total Abstinence Society had a strong presence in Cavan with many local branches established. These societies were voluntary associations that sponsored sobriety and encouraged and supported a withdrawal from alcohol. The local priest or reverend was often the energizing agent, the society's "spiritual direc-tor," and the president of the local chapter—each branch had a slate of officers and a supporting committee of six or seven members, and members took a pub-lic oath abstaining from drink at their moment of initiation.

The St. Patrick's Branch of the Abstinence Society was established in Cavan town by the early 1900s. At its annual meeting in January 1903, it was reported that "100 labourers, artisans, farmers, merchants, shop assistants and others attended at the old College, Cavan, on Sunday evening for the purpose of pay-ing their membership subscription."[82] The Maghera Total Abstinence Society cel-ebrated its first year of existence at its first annual meeting in January, 1903. This was a society of 118 members who were all required to take the pledge of total abstinence in front of their fellow members.[83]

There was a mass celebration of the abstinence movement in rural Cavan, the Great Total Abstinence Re-Union, which was held in the County Cavan town of Virginia in summer 1903.[84] This countywide event was sponsored by the Virginia branch of the union and featured a sports competition as a part of the celebration of abstinence. Gaelic football was played in a field near the town, and all of the branches of the Union were assembled in alphabetical order, fitted with "special badges" reflecting their local temperance association, and marched to the sport-ing grounds.[85]

TABLE 5.5

COUNTY CAVAN PARISH ORIGINS OF THE MEMBERSHIP OF PHILADELPHIA'S
CAVAN SOCIETY, 1907–1926

Parish of Origin	Philadelphia Cavan Society Members	Parish of Origin	Philadelphia Cavan Society Members
Annagh	2	Killeshandra	16
Bailieborough	1	Killinagh	3
Ballintemple	1	Killinkere	10
Ballyconnell	1	Kilmore	5
Castlerahan	4	Kinawley	6
Crosserlough	4	Knockbride	7
Drumgoon	4	Larah	9
Drumreilly/ Corlough	24	Lavey	2
Drung	6	Templeport	9

Source: "Minute Book of the Cavan Catholic, Social, and Beneficial Society
of Philadelphia, 1907–1926," Cavan Society of Philadelphia.
N = 114.

IDENTITY AND LONGING FOR CAVAN

One's home parish in Cavan resonated more brightly with members, which
added an additional layer of meaning and connection to the association in Philadelphia, which was an accumulation of smaller locales, from Killeshandra or
Drumgoon, that identified themselves with the Cavan parish as a place of origin and meaning. Table 5.5 displays the concentration of parishes with an iden-
tifiable population of Philadelphia's Cavan Society.

Cavan identity was local, tied to parish locations such as the Killeshandra
Insuppressible Wm. O'Briens National League branch, as were the Gaelic football clubs the Slashers, Erins and Celts, which were all parish-centric. The longing for the tradition of their previous village life, which was an active nostalgia,
sometimes assumed antimodernistic tones within the society. In 1912, the Cavan
Society joined other Philadelphia Irish associations in their condemnation of
Synge's play The Playboy of the Western World, which was scheduled to be seen
in Philadelphia.[86]

Cavan Discourse: Opposition, Militancy, and Masculine Pride

The Cavan Society did not ground its primary identity in the popular cause of Irish independence. However, the cult of opposition in exile was central to the common heritage of the Philadelphia Irish, and this legacy could not fail to permeate the inner workings and collective thoughts of the Cavan Society; it complied with the Diaspora Irish duty to redress, as Kerby Miller states: "Self-redemption re-emerged in the exhortations of many Irish and Irish-American nationalists."[87] In fall 1920, at the height of the Irish-Anglo guerilla war for independence, the association encouraged the purchase of a traveling pamphlet on the national Gaelic circuit entitled *Escape from Mount-Joy Prison*.[88]

The nationalist exile theme penetrates the educational sermons that were expected and accepted as truth and knowledge in the gatherings of the Cavan Irish in Philadelphia, which were delivered by ordinary association members or priests visiting the meeting or by a guest of the Cavan Society. It was suggested in 1907 that the Cavan Society research and reconstruct its own heroic history of Cavan militancy and military prowess for the education of its members, developing "a short history of some of our famous Cavan men . . . whose heroic deeds shed a luster on the County to which we are all proud to belong."[89]

The following Cavan history became part of the record of the society, a tale that affirmed the manhood of the pugnacious Celt and the embattled Catholic priest, all drawn from traditional Irish folklore in which the good fight would always be joined and only lost when alien forces were overwhelmingly superior in number: "Go back to the early days when Ireland was under the iron heel of the English oppression and when thousands gave up their life for faith and fatherland. In many of those battles were to be found true and tried Cavan men who gave up their life for their country and their God."

These lessons on history, nation and Catholicism were part of the identity apparatus of associationalism in the Diaspora, a popular ideology of Irish victimhood welded to an Irish masculinity of resistance. The defense of "Cavan soil" was the highest honor: "The great and noble Myles O'Reilly the slasher whose valour as a soldier is unequalled in the annals of warfare as one of Cavan's greatest sons, whose fighting for civil and religious liberty on the Bridge of Finea when his antagonist split his head in two he held the sword in his teeth and with one magic stroke cut the head of the English tyrant."

In its historical lexicon the society claimed the Union general Philip Sheridan as a patriotic warrior, the son of a "Cavan man whose deeds of valour shall hand his name to posterity."[90]

THE BUSINESS OF ASSOCIATION SURVIVAL

Philadelphia's Cavan Society had a system of fines that it developed and imposed and a list of unacceptable behaviors catalogued for the distribution of punitive sanctions, for infractions such as fighting with another member, getting drunk, failing to attend meetings, or disclosing associational secrets outside the club. The regular payment and collection of dues was a vital practical and moral matter to the men of Cavan and indeed to other Irish American associations.

Dues were $1 per month and paid at the monthly meeting. The $12 per year in dues, in addition to the 50¢ per meeting for refreshments or an occasional cigar at the meeting as well as the round-trip trolley ride, often with a transfer, added up to a sizable investment for the member earning worker's wages.[91] The termination of members was a blow to the fortunes of the association, so members in arrears were always given extra time to settle their debt; in 1926, the society agreed to "retain Bro. Peter Byrene, Bro. Patrick Sheridan, Bro. Frank McGuire on the books for 1 more month."[92]

Cavan members were guaranteed sick benefits of $5 per week, which could extend no longer than thirteen weeks. In March 1913, eight brothers received sick benefits for the month for a total of $145, exceeding monthly cash on hand and monthly revenue for dues by $70. At that rate, Cavan would have had to reach deep into its established investments to keep pace with its commitment to mutual aid. As 1913 turned out, however, Cavan would finish the year with $1,154 in the bank and $495 in its savings and loan.[93]

The Cavan Society, like Irish friendly societies and other Irish American associations, did not tolerate breaches of its disciplinary code or allow serious dissension within the public sphere that might threaten the fragile bonds of communal solidarity. The society was moved to action with serious breaches of conduct. In 1914 it recommended "the name of Hugh Monroe be stricken from the books of the Cavan Society for conduct unbecoming a member of the Association."[94] It also was decided that "no cards be played at any of our quarterly meetings after the meeting opened."[95] Things could also disappear from the society, like the beer donated for the annual Easter Ball in 1913, but such mischief involving property was not as serious as moral misconduct: it was decided that "the mislaying of Barrel Beer sent by Bro McKeon be left in the hands of the Ball Committee."[96]

THE ECONOMY OF LEISURE

In 1915 Cavan ordered tickets for the annual ball of the Catholic Sons of Derry and purchased 100 tickets from the Federation of Irish County Association for its upcoming field day. Cavan responded to a request from the Wexford County Association, purchasing an ad in their souvenir program for 1916.[97] At its height,

an ethnic, subterranean economy had been erected in Philadelphia in which various Irish American associations—county, political, neighborhood, and cultural—
all exchanged monies through the promotion of their events and sale of tickets.

Ticket sales for balls also counted as a currency of mutual support among the
various Irish associations of the city. In fall 1914, in the Cavan Society, twenty-
five tickets were set aside for the "Roscommon men" and twenty for "the Irish
National Forresters for the coming balls."[98] Event ticket sales were vital to the
associations' financial standing, and contests between members for the highest
sales made the chore less tedious: "division 11 of A.O.H. recorded that there was
much interest in the contest between the President and Brother Farroll, regarding the sale of tickets for their forthcoming ball."[99] Mutual support extended
across the Atlantic; Philadelphia's Cavan brothers donated to the building of the
"parish house" in Corlough, County Cavan, a gift of the "Cavan boys and girls
of Philadelphia."[100]

The care and compliance with alcohol at the ball during the period of American Prohibition was yet another example of the sensitivity to ethnic labeling that
the Irish associations struggled to avoid. For the ball of 1923, the brothers reluc-
tantly agreed that the restriction on "the use of liquor or beer at our Ball be complied with [and] no intoxicating liquors of any kind be handled at the Cavan
Ball of 1923."[101] A week later, the society seemed to be in denial about having an
annual ball with no liquor and debated once again whether to flout Prohibition.
Again, however, they decided that they would bring the refreshments themselves,
but they were strict that there should be "no intoxicating drinks of any kind."[102]

THE ETHIC OF MUTUAL SUPPORT

Disbursements for sick benefits were a constant threat to overrun the meager
resources of the association, but mutual support was the founding principle of
the ethnic association and sick benefits were a sacred condition of solidarity that
was rarely questioned in Cavan public settings. The most expensive item on the
monthly meeting balance sheet was sick benefits; in November 1911, $85 in sick
benefits were paid to Cavan members from a total monthly expense of $89.50.[103]
In February 1914, 90 percent of the monthly expenses was for brothers' sick benefits, commensurate with the Irish American civic value commitment to restore
the member to health.[104] In 1916, sick benefits of $75 for June nearly extinguished
the association's operating reserve, leaving a balance of just $12.[105]

Yet Cavan was steadfast in its commitment to extending financial aid from
its financial resources over and above a minimal commitment to health, and the
society often extended need to brothers caught in dire straits. After paying death
benefits for Joe Ward, the society decided to offer something extra for his surviving family—noting "it was brought to the notice of the chair about the financial condition of our late Bro. Joe Ward." Eventually, the society decided that

"$50 be taken out of the $100 sometime ago donated to the Irish Volunteers Fund and be given to Joe Ward as a Christmas present."[106] A committee of Cavan members was formed to visit "Brother Logan" in the hospital and dispatched in 1907.[107] And, in 1917, the society appealed to its members to "appoint a committee to decide on some way to raise some money for a Brother member who is in poor circumstance."[108]

The ethic of mutual aid was not just a Cavan principle; in general, the Irish American organizations privileged the provision of sick benefits and extra mutual aid because of its status as a sacred rite of the spirit of the commune. AOH Division 10, from 20th and Carlton Streets, stated that they had paid "sick and death benefits over $1,400" for 1898, a figure that the organization was proud of and committed to, and which it vowed to "ever continue to do whenever called upon."[109]

AOH No. 13, which met at 8th and Walnut Streets, in 1894 heard "appeals from two sources for help for widows and orphans of deceased members, and both were promptly aided by unanimous vote, the sum to be taken from the treasury."[110] And Camp 246 of the Clan na Gael extended its financial resources to come up with $50 for a "brother Harkins [who] was in a very low state and would not last long."[111] The Limerick Guards Patriotic, Social and Benevolent Association was an Irish nationalist association that cultivated a paramilitary public image. The Limerick Guards was also a society of mutual support; it donated "the sum of $25 for St. Joseph's House for Homeless Boys" in 1895. At the same meeting, the Limerick Guards decided to give an extra $50 to the widow of one of their former officers "in addition to the $75 to which his membership entitled him."[112]

The ethic of care and support for its people was also extended to Cavan workers stretched thin by industrial strikes in Philadelphia. Many Cavan men found work at the Baldwin Locomotive Works in Kensington, and Cavan men on strike against Baldwin Train in summer 1911 found support from their association as "all members employed in Baldwin and on strike be exempt from monthly dues until strike is ended." Yet, ever vigilant when it came to dues and correct procedure, President Brady intervened to make sure the striking Cavan members were not supplementing their incomes with side work: "the chair appointed a committee to find out if the strikers are employed anywhere else."[113]

Even as the Cavan Society struggled, at times, to meet the financial demands of mutual support it was, by May 1913, six years after its beginning in 1907, essentially a financially healthy Irish American association. For the month of May 1913, Cavan reported $52.25 in dues collected, which added to $81.45 cash on hand. May's expenses were a total of $78.90 for printing, for a deposit into the savings and loan, for meeting refreshments, and for the normal, but manageable, payout of sick benefits. In reserve and carried forward was $754.44 in a savings account and $445 in a building and loan, which produced an ending balance of $1,254. Cavan, like Donegal, used its surplus for investments, a conservative course of financial planning that eschewed immediate rewards in favor of a more secure association future.

CONFLICTING NATIONALISMS: THE WAR IN EUROPE

The United States entered World War I in April 1917, and soon Cavan men faced military duties in France. The Cavan Society sent a notice "to every member stating any member called on to defend the Country shall be entyled [sic] to death benefits."[114]

Yet the Cavan Society approached America's entry on the side of the Allies with a reluctant vigor, and the weight of the perpetual moral dilemma of the Irish fighting on the side of the British. The August 1917 meeting recorded "the sad heart breaking feeling of mothers and fathers, brothers and sisters parting with the ones they loved best going forth, some to get killed and buried on a foreign soil for a cause not wise to mention."[115]

Cavan also decided to purchase $500 in Liberty Bonds in support of the war in November 1917, a sizable amount when their total resources were just under $3,000. This amount was eventually reduced to $300 and finally to $100 as the society decided it was more prudent to invest $200 instead in its savings and loan.[116] It was also decided that men in uniform be allowed to stay "on the books" only if a friend paid their dues for them while they were away.[117] This stipulation was later ignored; when the war was over, Cavan men were welcomed back: "All members of our society returning from France [will] be reinstated on the Books of our society in good standing as soon as they report."[118]

THE WARS IN IRELAND, 1916–1923

The Cavan Society operated as a mutual aid and cultural organization, but like other Irish American associations, it was also an agency for news and opinion about native Ireland, an Ireland eventually embroiled in its own wars of independence and internal bloodletting after World War I. Unlike the Clan na Gael with its more overt mission to directly support Irish independence, the Cavan brothers were much more conservative in their politics, influenced by religious constraints and more narrowly focused on sustaining the identity of County Cavan descent in Diaspora Philadelphia.

Given the magnitude of change and disruption that would take place in early twentieth-century Ireland, beginning with the Easter Rising in 1916, through the guerrilla war with England, 1919–1921, and the Irish Civil War of 1922–1923, it is surprising how little of these momentous Irish events penetrated the second-story meetings of the society's rented space at 15th Street and Ridge Avenue in Philadelphia. Eventually, the Cavan Society would confront the dualism of supporting America in World War I in alliance with Britain and, at the same time, promoting Irish freedom, and the society was mobilized to support the wars for an Irish republic.

Cavan withdrew $100 out of its annual ball receipts in 1916 and forwarded it to the United Irish League.[119] This was granted after a plea from the United Irish League and a lengthy debate within the Cavan Society; it was only after a consensus emerged that the annual ball had generated a sizable surplus in 1916 that this donation was allowed to go forward. By 1916, the wave of revolt and support for Irish independence had reached the Cavan Society, and it too established a fund for the Irish Volunteers. However, the Cavan contingency always seemed to side with personal troubles over public issues, and $25 was taken out of the Irish Volunteers Fund to help a brother in need.[120]

A visitor to the March 1918 meeting of the Cavan Society, the president of the Federation of Irish County Associations, presented "an outline of the Irish Convention" and encouraged the brothers to attend Sunday night meetings "on the Irish Cause" held at 1628 Arch Street.[121] In 1920, the Cavan Society, "after hearing from Ex-Congressman Donohoe on the condition of things in Ireland and the persecution of the Irish at the hands of the representative of England, the Black and Tans, and of the work of the Friends of Irish Freedom," decided to send one of their own to the gathering convention of the Friends of Irish Freedom in Pottsville, Pennsylvania.[122]

In 1920, the Friends of Irish Freedom in Philadelphia sent "circulars" around to the various county associations describing the vicious guerrilla war in Ireland and the growing interest and support for the Irish fighters among the diaspora community in Philadelphia. The Cavan Society approved the contents, "endorsing every act" of the Friends of Irish Freedom platform in 1920.[123] The Sons of Irish Freedom, another nationalist organization born in Philadelphia during the years of Irish revolt, also attracted Cavan's attention, and the society sent a committee of four, Andrew McHale, James Kelly, Philip Brady, and Pat McBreen, to its 1920 gathering.[124]

In 1921, the brothers turned their attention increasingly to the guerrilla war in Ireland: "after a lengthy address by Father Campbell on conditions in Ireland [it was decided that] the Cavan Society stand by Father Campbell in his progressive movement of the Irish republic."[125] The Cavan Society, like other Irish American associations, became a source for funds to support the Irish cause in the war of independence. One hundred dollars in bonds for the Friends of Irish Freedom were purchased by the Cavan Society in early 1920. Individual members were encouraged to purchase bonds, and it was announced at a meeting that "every member of Cavan Society interested to purchase Bonds [should] purchase them through Cavan."[126]

Nationalism cut both ways in Irish American associations during and just after World War I, and the Irish in Philadelphia confronted a persistent tension that forced them, on the one hand, to support an American alliance with their historic British enemy and, with the other, lend financial and moral support to Ireland's war for independence. For the Cavan Society, a late arrival to Irish nationalist politics, the transition to the Irish cause represented a sizable leap for an association consumed by its more insular attention to preserving what Cavan memories they could reconstruct in industrial Philadelphia.

THE REQUIRED PARTNERSHIP OF CHURCH AND SOCIETY

The nexus of the Catholic Church and the Diaspora Irish of Philadelphia was unavoidable within the social milieu of the Irish American voluntary association; for the Cavan Catholic, Social, and Beneficial Society, the Church's bonds were formally declared and often acknowledged in Cavan's statements but control and adherence to Catholic authority in Philadelphia was always elusive. One of the first acts of Cavan existence was to appoint a "spiritual advisor," a Catholic priest who, in 1920, was paid $100 from the treasury of the society.[127]

The Cavan Society made a ritual excursion to attend a Sunday mass at St. Theresa's Church once a year. St. Theresa's was in the western suburbs of the city, and a special morning time was set aside to meet with the Monsignor; afterward, the brothers enjoyed a meal in the church's school hall. (Compliance with the required Sunday excursion and masses at St. Theresa's was not universal, however.) The society also designed and purchased a special badge of their society to be worn en masse in attending church.

In 1918, after a dismal showing at the Sunday communal mass, the following was recorded at the next meeting: "After hearing several remarks for the brothers who were present at the mass in St. Theresa's and several excuses from those who could not attend [it was stipulated] that any member absenting himself next year (without sufficient cause) be fined one dollar."[128] The following year, a circular was sent to the brothers reminding them of their commitment to the Holy Communion day at the church.[129]

The bonds cementing association members and the Catholic Church had eroded by the early decades of the twentieth century. E. J. Hobsbawm comments on the transformation to modernity, a trend that may have been operating on Cavan's new urbanites: "The historical or individual step from village to town, or from peasant to worker, has in general led to a sharp reduction in the influence of traditional religions."[130]

The Donegal Association of Philadelphia also made excursions on New Year's Day, and the archbishop of Philadelphia received those members who made the excursion.[131] The Donegal commitment to the Catholic Church required a test of member compliance; in a meeting in December 1907 it was recorded, "All who intend going to the Cathedral on New Year's Day should stand up, [and] every member in the Hall stood up."[132]

We have seen how the need to stay afloat financially occupied the energy and talents of the membership of the Irish American associations in Philadelphia. These societies were also seen as a convenient place for representatives from Irish parishes and American Catholic churches to visit and solicit funds and a personal appeal for funds from a priest was often a message the brothers could not resist.

Kerby Miller writes, "Catholic missionaries regularly visited the United States seeking alms from affluent emigrants for new churches and schools which their parishioners at home could not afford to build."[133] The meetings of the Donegal Association were regular recipients of visits from priests seeking aid for projects in Ireland. In 1897 Rev. P. H. O'Donnell visited the association in request for financial aid for poor farming families in Donegal; in 1905, a Father McCafferty dropped in on the association in search of support for St. Eunan's College in Letterkenny.[134]

A Father Cummins from Roscommon in Ireland was a guest to an AOH meeting, Division 52, at 13th and Columbia in north-central Philadelphia, and after "speaking on the mission on which he was sent from the other side, it was unanimously agreed to that he should receive $50."[135] AOH Division 68, in South Philadelphia, received "Fathers McFadden and O'Kane, respectively from Donegal and Tyrone. . . . The rev. gentlemen from the 'Green Isle' addressed the members on the object of their mission—a most worthy one, and to the credit of 68 be it recorded that its members gave generously."[136]

Cavan was on the circuit of roving Catholic priests and donated $100 "for Revd. Father Sherlock from Oregon who is soliciting aid in the East for the maintenance of Catholic Schools and Catholic education in the northwest."[137] The Church of the Precious Blood from Corpus Christi, Texas, was "given the privilege to go around our meeting to sell tickets," in support of that distant parish.[138] In Ireland, member-supported church projects were a tradition; the Killinagh Parish church in County Cavan took on a major renovation in 1890 to add a "Marble Altar, Side Altars, Erection of a Gallery." Over 160 members donated what they could, most often simply £1, to the fund, and donating members were identified in the local Cavan town press and inscribers to the church project.[139]

When Reverend McEnroe, Cavan's "spiritual advisor," died in 1914, the society sent out notices and arranged for the entire association to attend mass at St. Theresa's to "receive Holy Communion in a body."[140] The secular demands of Cavan, for mutual support and the rational ordering of an association, required discipline and control, but the emotional displays of traditional loyalties to the land of origin, the Church, and the priesthood, were also part of the identity mechanisms that made the Cavan Society whole.

President Brady died suddenly at age fifty-six, in mid-December 1922, not long after attending his final meeting of the Cavan Society. He had "arrived at the closing prayer just in time to wish the members a merry Christmas and a happy

new year, and today he is dead; Lord have mercy on his soul."[141] On hearing of
his death the brothers sent flowers and established a "vacant chair" for their
future meetings in honor of Brady's long body of work with the association.[142]
He had been elected president for twelve straight years, beginning his leadership of Cavan in 1910, yet another example of how longevity and the provision
of mutual aid marked the Irish American association in these years.

THE CAVAN AND DONEGAL SOCIETIES AS MODELS

There were social trends in the growth and consolidation of the Cavan Society
and the Donegal Association of Philadelphia that opened pathways for Irish identity within a narrow range of vision. These associations reached out to a certain
social type, one described as an emigrating man from a rural parish in Cavan
or Donegal, in his early twenties, with some prior knowledge and exposure to
minor industrial skills that could be used as transitory, personal capital in finding work in industrial Philadelphia. Many of the men who made their way to
these county societies were Irish emigrants with no industrial skills and continued their life of labor in Philadelphia as manual workers.

In the ethnic voluntary association, the other type of member was a group of
officers and men of voice and initiative who were more often trained as skilled
workers or owners of small businesses, grocery shops, or saloons. For the Cavan
Society, no manual laborer was ever elected as an association officer, and the leadership of the Donegal Association reflected men of modest achievement as well.
However, the discursive tone and pitch of policy of these associations was of the
working class; 86 percent of Cavan members between 1907 and 1926 were
recruited from labor.

The membership and the leadership had to attend to a number of influences,
from parochial concerns and traditional alignments with the Catholic Church
to secular Irish nationalism. For the most part, the Cavan and Donegal Societies were able to deflect the more rancorous content of the Irish Diaspora rhetoric of defiance and opposition, but they too allowed an ideological rendering
of Irish history as tragedy, a precursor to the next step of a separate nation. These
were, at times, insular societies by nature, focused on what meaning could be
distilled from a reconstructed vision of the narrow world of rural parishes and
town existence. Yet, as with the AOH branches, the Irish separatism of the Gaelic
public sphere was conditioned by the rules and codes of normative civic culture,
a remnant from institutional life and practices in native Ireland, much of which
was similar to previous civic styles and traditions, involving the democracy of
ordered agendas and proper behavior in public places.

The Cavan and Donegal Society men and women, many of whom were recent
immigrants, found each other in an industrial complex of vast space and complexity. They came together in search of companionship and mutual support and,

in the process, contributed to a public sphere of Irish meaning out of these modest motivations. There were many preimmigration models on the methods of local civic engagement in their native Cavan and Donegal Counties, from branches of the foresters and agricultural cooperatives to Gaelic football clubs, and all of these societies were learning centers that predated American influences, and gave Irish Americans a head start when it came to forming their own society in Philadelphia.

The Irish American association constructed its own path, which was different from the friendly society in Ireland with its minimal commitment to member health and well-being, its forced censorship on public debate of controversial material, and its primary focus on the Christmas division of its yearly surplus derived from members' dues. Irish Americans deviated from these transatlantic roots to value member health, a sound approach to financial solvency and support for causes of Irish meaning at home and across the Atlantic. The reverence for democratic processes was evident in the strict adherence to the rites of the meeting, the public record of the financial books and attention to debt management and investments. In addition, the Cavan and Donegal Societies pursued consensus on matters of group concern through the airing of opinion and the raising of formal motions; these associations dealt with the Irish curse of alcohol by confronting the problem, debating it, and agreeing on a course of action. In the tradition of societies of mutual aid organized by common men of working means, Cavan and Donegal found ways to conform to the ethic of self-education and self-reliance; in E. P. Thompson's words, the Irish American association in Philadelphia "made itself as much as it was made."[143]

CHAPTER 6

The Forging of a Collective Consciousness

MILITANT IRISH NATIONALISM AND CIVIC LIFE IN GAELIC PHILADELPHIA

John Sullivan rose at the annual banquet of the Ancient Order of Hibernians (AOH) in Philadelphia in 1894 and proclaimed, "Our race was at the forefront, never wavering in their duty or loyalty to the land of their adoption," in reference to the Irish contribution in the American Civil War.[1] The record of Irish combativeness in defense of the Union merged into a readiness for defense of the Irish nation in waiting: defense of the American republic and a militant stance on Irish nationalism were mutual pillars of the Gaelic sphere.

This chapter will trace the path of militant nationalism in Irish Philadelphia in the 1890s and early 1900s, whose legacy was captured in symbols and ritualized sentiments as well as the real actions of support for an Irish nation. The following pages also detail the ordinary mechanisms and methods that the Irish Americans developed to build and sustain their own institutions of the public sphere, particularly the disciplinary codes and practices of associational life.

THE CONSTRUCTION OF ETHNIC AWARENESS

By the 1890s, in the midst of the general awakening of Irish culture with its attendant, reconstructed myths, the Irish in Philadelphia had settled on a universal ideology that bound them as a displaced diaspora subnation. The search for labor defined real existence, but the tenets of this mission had ample room for nationalism, support for the late-century Gaelic revival and a loyalty to American democracy, a persistent Irish urge since the 1790s, which Brundage terms "the powerful Irish drive for acceptance in America."[2]

Symbols were a necessary part of the identity equipment of Irish American associationalism, and the business meetings and social gatherings of the divisions displayed their own version of Irish identity and American loyalty. A "fine green silk flag of Ireland . . . emblazoned in green and gold, with the harp of 'old Erin' occupying its proper place in the center" was draped over the president's chair of AOH Division 68 as this association held its monthly meeting in its own hall in South Philadelphia. After a singing of "God Save Ireland" and "three cheers for the Red, White and Blue," the meeting adjourned.[3] At the Irish American Club on St. Patrick's Day in 1890 preparations were made for a public statement on national loyalties, and it was predicted that the "large American and Irish flags [would] float in the breeze from early morn to midnight."[4]

Fraternalism and reconstructed traditions were reinforced in the associations as well as the rigid form of control exercised in public settings of the voluntary association, a discipline that served to expose the Irish to orderly codes and imprint a modicum of bourgeois discipline on the members. Writing on the American voluntary association in the late nineteenth century, Frank Beito states: "By joining a lodge, an initiate adopted, at least implicitly, a set of values. Societies dedicated themselves to the advancement of mutualism, self-reliance, business training, thrift, leadership skills, self-government, self-control, and good moral character."[5]

Joining an Irish American association in these years was a statement that could affirm values that meshed neatly with the disciplinary code of work in an industrial society, but also infused their organizations with their own selection of Irish traditions and reconstructed rites, with an ideological interpretation of their history and an emotional and deep resentment of past and current enemies. Simply "handling the gavel" to bring order to the meeting was an admired trait, a test of firmness and control and a marker of order among a people long derided as being disorderly.

John Boyce O'Reilly, a member of AOH Division 1, died in spring 1893, and his AOH brothers remembered him for his "loyalty, earnestness, self-sacrifice" in the formal gathering of their society. O'Reilly epitomized the values and style of late-century Irish Philadelphians, and his colleagues noted that "in sparring, he always wanted hard hitting. Pain, he did not seem to feel, but he wanted it earnest and strong."[6]

Kerby Miller describes a rural Ireland in the early 1900s as a set of conflicting influences, modern and traditional, the result a social structure of a set of interaction rituals that stifled individual initiative while supporting communalism. An ethic of individual achievement was naturally respected and followed in the industrial American city, but the orderly working of the society also reflected a pattern of communal rule; rarely do we see the individual voice coming forward to move opinion, to make an independent argument, or to risk questioning the consensus on stock Irish American assumptions on the righteousness of Irish nationalism, the sanctity of Ireland and its troubled history, and the role of Irish Americans as defenders of Catholicism in a hostile, nativist world.

The ritualized forms of coming together in Irish American groups replaced the tensions and dynamism of argument, in essence resembling Habermas's actors playing with reason and analysis within the liberated air of European cafés. The communal allegiances, the taboo on real debate on politics and religion as in the friendly societies of native Ireland, and a respect for an order of emotional control in the running of the Irish American societies, combined with the forced consensus on Irish nationalism, all served to bury the individual voice and its liberal protections in public settings.

Given multiple motivational models, the Irish ethnic association in Philadelphia came to have a strong aversion to individual action and initiative. The orderly and subdued society, however, was the perfect instructor, as it "represented the extension of such [Protestant] values within the immigrant working class."[7] Organizational rules and processes and strict adherence to a code of discipline and accountability were taken up by Philadelphia's Irish to counter persistent labels and images of an opposite historical imagery; this compensatory mechanism, this discipline, was also part of a transatlantic cultural imperative linked to associational methods that were previously observed and adhered to in Ireland. The Irish Philadelphians of AOH Division 46 located by the Schuylkill River docks took pride in the formal code of the meeting: "The regular business . . . was transacted up to the letter of the law, for both officers and men in 46 are strict parliamentarians and never under any condition is the constitution violated."[8]

Irish American associationalism in Philadelphia was defined by a competing dualism, an inherited, conscious commitment to formal rationality and control in the ethnic organization based on an instrumental strategy of prudent business practices balanced by the expressive agents of sentimental remembrance and lingering bitterness about colonial rule. Even the most radical revolutionary movements tapping emotional cores of national redress and devoted to social and political upheaval, the Irish Revolutionary Brotherhood, was a product of orderly, rational control in organizational structure; as Miller states, "James Stephens' conspiratorial Irish Republican [Revolutionary] Brotherhood was preeminently modern in its bureaucratic complexity."[9]

THE SCHOOL OF DEEP RESENTMENT

The meetings and gatherings of the Irish in Philadelphia were also moments for disseminating and validating cultural messages to the members. The message became an obligatory recounting of lament and longing for a faded, idealized vision of rural Ireland; it was a repetition of a discourse of deep resentment that the Irish carried with them into their diaspora, where it was renewed and cultivated as a singular signpost of the Gaelic public sphere. John Mitchel's writings,

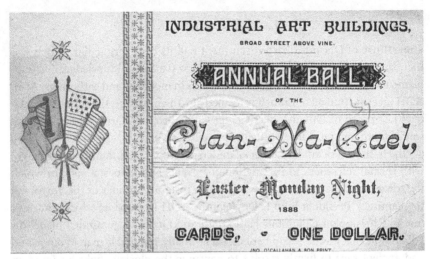

Ticket to the Clan na Gael Ball on Easter Monday, 1888. Source: CHRC.

including his work *Jail Journal* chronicling his time as a transportation prisoner of the British, which was released as a book in 1854, comprised a singular voice of popular appeal; Fenian intellectual John Leary described the influence of Mitchel's prose as "a record of hatred so intense, that it has earned a sort of immortality for the incandescence of its language."[10]

Mitchel, after his escape from Tasmania as an exiled prisoner of the British, arrived in New York City in 1853, where he was greeted by a popular street ballad available at the docks; it read in part:

> A welcome, brave MITCHEL, the champion of Freedom,
> Thrice art thou to the home of the brave,
> God be praised thou art free from tyranny's thralldom,
> To the power of Great Britain, no longer a Slave.[11]

The rhetorical position bombarding the Irish in Philadelphia was often one of physical and cultural banishment as a real reflection of Catholic Irish status in the diaspora nation.[12] For the Clan na Gael, it was exile with a renewed commitment to strike back, to move beyond the remnants of the sensational and flawed strategy of the Fenian border raids into Canada of the 1860s and early 1870s into a more determined nationalist opposition. This worldview was suspicious of outsiders, a group that at times was extended to bosses and men of privilege, an acceptance and language of opposition that E. P. Thompson describes as the vague origins of class consciousness: "an identity of interests . . . against the interests of other classes."[13]

The Language of Discontent

The culture of Diaspora Irish resentment had its own vernacular, which was incubated in the ethnic press, passed along as truth and knowledge, and supplemented by multiple communicative means in meetings and gatherings. At an AOH meeting in 1898 of Branch 15 located at 13th and Ridge, the warehouse district just north of Philadelphia's Center City: "Brother Harry Boylan spoke at some length and most forcibly against Anglo-Saxonism."[14]

The Irish Americans had a special understanding, a "community of language" with special references to past nationalist events and heroes, a code in which the town of Skibbereen and its song was an instant reminder of the horrors of the Famine.[15] President John F. Doyle of the AOH Division 49 which routinely met in Christopher Columbus Hall at 8th and Fitzwater, reminded his fellow Hibernians that it was "incumbent on every manly, honorable man of our grand and ancient race to firmly resolve to continue the glorious fight for freedom until the last vestige of English tyranny had been forever obliterated, and until the last red-coated myrmidon had ceased patrolling the land of St. Patrick's Shamrock."[16]

In 1899, at a Board of Erin meeting, the group's president. John Doherty. "delivered a forcible address on Unity." This meeting ended with the singing of "old time Irish songs in a manner that aroused those present to follow in the footsteps of the men who made a sacrifice in the cause of Mother Ireland."[17]

Irish ballads of nationalist content were a vital mechanism for maintaining a separatist edge to Irish American thought and a cultural treasure carried forth from revolts and risings in Ireland. Smyth notes the influence of ballads in rousing the United Irishmen in the 1790s in Ireland, with songbooks distributed among the clandestine meetings and gatherings of the movement, circulating copies of *Paddy's Resource* containing over "100 political songs, 'set to traditional' airs." One verse of a rebellious toast read, "May the potato-beds of Ireland be manured with the blood of its tyrants."[18]

Max Weber described the binding power of nationalist language and imagery among exiled communities:

> Whenever the memory of the origin of a community by . . . emigration . . .
> from a mother community remains for some reason alive, there undoubtedly
> exists a very specific and often extremely powerful sense of ethnic identity,
> which is determined by . . . shared political memories . . . persistent ties with
> the old cult, or the strengthening of kinship and other groups, both in the old
> and new community.[19]

The Irish American language of discontent also received support from high places. A professor of Celtic languages at Catholic University (in Washington,

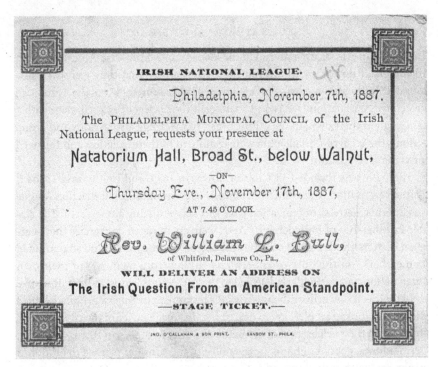

Admission ticket for an evening lecture on Ireland, 1887. Source: CHRC.

D.C.), P. Henebry, wrote in the Philadelphia Irish American press in the late 1890s, "I have struggled through the dreariness of dull years in 'National' schools whereof the 'Nationality' was stark foreignism, and their function the hiding, the covering up, the beslaving of the real Nationality of this country with the revolting slime and sediment of Englishism, and I saw no gleam of intelligence there."[20]

At a meeting of the Parnell Branch of the Irish National League of Philadelphia, Charles Griffin emphasized to the crowd that for "seven centuries the Irish people have been kept in abject misery and subjected to indignities that would do injustice to the most uncivilized nations. Very few Americans properly understand the Irish cause."[21]

The language movement of the Gaelic League eventually intertwined with Philadelphia's Clan na Gael traditional celebration of Robert Emmet's birthday. Thus we find Margaret MacDonough of the Philo-Celtic Society contributing to the Clan's event at the Academy of Music in 1911; MacDonough performed, in Gaelic, the song of the National Gaelic League, "Clan na-Gael Go Deo" as well as "O'Donnell Abu" and the "Green Hills of Ireland."[22]

ENEMIES AT HOME AND ABROAD

The revival of American nativism in the 1890s supplied the Irish Americans with all the proof necessary to remind their community that they were still surrounded by hostile agents. Philadelphia's Hibernians took on the American Protective Association (APA) and a late-century resurgence in nativism with a campaign of their own; in the ethnic press, in meetings, discussions and group actions, the Irish of Philadelphia were reminded of their isolation and the need for vigilant opposition.

The APA was founded in Clinton, Iowa, in 1887, and by the mid-1890s it counted 2.5 million Americans in its ranks. The Immigration Restriction League was another nativist organization that was active during these years. The sizable membership of Philadelphia's AOH were encouraged to exercise that cherished Irish method of rural communal control—the boycott—and so reminded its members "on the duty of Hibernians buying from members of their own organization and particularly referred to the A.P.A. as the most to be shunned."[23]

In their war of words with anti-Irish Protestantism in America, Philadelphia's Hibernians took great pleasure in describing the misbehavior of the city's Orange Order when their celebration of the Battle of Boyne in of 1895 in Rising Sun Park, Germantown, got out of hand. In the midst of the summer picnic celebration, a minor row with police turned into a melee as seventy-five Orangemen were reported to have descended on the outmanned city police: "The police were overwhelmed and beaten to the ground [and] rolled in the dust and were stripped of their badges."[24]

Enemies, both real and contrived, were everywhere; the Catholic Irish American response was to confront public insults and unify the public sphere through conflict. Theirs was an inherited sense of conflict, sewn into the texts, oral reports, traditions and politics of Irish opposition. Renato Rosaldo reminds us of the enduring, persistent quality of conflict as identity, and of its instrumental value as a motivating force; he writes, "Cultural traditions, understood as actively selected versions of the past, constitute and reconstitute themselves through social conflicts that project themselves from the past into an imagined future."[25]

The *Philadelphia Times* had written a few columns that were perceived as anti-Irish in the late 1890s, and the AOH responded with their own attacks against "yellow journals." The offending press reports in Philadelphia's mainstream media were read in local association meetings, condemned by members and were followed by the passing of defensive resolutions and the issuing of bans and boycotts.

Kensington's AOH "Division 56 . . . resents the mis-statements, malicious falsehoods and deliberate lies with which the columns of the newspaper press of the country" have engaged and "will refuse to encourage in any manner the circulation of such journals."[26] Division 78 in South Philadelphia decided to boycott the *Philadelphia Times* as well because of their "recent scurrilous attack on the ancient order 'The Molly Maguires' a rehash of Megargee's Fairy Tales."[27]

Labor concerns and troubles could not completely be filtered out of the meeting rooms of the public sphere, the AOH for example, its memberships so heavily laden with working-class Irish. The 1893 Depression took its toll on industries, a condition noted in AOH Division 55: its president acknowledged that "trade depression had its direct effect upon us, most of our members being employed in the textile industry."[28]

In a pamphlet that circulated among the Catholic societies of Philadelphia in the early 1900s, *Why the Catholic Church Cannot Accept Socialism*, readers learned that social organization was primarily "subject to the law of God."[29] The social was not always avoided or deleted from the agenda of Irish men and women gathering in public forums and attention to class and the nature of industrial work surfaced in odd associational settings. President Edward Murphy of the Irish Catholic Benevolent Union wrote to his constituency on the eve of the society's impending gathering in March 1890. He announced "the creation of a Labor Bureau, formed for assisting members in obtaining employment." He went on to remind his fellow Catholic members that "it is to be hoped that the various societies will take a more active interest in the Labor movement."[30] Socialism may have been a taboo topic in gatherings of Irish American working men in Philadelphia in the 1890s, but labor and its troubles were never far removed from the minds and voices of working Irishmen.

However, British militarism and cowardice were always welcomed topics in the ideology of Irish memory celebrated in the Irish public sphere. A member rose at a meeting in AOH Division 31, deep in South Philadelphia, and "delivered a scathing speech" against the British in the American Civil War, "who during the war of rebellion sent the Alabama on the high seas to destroy the commerce of this country."[31] At another AOH meeting, "Brother O'Malley . . . made quite a historical speech, in which he amusingly referred to the 'Castlebar races,' a ridiculous exploit of the red-coated soldiers of England in '98, who, when attacked by the French soldiers under Humbert, never ceased to run until they arrived within the military barracks in Tuam."[32] This reference was to the United Irishmen rebellion of 1798 and the landing of French troops in the west of Ireland in support of the Irish rebels, a bold strategic move that met with initial French and Irish success only to end with another Irish national loss. O'Malley's home association was 15th and Ridge, and he was a visitor to this meeting at 11th and Anita, a distance of a couple of miles, and judging by his frequent guest appearances and public pronouncements, he was something of a traveling oral historian among the Irish associations of Philadelphia.

The Irish American defense mechanism in these years was tuned to the slightest insult generated by ethnic heritage or social class; this hypervigilance militated

Reception to Michael Davitt,
THE FATHER OF THE LAND LEAGUE,
Under the Auspices of the

Municipal Council, I.N.L.
AT THE ACADEMY OF MUSIC,
Saturday Eve'g, January 15, 1887.

Doors open at 7, to commence at 8 o'clock.

GENERAL ADMISSION, 25 CENTS.
Reserved Seats, 50 Cents.

JOHN F. MURPHY, PR. 2274, FIFTH ST., BELOW WALNUT.

Ticket to a Philadelphia reception hosted in honor of Michael Davitt, an Irish nationalist activist. Source: CHRC.

against methods of compromise, undermined the growth of a generalized public trust, and made Gaelic unity a safe and secure bunker for Philadelphia's Irish.

DEFENDING THE PUBLIC SPHERE: THE ANCIENT ORDER OF HIBERNIANS IN PHILADELPHIA

The AOH in 1890s Philadelphia was affiliated with the national order and followed the dictates and politics of this organization, including its steadfast opposition to nativism and its support of Catholic education. The Philadelphia AOH purchased a building in 1895 on 8th Street, a central location in Center City, a place President McKernan describes as "a place they could call their own."[33]

The AOH accommodated and made room for Catholic support, by moderating its positions and aligning itself with popular causes such as the Land League agitation in Ireland. By the 1880s, the AOH had softened its revolutionary image, recanted any connection with secret societies and reached an accommodation with the Catholic Church. As Kevin Kenny notes, the AOH in Pennsylvania in 1880 was "thoroughly respectable."[34] The AOH was also a mutual aid society and offered insurance benefits for its memberships like any beneficial organization; its motto was "Friendship, Unity and true Christian Charity."[35]

AOH Division 43, located at 9th and Spruce in the old city, boasted 140 members. The year 1895 was a good financial year for this AOH division; its membership was healthy, and the association laid out only $25 in health benefits, leaving $404 in the bank for the next year.[36] Some years taxed the financial solvency of the local associations and the commitment to mutual aid; for Division 10, which was located in the warehouse district (formerly known as "Corktown"), 1890 was reported as a trying year, with $1,600 in sick benefits doled out and an additional $600 spent on funerals.[37] The capillary nature of the citywide AOH in the 1890s was held together by a number of supports, which made it a solid organizational structure with a centralized hierarchy, which allowed for local autonomy, neighborhood bonds, and the communicative network of a citywide circulation of a message loyal to an AOH vision of Gaelic purity.

In 1893, there were 55 branches of the AOH spread across Philadelphia, which put the city's total membership at over 10,000.[38] By 1894, there were 57 divisions, and in 1895, there were 62 divisions with over 12,000 members. By the end of the century, in 1899, Philadelphia's AOH had expanded to 87 divisions.[39]

The Hibernians for 1888–1889 recorded paying out $15,194 in sick benefits and $2,559 in death benefits. Division 7, located south of Center City, was the third largest division, with over 250 members on the 1888–1889 rolls and paid out the most sick and death benefits for the year.[40] The membership populations of the branch divisions in 1888–1889 were variable, but many local division associations had high numbers of members, whose dues-paying potential supported the local autonomy of the neighborhood divisional societies. The AOH divisions with high populations were also dispersed across the city, reflective of Philadelphia's wide industrial span and connected to areas of high Irish residence—Kensington, South Philadelphia, Germantown, and Manayunk, which were neighborhoods close to industrial works.

Divisions thus strove to keep their memberships high, a necessity in a city with a mobile working-class population that witnessed the coming and going of association members with changes in job location or financial resources. The figures in Table 6.1 depict the city's AOH divisions from 1888 to 1889, including the number of members per division and financial resources at the end of the year for the AOH. The sizable population of AOH members was dispersed across Philadelphia, being spread among thirty-seven divisions at the time, but it also recorded 1,000 men "dropped from the rolls" during the year.[41] The branch associations were always engaged in recruiting drives for new members. In one case, "two beautiful emblems of the Order were presented to Joseph O'Leary and James D. Farrell for bringing in the highest number of members during the preceding six months." O'Leary and Farrell enlisted forty-four new people for Division 53, which was located at Broad and Catharine Streets in South Philadelphia.[42]

The AOH and its numerous branches in Philadelphia in the 1890s were indeed a voice for a resurgent and militant nationalism embraced by ardent supporters of the cultural revival, but they were voluntary associations first, which demanded organizational order and financial solvency. If the Irish were well schooled in their native nationalism and opposition to modernism, they were not opposed

TABLE 6.1

A.O.H. DIVISION MEMBERSHIPS AND FINANCIAL RESERVES, 1888–89

Division	Number of Members	Value of Cash and Property	Division	Number of Members	Value of Cash and Property
1	207	$1,894	20	62	$379
2	115	$671	21	334	$1,676
3	205	$1,182	22	94	$758
4	137	$2,031	23	40	$800
5	250	$2,600	24	113	$652
6	163	$1,275	25	66	$185
7	256	$1,732	26	148	$760
8	207	$957	27	57	$241
9	—	—	28	80	$480
10	292	$1,469	29	216	$982
11	48	$502	30	30	$300
12	169	$1,305	31	48	$208
13	195	$907	32	71	$305
14	138	$852	33	—	—
15	127	$1,017	34	77	$545
16	140	$582	35	93	$584
17	90	$640	36	58	$329
18	76	$569	37	43	$105
19	196	$769	Total	4,641	$30,243

Source: "1888–89 Secretary's Annual Report of the Philadelphia A.O.H.," *Freeman and Irish American Review*, August 10, 1889.

to mainstream methods of group cohesion, and their ethnic associations developed into bureaucratized examples of institutional control.

The first phase of AOH meetings involved scripted events and were brought to order with the business of the group's finances. Dues were to be paid on time, and even though allowances were made for late payments, eventually the non-payment of dues would earn a member a dismissal notice from the organization. The accounting of sick and death benefits was always a priority of collective fiscal health.

AOH No. 10, at 20th and Carlton Streets in Philadelphia, revealed that it had paid $1,600 in sick benefits as well as $600 for funerals in 1890.[43] AOH No. 43 gathered at the end of 1895 at 9th and Spruce to go over the year's expenses; it took in $659 in dues for the year, and after using much of its dues money for sick benefits with a miscellaneous spending of $216 for meeting refreshments, this AOH branch association reported $404 in bank funds to face the next year.[44] Flu epidemics could wreck an association's coffers; one, the Sourin Beneficial Society, reported that its "society suffered heartily from 'La Grippe' last winter."[45]

AOH meetings were held in various locations, as central for the branch membership as possible, and some divisions were able to purchase their own buildings for meetings. Division 78 had its own hall at 20th below Reed, as did Division 63 at 11th and Anita Streets. The Sheares' Club, named after two "patriot" brothers of the 1798 Rising in Ireland, was a permanent location that was home to two divisions, its interior a shrine of Irish American nationalism: "behind the President's chair recline in graceful pose two beautiful silk flags representing Ireland and America, while at either side are paintings of Robert Emmet and C.S. Parnell, and busts of O'Connell and Mitchel add additional glory and halo to the surroundings."[46]

The goal of every AOH division was its own hall, and the associations kept their eye out for real estate bargains. Division 31 had its sights on a building at 21st and Wharton at "a very reasonable price." Division 24 would eventually own its hall in West Philadelphia, at 37th and Market Streets, and proudly acclaimed: "In the near future this division will possess their own hall, which will be so large that they can accommodate other divisions less fortunate, thereby proving that they are true exponents of their . . . motto, 'Friendship, Unity and True Christian Charity.'"[47]

The Daughters of Erin was the women's auxiliary branch of the men's AOH. The Daughters also divided the city into branch associations and had identical administrative structures to the men's associations. Meetings were held on Thursday evenings, at 8:00 P.M., to avoid the Tuesday and Sunday afternoon time conflicts with men's meetings. There were at least thirteen branches of the daughters in late-nineteenth-century in Philadelphia.[48]

WINTER SPLENDOR

Winter was the season for the annual balls of the Irish American associations. It was a slow time in the building trades, and a time for extravagance and fundraising. The AOH sponsored a grand ball in February 1895 for all of its fifty-eight divisions, which was held at the Academy of Music. It combined a number of cultural icons in its décor that merged American democracy with Irish nationalism: "The national colors that decorated the fronts of all the galleries, gracefully diversified with shields of the national flag, and the green banner of Erin; while the names of Irish counties were emblazoned on bannerettes."[49]

The AOH Ball was the place to be seen in your best attire, a moment during the height of winter for an urban excursion among your people, a brief display of bourgeois pretensions. The evening's "grand march began promptly at 10 o'clock, led by President O'Neill and his pretty daughter Maggie, charming in a magnificent gown."[50] The other officers and their wives joined the promenade, including "Mrs. Maurice F. Wilhere, in a handsome costume of pale blue surah, black velvet and diamonds." In addition, AOH's paramilitary division, the Hibernian Rifles, who were dressed in their finest martial regalia for this event, were noticed and appreciated for "their thoroughly military looking uniforms."[51] The *Philadelphia Record* wrote, "The Academy was decorated for the occasion[,] . . . the equal love of the members for their native and adopted countries being forcefully exemplified in the intertwined Irish and American colors which draped the balconies and galleries."[52]

Yet the AOH never lost sight of Ireland and its struggle for independence and embraced just about every nationalist cause and movement that appeared in the decades leading up to World War I and beyond. The symbols of a Gaelic defiance, its martial nationalism, were more vital than actual readiness and always in demand at mass gatherings. The limited presence of the Hibernian Rifles was noted at the February 1895 AOH ball held at the Philadelphia Academy of Music: "[there were not] more soldierly looking men than the few who were in attendance dressed in the Rifles' neat uniform and pity was expressed by many that Philadelphia, instead of having a mere shadow of an Irish military organization, had not a regiment, with its full complement of men, who could march under the flags of their adopted country and the country of their birth."[53]

The AOH supported many of the new cultural initiatives of the 1890s, such as the Gaelic-language movement, the American branch of the Gaelic League, Irish history in schools, and Catholic education.[54] The AOH in Philadelphia aligned itself early on with the emerging Irish language movement of the 1890s; the following statement from an AOH division meeting in 1898 testifies to the commitment:

> However much we allow for the dire persecution with which the speaking of the soft and mellow Gaelic was pursued by cruel and craven invaders, and whatever force be attributed to the relative necessity for acquiring the commercial legal tongue of the stranger, it still remains a problematic fact, which is little to the credit of the Irish people, that, while preserving intact their ardent national aspirations, they did allow the grand native language to be wrested from them.[55]

This statement reflects the chain of causation in language preservation, the damage inflicted by the "commercial legal tongue of the stranger," and Irish culpability for allowing Gaelic to wane.

Second Grand Ball

GIVEN BY THE

Catholic Sons of Derry

MUSICAL FUND HALL, Locust Street above Eighth

Wednesday Evening, April 19th, '11

TICKETS - - - - FIFTY CENTS

This Society meets the Fourth Sunday of every month, at INDUSTRIAL ART HALL, 314 North Broad St., at 2 P. M. Membership is open to all practical Catholics born in County Derry, or by descent through birth of either parent in said County. Believing in union, this Society belongs to the Federation of Irish County Societies. The objects of this Association are PATRIOTIC, Social and Beneficial.

OFFICERS:

JOHN A. GILLAN, President   JAMES MURRAY, Vice-President
GABRIEL J. WILSON, Rec. Sec.   FRANK J. DEVLIN, Fin. Sec.
PATRICK McANALLY, Treasurer

Lines dedicated to the faithful sons of the 32 Counties of Ireland in the struggle for Freedom, at the instance of the Catholic Sons of Derry, at their Second Annual Ball, April 19th, 1911:

AIR—" COLUMBIA, THE GEM OF THE OCEAN."

O sweet "Derry," far o'er the wide ocean,
    The homes we e'er long to see;
The hope of each son's devotion
    Is from bondage you will soon flee;
An antedate makes us assemble,
    For victory gleams on our view,
Whose matters made each heart tremble,
    But our battle is very near through.

Chorus: When "dawn" shed a new light on you,
    The worn course of "right" to pursue,
    A banner of freedom did assemble,
    What dawn will the dread fight subdue?

When war waged with wide devastation,
    And their army was found in poor form,
"Old Derry's" one animation
    Was in thousands your ranks to adorn;
And the land where liberty hangs over,
    Can plainly point her way through;
To the "arms" that wrought victory for her,
    We ask justice in lieu.   Chorus.

Then, "County and County," come hither,
    Your hearts fill up with the vim
That makes your wreaths never wither,
    Nor your path to victory grow dim.
"Derry's Sons" from you will ne'er sever,
    But holds to one cause as true,
"Freedom of Ireland," for ever
    Each year shed bright laurels on you.

GILBERT A. FAHY, R. C. H. S., '07.

O'FARRELL PRINT, 1630 S. TENTH St.

Handbill for the 1911 annual ball of the Catholic Sons of Derry. Source: CHRC.

LIGHTHEARTED GATHERINGS

Once business had been finalized, time was set aside for leisure and monthly meetings closed with Irish songs or poems, the sharing of a joke, refreshments, and informal conversation among members. Such songs as "Gems of the Emerald Isle," "Joe Hardy," "Emmet's Grave," "Heroes of the Past," and "Poor Pat Must Emigrate" punctuated the evening air at the close of Hibernian meetings.[56] The monthly meetings were popular locations for visiting friends and associates from outside the host association who often pitched in with a few words on politics, a joke or a song.

If winter was the season for society balls, a time for dressing up and display in the company of women, during Philadelphia's stifling summer months Hibernians took to the water. During these excursions outside the city, to the ocean, Atlantic City, or the nearby Delaware River, the Irish celebrated their culture. As an example, in 1893, the AOH organized a day trip down the Delaware to Bay Head, where the river meets the ocean. As always, "a good piper rolled out the jigs, the reels and the hornpipes" during the journey.[57]

The Turf Cutters' Leagues were auxiliary societies of the AOH, a lighter version of the parent organization in which divisions were "bogs" and members were "turf cutters." President of Bog 4 Frank McGuckin testified at the meeting: "though it has not been my good fortune to be born in the 'Green Isle,' I am fully aware of her history, the wrongs she has so long endured, and as a consequence my heart yearns for the day when the land of my forefathers shall be . . . great, glorious and free."[58] The Turf Cutters were prevailed on, at the conclusion of this meeting, to commemorate "the memory of the 'noble-hearted three' who died for their country on an English scaffold thirty-one years ago," a reference to the Manchester Martyrs.[59]

A gathering of Philadelphia's Turf Cutters was also an opportunity to poke a little fun at everyone's Irish heritage, as President McGuckin went on to "give a cheering report of the league of Turf Cutters over which he is chief." He reminded his fellow bogmen that "when the more serious business is o'er, the usual sociability will reign supreme."[60] And, at the meeting of another Philadelphia bog, "Financial Secretary Quigley entertained the members by giving a comical and confusing dialogue between an Irishman and a Dutchman amid roars of laughter."[61]

The ultimate comic relief was always reserved for Ireland's ancient enemy. For example, at the Board of Erin meeting in 1899, a little fun was had at the expense of the Anglo-Irish and the British monarchy in the singing of the song "The Dawning of the Day." One verse went:

"Is that your Queen, my Lord?" she said
"That auld and burridly dame?
I see the Crown upon her heid,
But I dinna ken her name."[62]

A MOVABLE URBAN SOCIABILITY

Out-of-neighborhood guests were a welcomed feature of the monthly AOH meeting, and these visitors were publicly acknowledged and often called on for an
observation or a song at the close of the meeting. The associations considered
the convenience of location in planning their events, as when the Hibernian Ball
in November of 1889 was promoted as an event that was easily accessible, in order
to "enable many persons living in distant sections of the city to attend."[63]

Rituals in the Gaelic zone were also political, reminders of past rebellions
serving as mechanisms of remembrance that kept the British Empire in focus.
The public recital of Robert Emmet's speech from the court dock was such a rite,
as described in a reading at an AOH gathering in 1895: "where the brave and
youthful Emmet hurled defiance at . . . the personification of all that was cruel
and bloodthirsty in England's misrule."[64]

Halls were also loaned out to other divisions in need of a meeting place: the
Brothers of Erin met in the hall of AOH Division 78, 20th Street below Reed in
South Philadelphia, and AOH guests from Division 11, at 3rd and Poplar, and
Division 59, at 26th and Wharton, were present.[65] At this meeting in summer
1898, after each new officer rose and gave a speech, the visiting president of
Division 59 "delivered a very important address, relative to the necessity and
advantage of naturalization. The Brother is the Father of this idea which since
its inception has been the means of enabling several Irishmen to go success-
fully through the trying ordeal of the Naturalization Courts." The meeting
then set up a committee and a class schedule to help those born overseas
through the process of becoming American citizens; class was held on Monday
evenings.[66]

Officer election night was often a time for celebration and visiting friends.
At Division 24, at 37th and Market Streets, "a number of visitors came to congratulate Brother Stone on his election. Singing, dancing and recitations figured
largely on the programme, contributing to a successful and joyous evening."[67]
During an election Sunday afternoon meeting of Division 11, which was at
15th and Ridge by 1899, "the usual number of visitors were present and the cus-
tomary sociability reigned during the later part of the afternoon."[68]

Visitors were called upon for their speaking and singing abilities. At an AOH
Division 31 meeting, "Dunn, of eleven, gave some very excellent renditions, both
in prose and poetry. Bracken, of thirty-four, gave a parody of the three tailors of
Tooley Street" and also sang "Wolfe Tone's Grave," and they closed the meeting
by singing the American national anthem.[69] AOH Division 86 met and finished
with a long set of songs and recitations; visiting "Brother Clarke of 83 gave a recitation entitled 'The Forging of the Pikes,'" and "Financial Secretary, John
McShea, sang in fine form 'Death to the Tyrant, Our Land Shall be Free' as the
evening concluded."[70]

A movable Irish American sociability in the associations required spending extra personal funds for the trolley fare and tested multiple allegiances as members moved about the city to meet and engage with colleagues and friends in the monthly business meetings. While the primary attraction was personal, relaxed association with friends and the fellow Irish, there was a satisfaction gained in reconfirming their faith in Irish identity, sharing in sentimental songs about Ireland, and lifting their voices together for the obligatory singing of the Irish and American anthems to close the affair.

A CONSENSUS OF FORCED LOYALTY

Within the open forum that was the life of the public sphere, there also emerged a tight collective acceptance for the Irish way, a communal understanding of a diaspora identity that afforded scant room for individual opinion or tolerance for dissent. As an example, at an AOH meeting in 1898, "a motion [for consensus] was at once made . . . which was carried unanimously, almost, for one individual who displayed his unIrish animus made a very feeble objection, in which he was totally alone in his glory."[71]

This forced consensus was followed on matters affecting Irish culture and meaning, less so on the more mundane details of running the association. In business affairs, for example, whether to purchase a hall or make a move to another location or to float a fundraising scheme, there was often much debate. "Joseph McLaughlin spoke, who showed in plain and calm language the necessity of a large hall or headquarters for the united divisions of the A.O.H. in Philadelphia. The brother told some plain truths regarding the premises at 243 S. 8th St.," and so the debate continued about the prospect of purchasing a large building and property.[72]

Group unity was a high value of the public sphere; failure to attend meetings and functions was a breaking point for many brothers who had to extend themselves to attend. "Mr. O'Byrne, a guest . . . thrashed with a heavy flail 'the laggards who are not with us,' at a meeting of 63."[73]

Guest speaker, Rev. Cummins from Roscommon, Ireland, to AOH Division 61, "took for his theme 'Unity,' and spoke upon its effect on the Irish people, demonstrating the power they could wield in this country if they were united and determined to stand by each other." The guest spoke on history, the unity of the Germans and Irish in Philadelphia during the American revolutionary war, "in olden times . . . the Irish and Germans fought side by side to drive England's soldiery from this land."[74] A consensus on Irish history and Irish victimhood was confirmed at AOH gatherings, in formal discourse and educational sermons and lectures, and informally, in song and poem as members closed the meetings and prepared to return home.

THE RESPECTABLE ETHNIC ASSOCIATION

It has been proposed that the AOH was an association in which many of Philadelphia's Irish working class joined and felt comfortable in its numerous divisions spread across the city's neighborhoods. It has also been proposed that the Irish who joined associations in Philadelphia were a different breed, a self-selected cohort of immigrants with a particular attraction for orderly, respectable norms of behavior.

In this study, the communal setting of the ethnic association drives a wedge between layers of the working class, a top layer of Irish American skilled workers, an ethnic "labor aristocracy" of sorts, and an underlying mass of unskilled Irish American workers; the voluntary association was the social site of this cleavage and the attraction of an achievement ethic the clear victor over a rougher brand of working-class influence that had no vocal constituency, no set of leaders or spokesmen to articulate a defense against the encroaching civilizing processes. Irish ethnic associations were, in this view, little schools for the unconscious dissemination of greater social norms, and late-nineteenth-century Irish ethnic awareness tagged along and attached itself to the primary moral messages of an aspiring, achieving Irish American.

To be a member of an Irish American association in the late nineteenth century in Philadelphia was to attain a certain ethnic citizenship—as Max Weber writes, "the sense of ethnic honor is the specific honor of the masses, for it is accessible to anybody who belongs to the subjectively believed community of descent."[75] The mere fact of this citizenship, conferred by membership in an ethnic association, was sufficient motivation for the average association member; it provided a measure of status differentiation that was satisfying in itself.

Yet, there was a tension about class privilege and Irish identity in the ethnic associations that surfaced in the cracks of bourgeois aspiration and the struggle to move upward. Describing an Irish American woman who had taken an interest in the Gaelic League, "unlike most of our countrymen and women who occupy a high social position and command wealth in the United States, she proudly boasts of the Old Land and her ancestry."[76] It was an allegiance, a worldview of opposition to rank and privilege and a distrust of established power, that also defined the world of the Diaspora Irish in their associations in Philadelphia.

THE NORMALIZATION OF MILITANT NATIONALISM: PHILADELPHIA'S CLAN NA GAEL

Philadelphia's Clan na Gael was a voluntary association with a mission; it was intended as a revolutionary outpost in the Irish Diaspora to provide support, especially financial, for the moment when Ireland would strike back at England.

The Fenian Brotherhood of the 1860s was the precursor to the Clan na Gael and both organizations had a sizeable presence in Philadelphia.[77] Its public name was the Clan na Gael but to members it was the United Brotherhood, a society with rites and codes modeled after Irish secret societies in the nineteenth century. It was all that, but through the course of organizing along the normative lines of Irish American voluntary societies, in Philadelphia it turned itself into a vast set of urban mutual aid societies. The Clan na Gael in Philadelphia peppered the Irish American public sphere with a separatist message, espousing a militant tone in a steadfast denunciation of Britain's role in Ireland, allowed its Irish Americans an evening of real and imagined revolt at the monthly branch meeting.

The Clan na Gael in Philadelphia embraced a public posture of military preparation; it was noted during a meeting in 1888 that America allowed arms to be displayed in public stating, "for centuries the Irish had been living under foreign domination and had no free military units of their own."[78] This call to arms had already been answered by the formation of various guard units of Irish Americans who performed at various Irish functions in the city. On St. Patrick's Day, 1859, Philadelphia's *Public Ledger* reported on the parade's march of Irish units: "the following companies participated: Montgomery Guards, Irish Volunteers, Hibernia Greens, Emmet Guards, Meagher Guards, Shield Guards . . . after marching through the principal streets the Regiments proceeded to a body to hear a lecture."[79]

In Philadelphia, the Clan na Gael never lost its posture and militant style, but as the 1890s gave way to the new century it assumed a more supportive role to Irish nationalism. The Irish American Club, located in Center City Philadelphia, came to resemble something of a reserved gentlemen's club for Philadelphia's Irish Americans. Like the AOH, Philadelphia's Clan na Gael had a capillary structure with "camps" distributed across the city; in 1889 there were thirty-seven camps recorded, fifty-one in 1903.[80]

The American Clan na Gael was founded in 1867 in the aftermath of the decline of the influence of Ireland's revolutionary Fenian Brotherhood. The Fenian Brotherhood was established in 1858 in New York, a body of men determined to gain Irish independence through the force of arms. It was a secret society that operated by the system of autonomous small circles of committed revolutionaries scattered in geographic zones of influence and concentrations of Irish population.

The Philadelphia Fenians in the late 1860s had thirteen circles with an estimate of 800 men in each circle.[81] After two disastrous escapades involving botched invasions of Canada by Irish American Fenians and a failed rising in Ireland in 1867, the group withered away in the United States only to be replaced by the Clan na Gael. James Gibbons of Philadelphia was a leader of the Fenians, rising to become president of the Fenian Senate in 1865. From his printing business on Chestnut Street he advocated a more militant approach to Irish freedom supporting armed revolt in Ireland as well as the military advances into Canada, helping to secure guns from Philadelphia's Frankford Arsenal in 1866.[82]

The Clan na Gael was designed to be the American outpost of the Irish Revolutionary Brotherhood (IRB), the militant successor to the Fenians, and it achieved a shifting of the impetus for Irish revolution to the United States.[83] It earned fame by organizing the spectacular rescue of six Irish Fenian prisoners on board the ship *Catalpa* out of Australia in 1875, but its revolutionary élan drifted into periods of inactivity, and it settled in the late nineteenth century into a patient wait for the right set of circumstances and the right time for active rebellion in Ireland.

Events in Ireland would reinvigorate Irish militant nationalism and America's Clan na Gael. In the 1890s, Irish cultural nationalism swept across the Atlantic to ignite the movement to save Gaelic language and culture and, at the same time, rekindle the flames of political nationalism, and the Clan na Gael found renewed purpose in its existence. Later, the rise of Protestant-backed Unionism in the North of Ireland, Carson's own armed volunteers, led Philadelphia's Irish once again to the conclusion that force was the only way to gain any type of Irish independence. Fundraising for the Irish Volunteers, dominated by the IRB, became the exclusive province of America's Clan na Gael, and Philadelphia's branch was in the thick of the movement.

The Clan na Gael in Philadelphia boasted thirty-seven divisions in 1888 and was overseen by a Board of Directors which met the third Sunday of each month at the Irish American Club at 1708 Race Street.[84] Philadelphia's Clan na Gael also sponsored a debating club meeting every Wednesday evening at the Irish American Club. The Clan na Gael enjoyed its image as a semi-secret society with insurrection as its mission; it was announced at a meeting in 1891 that "new members should be guarded in their expressions regarding the affairs of the Club" and reminded its men to "guard against the presence of strangers in the house."[85] This obsession with secrecy was a Philadelphia Irish tradition: the Society of United Irishmen of Philadelphia reminded its members in 1797 to "never, from fear of punishment, divulge any of its secrets. . . ."[86]

The Irish American Club was originally the exclusive home of the Clan na Gael, the club's board of governors doubled as the organization's administrative board, each member issued a private key for entrance. The club was the ideological center of Gaelic identity in Philadelphia; by the late 1880s, the club had gone into debt to support its quasi-bourgeois lifestyle. The club board considered admitting outsiders of the Clan na Gael to offset the debt, the brothers moving that "the portion of the constitution requiring members of this Club to be members of the Clan na Gael be amended and that membership in this club be open to every person of Irish nationalist feeling and tendencies who shall be proposed and elected in the form at present set forth."[87] The motion was debated and defeated and Clan members were obliged to dig deeper in their pockets as "a voluntary subscription list was opened and $400 subscribed in a short time."[88]

The spaces of Philadelphia's Irish American Club were often rented out for divisions of the Clan na Gael and others to hold their monthly meetings. In the case of the Literary Societies, the Philo-Celtic Society, its premises were provided rent-free. The Philadelphia Clan na Gael, in the late 1880s, also grappled with the murder of the prominent Clan na Gael figure, Chicago's Dr. Cronin, the suspects in this Irish American drama the Clan na Gael's Chicago-centered "Triangle" leadership—Philadelphia Clan President Ryan "made an exhaustive statement concerning the tragedy . . . listing the name prominently mentioned" as the guilty party.[89]

Financial solvency was a constant problem for the Clan na Gael, and fundraising and the collection of dues were of primary importance for the association. A "collector of dues" was appointed who would go directly to the homes of members and solicit the funds; for his troubles, the collector received 10 percent of the remittances.[90] In 1904, collector Brother Kearns of Clan na Gael Camp 246 reported that he had personally "visited all the brothers he knew" to collect dues owed this branch.[91]

The individual branches or "camps" of the Philadelphia Clan na Gael had a great deal of autonomy and ran their organizations as separate voluntary associations, but the Central Board had a voracious appetite for funds. There was a constant tension over the distribution of funds and the board's request for contributions from the camps; the divisional "camps" faced punitive sanctions for actions judged too independent for the board, but the branch camps were most often suspended for the simple fact of non-payment of Clan na Gael dues to the Central Board.[92] For Clan na Gael summer sports picnic and balls, 75 percent was expected for the board, and 25 percent went to the camps. In 1891, "brother" James Mulgrew was asked to leave the Irish American Club because his camp had been suspended.[93]

ENTERTAINMENT AS NATIONALIST MESSAGE

The Clan na Gael in Philadelphia organized large events that would focus attention on Irish nationalist causes. The twenty-second anniversary of the "Manchester Martyrs, Allen, Larkin and O'Brien" was the theme for a Saturday evening in 1899 of Irish music and history at Horticultural Hall, Broad and Spruce Streets, Center City Philadelphia. Solos in baritone and soprano were presented for songs such as "Our Land Shall Be Free," "Paddies Evermore," "Green Old Flag," and "Erin Weeps Forsaken." Edward O'Meagher Condon, editor of Philadelphia's *Freeman and Irish American Review*, delivered the keynote speech in remembrance of the Manchester three.[94]

Handbill for the Clan na Gael's 1891 celebration of the Manchester Martyrs. Source: Digital Library@Villanova University.

Ticket to the Clan na Gael's 1889 annual ball. Source: CHRC.

The notation of the birthday of Ireland's revolutionary patriot Robert Emmet was an opportunity the Clan na Gael seized in 1891 in Philadelphia when it hosted its Emmet Evening at the Academy of Music. Emmet celebrations were a tradition carried to Philadelphia from rural Ireland—the 1903 Emmet Centenary held in Bailieborough, County Cavan, in Mr. Farrelly's farm field, attracted over 400 people from the surrounding parishes of Killeshandra, Killann, Killinkere, Termon, Laragh and Knockbride. This rural gathering listened to William Redmond, the leader of the Irish Constitution Party, as he recalled the sacrifice of Emmet, "the bravest patriot and greatest soldier that ever gave his life for the liberty of any land."[95]

In Philadelphia's Irish community in 1891, five thousand ticket-paying Irish Americans were reported to attend the Emmet remembrance located not in a cow pasture but in a somewhat more elegant setting at the Academy of Music—"the Academy was beautifully decorated with the green and the orange, appropriate mottos, shields bearing the names of the four provinces, the counties of Ireland, eminent Irish patriots, and the Stars and Stripes."[96]

After such an important event in Philadelphia, there was the usual reception at the Irish American Club House, 1708 Race Street, in which 150 people were served a midnight dinner followed by "songs and recitations . . . [that] did not terminate until about 4 o'clock in the morning."[97] Such was the nature of the grand Irish American spectacle in the early 1890s, part nationalist rally, a lesson in Irish culture and history, and a grand night on the town.

TABLE 6.2

OCCUPATIONAL STRUCTURE OF
PHILADELPHIA'S CLAN NA GAEL, CAMP 246,
1892–1895

Occupation Category	Share
Professional[a]	1.5%
White collar[b]	11.5%
Skilled labor[c]	39.0%
Unskilled labor[d]	48.0%

Source: "Minute Book of the Clan na Gael,
1889–1923," MSS 37, box 1, Historical Society of
Pennsylvania, Camp 246, 1892–1895.

N = 181.

[a] Includes attorneys and physicians.

[b] Includes shopkeepers, grocers, and saloon
keepers.

[c] Includes machinists, textile workers, and
railroad men.

[d] Includes manual laborers.

A Mobile Public Sphere

Like clandestine meetings of the United Irishmen in Ireland and the branch meetings of the AOH in Philadelphia, the monthly Clan na Gael "camp" meetings were neighborhood gatherings with an open invitation for outside brothers to drop in and participate. Camp 246 of the Philadelphia Clan na Gael had its headquarters on 814 Girard Avenue in the river district of the Kensington section just north of central Philadelphia.

Tables 6.2 and 6.3 describe the occupational structure and ethnic descent of a sample of the membership of Clan na Gael Camp 246; the portrait is derived from the information supplied by new members initiated into the society between 1892 and 1903 recorded in the minute book. This one branch society of sizeable membership reflected the working-class nature of the Clan na Gael and Irish American societies of the 1890s, early 1900s, 87 percent working in skilled and unskilled sectors of the industrial economy. Camp 246 was also populated through the steady stream of emigration from Ireland throughout the nineteenth century, 84 percent of its initiated members born in Ireland.

TABLE 6.3

ETHNIC DESCENT OF MEMBERS OF THE CLAN NA GAEL,
CAMP 246, 1892–1895

Ethnic Background	Share
Irish (parents born in Ireland)	84%
American (parents born in United States)	16%

Source: "Minute Book of the Clan na Gael, 1889–1923," MSS 37,
box 1, Historical Society of Pennsylvania, Camp 246, 1892–1895.
N = 280.

The Clan na Gael as a Gentlemen's Club

The Clan na Gael in 1890s Philadelphia was still a militant, conspiratorial, secret society, raising funds for Ireland and intent on helping to seize control of Ireland from the British. Yet its headquarters, the Irish American Club, had also acquired some of the trappings of an Irish American gentlemen's club, which rendered it a nineteenth-century heterotopia of ethnic-centered meaning.

The concept of heterotopia allows us to understand a space like the Irish American Club, with its juxtaposition in Center City Philadelphia among the brick buildings of the city's Anglo ascendancy; this spacious town home was "another space," functioning as a gentlemen's club within the context of militant revolutionary action on behalf of the emerging Irish rebellion and its eventual wars of liberation from England. Irish American members used their status as private citizens to gain entrance to a building on one of Philadelphia's stately boulevards and in this way to join the public realm of Irish culture, revolutionary politics, and nationalism, all oppositional movements of the imagination as well as real politics. Foucault's heterotopia construct confirms the multiplicity of social sites in a public, brings together "several sites that are in themselves incompatible," and opens the door for counterpublics like Gaelic Philadelphia.[98] These are zones of influence that exist alongside and in opposition to norms backed by practices of long validation that elite ethnic groups used to exert power and control.

Members of the Clan na Gael's Irish American Club at 1708 Race Street each received their own club key, and a pool table was available on the third floor. In looking at the monthly treasurer's report for 1890 prepared by the board of directors for the Irish American Club, we can see how the resources were distributed, which commodities were purchased, and ultimately, where the members' values lay. Club bills were paid for cue tips, pool balls, cigars, beer, ice, glasses, playing cards, ice cream, lamps, carpets, paper hangings, plumbing, bookcases, liquor supplies, and whiskey.[99] A sideboard of food was available for members to order from, and a steward was on staff every Saturday evening and Sunday afternoon to take care of drink and food requests. A waiter was also on the premises to carry drinks and cigars to the third-floor pool room. In addition, expenses were paid for a front doorman and watchman as well as a janitor.

In 1917, the business of leisure was paramount at Irish American gatherings at the club at 17th and Race Streets. A poker room was established in the front parlor while $175 was spent for cigars in the spring of 1917 and 100 folding chairs were purchased for events. The club had purchased a revenue license in 1891, which legalized the selling of beer, whiskey, and cigars, and they kept a healthy stock of these items on hand at the Irish American Club.[100] The closing hour would even be pushed back to 1:00 in the morning from midnight.[101]

The Irish American Club at 1708 Race Street was the place to adjourn to for Irish American events in Philadelphia. At the Clan na Gael Games in August 1890, an event that attracted 45,000 spectators to Rising Sun Park in North Philadelphia, a post-sport reception was held for out-of-town guests in which speeches were made and "patriotic songs" filled the evening air as the day of sport and Irish festival wound down.[102] The leisure of the association in an atmosphere of nationalism and remembrance was an assumed benefit for many Irish American associations; the members AOH Division 54 on North Broad Street were said to be pleased with their new hall "where they can enjoy themselves in harmless amusement during their leisure hours."[103]

DISCIPLINE AND NATIONALISM

The Clan na Gael, like other Irish American associations, adhered to an ideal model of respectability and control and expected its members to be restrained in emotion, disciplined in speech, and courteous to colleagues. Hobsbawm outlines the ritual practices of societies devoted to movement from the initiation to the "ceremonials of public meeting," and the "practical rituals" of coming together, with the secret handshake an example of these practices. Public symbols and flags adorned the outside of the Irish American Club, which displayed the Tricolor of Ireland prominently just below the Stars and Stripes.[104]

The meeting of any Irish American society in the 1890s was sacred, but rites of initiation and assembly by the Clan na Gael were loose given the militant nature of this association, for which secrecy was naturally of high value and the oath a less cherished formality. On occasion a potential member was not admitted, being cast as a potential disruptive force within the collective. As an example, one Pat O'Hara was denied admission in 1894 "having received 3 black balls."[105] It took two "black balls" to be denied membership, a process of initiation that required secrecy to protect the identity of voting members; anyone found guilty of exposing the authors of black balls was himself expelled.[106] Black balling members was a common practice of associational life, from the early

Freemasons to the Friendly Societies and Tontines of Dublin. In Ireland it was "black beans" and members from St. Jerome's Tontine Society, for example, and others in Dublin could be fined for "exposing the beans" or the outcome of an initiation procedure.[107]

Even with the social discipline expected of members and the attempt at secrecy required for a revolutionary group, the Clan na Gael in Philadelphia had all sorts of distractions related to personal troubles. There was a lawsuit in 1903 against the Irish American Club, and funds were borrowed from the Clan na Gael's Defense of Ireland fund "to defray the expenses of the lawsuit in defense of the club."[108] Bad behavior at the Irish American Club surfaced from time to time; in 1905 "a charge of conduct unbecoming a member of this organization was proffered against Wm. Carroll of [Camp] 220" and a "trial committee" was appointed to hear the case.[109] A Brother Tennyson was involved in a brawl with another member at the Irish American Club and "suspended from the privileges of this club until trial by proper authority." Moreover, "it was regularly moved and seconded that the Directors of the Irish American Club pay for the glasses of Ed Walsh which were broken by the assault of Mr. Tennyson."[110]

Squabbles between brothers naturally arose but were tamped down quickly. Inside the Clan na Gael camps, "a discussion arose about Brother Brady accusing Brother Murray of slandering him . . . it was moved and seconded that this be laid over for two weeks. After some further discussion the whole matter was dropped."[111] Part of the disciplinary code of the Clan na Gael was the requirement of silence with the outside world about internal affairs, as when Division 246 "moved that Brother McIntyre be suspended for one year being found guilty of slandering the order."[112] In winter 1903 the Irish American Club moved to 726 Spruce Street, the headquarters of the Clan na Gael. At the meeting in 1903, there were fifty-one "camps" represented by delegates to the board's meeting.

The Clan na Gael moved the Irish American Club again, this time to 1428 South Broad Street, in 1922; the organization had entered a period of stagnation. For the March 1923 Board of Directors meeting only seven camps sent delegates; the next month, a discussion was held "on ways and means to make this club more popular." During the summer a decision on reducing the price of refreshments was deferred because not enough delegates were in attendance.[113] Interest in Irish nationalism waned in Irish America after the Anglo-Irish War, the 1921 Treaty with Britain which established a fledgling Irish state; even though the Civil War in Ireland would rage into 1923, some form of Irish freedom had been secured in the early 1920s, thus satisfying a part of the Clan na Gael's mission.

STRIDENT NATIONALISM IN THE PUBLIC SPHERE

The Clan na Gael in Philadelphia preferred the nationalist version of Ireland's past and created their own interpretive framework and language that members

mastered as they settled into the society, taking part in meetings, voicing opinions during debates, sharing cultural bonds and vilifying enemies. Association
officers often closed meetings with a meaningful word or two, as did camp "Treasurer McConne [who] entertained his audience by giving the 'Croppie's Grave'
and referred to the great meeting of 'Tara' in the time of O'Connell and to the
struggle for freedom in '98."[114]

Meetings of branch camps ended with didactic reminders and resolutions of
nation: "the necessity of carrying their nationality with them at all times" and
the hope that "we will all go home to Ireland when the landlords go." Often, the
final words were reserved for the fallen men of the diaspora and the "memory
of men who are gone."[115]

An opportunity to reinvent and live Irish nationalism was rarely lost in the
1890s, and the monthly meetings of the neighborhood branches of the Clan na
Gael were ideal locations for remembrance and distribution of the image of Philadelphia's Irish as "exiled fellow-countrymen."[116] The following ballad of longing, "Poor Erin," closed a Clan na Gael meeting in Philadelphia in the late 1890s:

> Oh! She's a rich and rare land;
> Oh! She's a true and brave land.
> Yes, she's a rare and fair land
> This native land of mine.
> No sons than hers are braver,
> Her daughters hearts ne're waver,
> I'd freely die to save her
> And think my lot divine.[117]

This study states that in the late nineteenth and early twentieth centuries in
Philadelphia, ordinary Irish men and women constructed a Gaelic public sphere,
a web of communicative content and meaning on the nature of Irish identity,
which constituted a civic world of complex organization and high meaning. This
accomplishment was based on a number of factors, including social learning,
Irish heritage, transplanted cultural knowledge from native Ireland, contact with
the associational spirit of the times, and American democracy in small groups
and organizations. This public was supported by the surplus derived from wages
earned by ordinary working-class men and women in Philadelphia's volatile but
expansive industrial economy. It was also based on an unchallenged loyalty to
late-century Irish nationalism, an ideology of distrust of imperial Britain dating back to the United Irishmen through Young Ireland and the Fenians, resulting in a steely consciousness of opposition to those opposed to the rise of a free
Irish state.

CHAPTER 7

Sport, Culture, and Nation among the Irish of Philadelphia

The 1890s and early 1900s in Ireland and Philadelphia were the years of the Irish cultural revival, a movement that asserted itself in these transatlantic locations, part of a rising constellation of Irish national forces casting their gaze backward to ancient and traditional symbols of Irish autonomy and pride. At the same time, the Irish in Philadelphia followed a modernist impulse to settle, achieve, and construct an ethnic community out of the dislocation of emigration and adjustment to labor in a vibrant, vast, industrial city. The revival embraced many forms of culture and expression and was seen in many shapes, including in the Irish agricultural cooperative movement and prominently in language, and it was also seen in the rise of the Gaelic League in Ireland and in the United States, in theater, in literature, and in sport.

The sports club was an emerging type of voluntary association in the late 1890s, and this new institution was changing the nature of leisure. E. J. Hobsbawm observes that sport had become "a mass spectacle . . . transformed into the unending succession of gladiatorial contests between persons and teams symbolizing nation-states. . . . The imagined community of millions seems more real as a team of 11 named people."[1]

Philadelphia's Irish Americans in the 1890s were busy constructing their own "imagined community" born of an ethnic confidence based on long-term settlement in Philadelphia, a sense of arrival that allowed for cultural excursions outside the world of labor and work and for experimentation in rediscovering and reinventing Gaelic pastimes.[2]

This chapter focuses on the short-lived rise of Gaelic sport in the 1890s and early 1900s in the Irish American community of Philadelphia, a broad ethnic network dispersed throughout this sprawling industrial metropolis, which was integrated by Irish efforts to forge bonds and bind the vast ethnic population, as

174

evidenced by the extraordinary number of Irish voluntary associations that circulated throughout the city.

The Gaelic sport revival also seemed to meld easily with an Irish Catholic masculinity that took pride in the public posturing of a Celtic paramilitarism in the form of Hibernian Rifle regiments, encampments, and other displays of the revived and armed Celt of the late nineteenth century. Irish sports such as hurling and Gaelic football, which were reconstructed from native origins, were a public reminder that Gaelic culture had arrived in Philadelphia in the 1890s; baseball was the sport of choice for most Irish Americans in these years, but an allegiance to the Gaelic games required a determined choice to affirm membership in the Irish sphere—to engage in an active and symbolic opposition to the given.[3]

The Mobile, Multiple Visions of Irish Nationalism

Mike Cronin suggests that nationalism can be "formalized, imagined or challenged by forces, groups and individuals both within and outside of the projected vision or reality of the nation."[4] This pliant typology, in concert with Benedict Anderson's concept of "an imagined political community," is a compelling heuristic for probing the inventions and practices of the national fervor of Philadelphia's late-nineteenth-century Irish residents.

Language played a vital role in the Irish American acceptance of the many shapes and forms of nationalism, producing a narrative in which cultural and political borders had been violated by outsiders—colonial invaders—a vernacular purveyed less by an intelligentsia, an Irish Catholic refined elite, but promoted by a coterie of popular journalists, amateur historians, traveling priests, and commentators who filled the halls of the ethnic society meeting rooms and the pages of the ethnic press in Irish Philadelphia.

The ethnic press in Philadelphia bound the local community as well as the Gaelic public sphere, offering details on local Irish events and reprinting national and international stories, all supporting the ideology of the violated Gael and suggesting that the Philadelphia Irish needed to defend its national icons and reconstructed images. Both Gellner and Anderson extol the influence of literacy and a common language on the rise of nationalism.[5] This ideal-based community had its symbolic defenders, and they became the sporting warriors of hurling and the mock soldiers of the Irish paramilitary brigades.

The cultivation of purely Irish sporting forms and paramilitary Gaelic imagery in the 1890s seemed, as John Hutchinson states, directed toward "the moral regeneration of the national community rather than the achievement of an autonomous state."[6] The statements and public postures on the shape of Irish identity being debated and hammered out by Philadelphia's Irish residents in

these years seemed more cultural than strictly political, a nationalism that oper-
ates within an exclusive idealistic framework intent on resetting a public image
rather than creating a new national state in Ireland. Patrick McDevitt's reading
of Gaelic nationalism also sees it as pitched toward cultural rebirth, in a constellation of "symbolic constructs created via cultural imaginings."[7]

Still, with all the cues bombarding Philadelphia's Irish at century's end and
stirring them to action, the result was the construction of an image and a style,
a more masculine, assertive, militant Celt. This was an Irish identity with strict
boundaries, identified by those in favor of a separate Catholic nation and all those
opposed, a united front of nationalism as stern opposition. As Cronin states, "The
Irish often seek to define themselves in a manner that is oppositional to Britain . . .
[reveling in] the rejection of anything British."[8] Sport simply became part of the
oppositional identity the Irish adopted in the late 1800s, a cultural appendage of
this defiant stance.

The Gaelic Athletic Association (GAA) ban on British games, which in essence
was a boycott of Anglo influence on sport and a historical brake on the easy diffusion of British cultural influence, represents opposition to British influence in
sport drifting across the Irish Sea in the late 1800s and early 1900s.[9] Writing on
the expanding imagery of Gaelic sport, Eoin Kinsella states, "It was in the nineteenth century that hurling, and specifically the hurley, became loosely associated with Catholic political agitation and support for Irish nationalism, both
cultural and political."[10]

For an Irish American working class intent on educating itself on ethnic
meaning in the wake of its exile from Ireland, endowed with the material
resources derived from employment in the industrial colossus of late-nineteenth-
century Philadelphia, organized in an interlocking maze of Irish American voluntary associations, they registered an ethnic pride in the past while embracing
the modernism of the new world wherever it appeared.[11] Their reconstructed
Gaelic games eventually assumed the shape of popular sport in their deep structure, but the meaning was attached to an emotional core of remembrance and
revolt, which was defined by the popular rhetoric of an Irish American public
realm.

SPORT, MANLINESS, AND THE PROTO-IRISH NATION IN PHILADELPHIA

Philadelphia was an Irish city in the late nineteenth century, the location of a
burgeoning spirit of Irish awareness and the home of ethnic voluntary associations and its own lively ethnic press, which made it an ideal location for the transatlantic planting of hurling and Gaelic football. Philadelphia's Irish community
adopted the athletic, nationalist creed, which they then applied to their concept
of the athletic Celt, a heroic masculinity based on "honor, pluck and ability," in
a sort of a Hibernian Social Darwinism.[12]

In the capillary branches of Philadelphia's Ancient Order of Hibernians (AOH) and the multitude of the city's Irish American societies in the 1890s, there was a warm sympathy for the language-revival movement, encouragement to attend the evening classes in Gaelic offered at various locations in the city, and even a gentle suggestion for members to purchase Gaelic grammar texts. Judging from the turnout at the sport picnics and the proliferation of these sport events—a mix of Gaelic and American games—on the social calendar of Irish American voluntary associations, many more Philadelphia Hibernians turned their attention to sport as leisure and also as an expression of nationalist sentiment.

There were multiple reasons for the rise of the Gaelic Athletic Association and its successful seizure of the Catholic sporting turf in Ireland in the late 1800s. Modernism itself allowed for the appeal of the new games in Ireland and, as Cronin and Mandle both argue, the reconstruction of Irish sport was enervated by images of ancient Ireland but constructed on the model of existing British sport structures.[13] However, dependent as the Irish were on existing sport forms and practices, opposition to British sporting tradition was an unquestioned mantle of Irish identity both in Ireland and in overseas Irish settlements.

THE GAELIC SPORT REVIVAL IN IRELAND

Michael Cusack, an athlete, sport organizer, headmaster, journalist, and literary man about Dublin, is credited with the inspirational vision and organizational energy behind the founding in 1884 of the GAA in Thurles, Ireland.[14] Renowned as the character of the citizen in James Joyce's *Ulysses*, Cusack was an eccentric figure in Dublin's Gaelic revivalist drawing rooms for his embrace of the language movement as well as sport.[15]

Cusack, who was experienced as a rural secondary teacher, arrived in Dublin in the early 1880s and assumed a teaching position at Blackrock, a Catholic college.[16] Three years later he established his own civil service academy in Dublin and, for ten years, achieved an enviable record of success in preparing students for civil service examinations. Cusack was also a versatile athlete, who was at one time or another a footballer, hurler, cricketer, track athlete, and rower.

He enthusiastically endorsed a Catholic "muscular Christianity" among his students at Cusack's Academy, sponsoring a football team of high standing. In the football championships of 1880, Cusack's Academy won twelve matches against teams including Catholic University, Kingstown School, Santry School, and the Hibernian Club.[17]

An exceptional athlete, who was first a cricketer, then a rugby player, and eventually a hurler, Cusack had joined the Irish Champion Club in 1878, but he had become disillusioned with Victorian sport in Ireland, tired of British influence, and disenchanted with the class exclusion that forbade working men access to Dublin Victorian sport, with club clauses that reserved sport for "amateur gentlemen," banning the laboring classes, the "tradesmen, laborers, [and] artisan."[18] Cusack also criticized the Anglo-Irish preference for foot races over the weight events at track meets, stating that the slightly framed, urban Englishman had an advantage over the native Irish competitor, who was conditioned by the hard labor of rural farm work and heavily muscled.

While Cusack and his GAA were carving out an Irish sporting nationalism for their reinvented games in the 1880s, W. F. Mandle suggests that they were only following a British precedent. Mandle writes of the new Gaelic sportsmen and their appetite for a sporting press as "unconscious imitators of the English writers who were doing the same thing in an English context for a Saxon tradition, for a Protestant faith."[19] Paul Rouse also acknowledges the hidden influence of the modernist urge upon the nascent Gaelic sport revival, "the proximity to Britain, the ties of kinship and commerce," which was not easily admitted nor erased even by determined sport separatists eager to distinguish their games from existing models.[20]

EARLY GAELIC SPORT IN PHILADELPHIA

"The Irish and Irish Americans are the greatest athletes in the world," writes Malachy Hogan in the *Philadelphia Ledger* in 1908. He goes on to say that they have a "phenomenal reserve of energy, such as quickness of thought and action and concentration of alertness, grit, nerve, and lightning speed." In all, Malachy states, the "Irish Celts . . . stand pre-eminently alone," their success in sport a testament to their racial separatism.[21] This statement of sporting Darwinism could just have easily been made at any meeting in any camp of the more militant Clan na Gael in Philadelphia, or a division of the Ancient Order of Hibernians (AOH), and it would have been accepted and applauded by the Irish Americans as public knowledge in the early 1900s, ideological support for an American GAA.

Ireland's GAA envisioned an American support system similar to the Land League branches that spontaneously surfaced in the 1880s and 1890s in American cities and, in fact, GAA sport sprouted in Boston, New York, San Francisco, Chicago, and Philadelphia.[22] The GAA in Ireland was struggling with its own nascent association in the 1890s, yet it endeavored to encourage the Gaelic sport revival in the United States, as we can see from this open letter in 1890 to Philadelphia's *Freeman and Irish American Review* from Limerick, Ireland:

> But what about the Irish abroad? Are not the exiled sons of our race, who are
> breathing the free air of the great Western Republic, as Irish as we are? Are
> they not in position to raise the standard of the Gael in the land of their adop-

tion with as much ease and with much lighter hearts than we at home, galling under the iron heel of alien oppression?[23]

The Philadelphia Irish were well informed on GAA events in Ireland through the association's extensive coverage in the city's ethnic press and may well have been inspired by the contemporary tales of Gaelic sport clashes. One could have read in *The Hibernian* about the 1895 All-Ireland football championships between the Young Ireland Club of Dublin and the Desperandums of Cork, in which the presence of 10,000 fans testified that there was "still an enormous amount of vitality in the Gaelic Athletic Association."[24] In addition, Philadelphia's Irish Americans would have learned about the modernization of this ancient Irish sport, the limit of seventeen players to a side and new safety rules, such as no "nails or iron tips . . . on the boots of the players" and rules against "collaring and holding and running with the ball"[25] and "pushing or shouldering from behind, tripping or kicking, catching, holding or jumping at a player."[26]

Most of all, however, Philadelphia's Irish Diaspora would have learned about Gaelic sport by watching the games among the burgeoning Gaelic sport clubs in Philadelphia. The GAA in Philadelphia received a boost through the GAA's "invasion of America" tour in 1885; the tour was centered in New York, but the Irish hurlers and Gaelic footballers came to Philadelphia for an exhibition in fall 1885. This exhibition was promoted through the Irish American associations in Philadelphia, especially the Clan na Gael and the AOH, and the Irish GAA played a team of Irish Philadelphians recruited from the various city hurling clubs at Philadelphia's Pastime Park.

THE PHILADELPHIA HURLING CLUBS

The Limerick Guards Hurling Club of Philadelphia was established in 1889, five years after the beginning of the GAA in Ireland, and the Guards eventually affiliated with the GAA in Dublin. The hurling club was formed from members of the Limerick Guards Patriotic, Social and Benevolent Association, a mutual aid society located at 9th and Spring Garden Streets in Philadelphia.[27]

The Limerick Guards played exhibition matches—there were not enough teams to organize a league—with the typical style of arrangement being a public challenge to a club for a match on an agreed-on date. On Thanksgiving Day 1889, the Limerick Guards hosted New York's Gaelic Athletic Club and its captain, Dr. M. D. Griggin, in a hurling match at Philadelphia's Pastime Park.[28] Hurling was indeed a new sport for many in the Irish American community of Philadelphia; indeed, it was noted that "a large number of those present saw for the first time a genuine hurling match."[29] The game's speed and potential for collisions were also evident as one of the New York hurlers had to leave the field after he slipped and hit his head "against the drawn hurley of a member of his own club."[30]

After the sporting event, Philadelphia's Limerick Guards hosted the Gaelic Club of New York at a reception and the ritualistic round of speeches at their association hall. Edward O'Meagher Condon, the editor of a Philadelphia Irish American newspaper, spoke on the martial imperative of Irish hurling. Recalling the Irish American commitment to the American Civil War and the need for readiness in the coming Irish war for liberation, Condon

> referred to hurling clubs that were in existence in this country thirty years ago, and of which he was a member, having in those days played games at Niagara Falls witnessed at times by 20,000 people. He said that the war coming on soon after that broke up the clubs, the hurlers being the first from their localities to fall in line and fight for the preservation of the Union. He hoped the hurlers of today would have an opportunity to use the supple limbs and strong muscles . . . for the attainment of Irish independence.[31]

Every occasion when the Irish gathered in late-century Philadelphia seemed to be a moment for building Irish culture and nationalist feeling, and the presentation in Philadelphia of hurling with its violent clash of athletes affirmed the growing popularity of these martial symbols. The Limerick Guards, led by Captain Hogan, returned the favor when they traveled to Brooklyn a few weeks later to play the New York Gaelic Athletic Club on their own hurling turf.[32]

By 1893, the Thomas Francis Meaghers and the Charles Stewart Parnells joined the Limerick Guards in Philadelphia as established hurling clubs.[33] Philadelphia GAA clubs took their names from fallen Irish Republican heroes or molded their public images on republican themes: nationalist icons such as Thomas Davis, Charles J. Kickham, Thomas Francis Meagher (a Civil War general of the Irish Brigade), John C. Cosgrove (who was convicted of treason and hanged for gun running), William Smith O'Brien (an elected Irish representative of Parliament), and James Stephens (founder of the Irish Revolutionary Brotherhood, the precursor to the Irish Republican Army) all merged sport and militant nationalism in the iconic imagery of their clubs.

At the 1890 Clan na Gael Games in Philadelphia, a game of Irish football was organized between the William Smith O'Brien and Terence Bellew McManus Clubs, with the winner taking a $300 prize and a banner.[34] The Shamrock Football Club of Philadelphia was another Irish American contender in the city's canopy of Irish football teams.[35] The AOH Irish National Games were held in summer 1895; they featured a "Grand Hurling Tournament for the American Championship" that brought GAA teams from Chicago, New York, and Boston to Philadelphia.[36] In their pre-match ritual, the Philadelphia hurling clubs, like their Irish brethren across the Atlantic, seized the public space of a quiet Sunday afternoon to march military style through the town square with their hurling sticks sloped on their shoulders like weapons, thus conveying the style and imagery of a resurgent Celtic masculinity as they gathered for a Sunday afternoon of Irish sport in the 1890s.[37]

The Nineteenth-Century Irish American Sport and Cultural Festival in Philadelphia

The Irish communal associations in Philadelphia used sport as a mechanism of appeal for their ethnic cause and a way to bring large crowds together in one location for fundraising events. These summer spectacles were massive urban picnics, part nationalist rally, part cultural lesson, and most of all a moment away from work in the industrial city for leisure and entertainment. The spatial component of these mass gatherings required expansive grounds subject to enclosure set within a trolley ride or two for the scattered Irish of the city, parks, and ball fields in North Philadelphia, "other spaces" that for 25¢ Irish Americans could enter, enjoying, for a day, their own Hibernian territory.[38]

Cultural events accompanied the sporting attraction and were presented according to the American competitive ethos, with competitions in the Irish jig, Irish reel, and the popular, "mirth provoking" tug-of-war matches among the numerous branches of the AOH.[39] The "ring" at Rising Sun Park in North Philadelphia became well known in Irish American associational circles as it was identified with Irish American track races in the 1890s.[40] Winning the AOH tug-of-war match among the competing divisions insured bragging rights in the victorious association for the entire year, and club teams with colorful titles such as the Richard Barrys, Daniel O'Connells, Free Soils, Larkin & O'Briens, Emmets, and Speranzas all battled for the coveted trophy and money prize.[41] The games also attracted massive crowds, and the financial rewards for the association could be substantial. For the AOH Memorial Day picnic in 1894, 20,000 tickets were printed and distributed among the divisions to sell; a "special paper" was printed and distributed to promote the games, and posters hung around the city two weeks in advance.[42]

The 1895 Gaelic Games sponsored by Philadelphia's Irish American associations attracted top athletes from across North America: the 1895 "Irish Nationalists" Games in Rising Sun Park were attended by runners from Canada, Pittsburgh, and the Manhattan Athletic Club and featured Peter Cummings, "the champion 56-pound thrower of the United States."[43] The entrance fee was a manageable 25¢, and the site was chosen for its proximity to the trolley lines that ran north and south.[44]

Urban transport was crucial to the success of the Irish summer sport picnics, and the park sites just north of the central city were the most accessible by trolley from all parts of the city, with direct routes north requiring a simple transfer from the western sections of the city. The 1894 "Games of the Emerald Isle" sponsored by the "Irish Nationalists" were held at Washington Park in North Philadelphia, while the AOH held its mass games in the same summer, Memorial Day 1894, at Forepaugh Park, a baseball park in North Philadelphia at Broad and Dauphin Streets, which was the home of the Philadelphia Quakers baseball team.

The 1889 Nationalist Games sponsored by the Clan na Gael were held in Rising Sun Park where "the immense crowd [was] estimated at from 45,000 to 50,000" and the city's Irish "came on the railroads, in the street-cars, in wagons and carriages and on foot."[45] Eager to avoid the stigma of rowdiness at any Irish gathering in Philadelphia, public order was a priority and on-duty police Lieutenant Brode was quoted as observing, "I never saw so much enjoyment, so great a crowd, and so little disorder."[46]

The games themselves, the many sporting events, the tug-of-war, the reel and jig contests, the cultural events, and the music and dancing were also a way of promoting the Clan na Gael as less secretive and conspiratorial, a more respectable Irish American association unlikely to do public harm. Indeed, it was reported that "the whole body of the citizens of Philadelphia approve of the Clan na Gael . . . it represents the Irish-American People."[47]

In 1890, the Clan na Gael's Nationalist Games were again held at Rising Sun Park, and the attendance was estimated to be 45,000. The athletic events, the jig and reel competitions, were the main attraction, but this was just as much a total Irish cultural festival: "The dancing pavilions were crowded all day. A large brass band and several orchestras discoursed sweet music and scattered throughout the grounds were a number of fiddlers and piccolo players, to whose inspiring music even the old people were tempted to dance the reels, jigs and horn pipes of the old land."[48]

Philadelphia's Clan na Gael followed the summer extravaganzas with a massive Labor Day event in 1890 that was a combination of picnic, track event, and nationalist political rally, which 40,000 people attended: "Men and boys, young women and old women, grandsires and babies. It was a family gathering. The people scattered through the park and enjoyed themselves in various ways. Of course the games attracted the greater number."[49] For those with stamina, at the close of the athletic games there was a reception at the Clan na Gael's Irish American Club on Race Street, more speeches, and the singing of "several patriotic songs" well into the evening hours.[50]

Irish American ethnic associations copied the grand model of the Clan na Gael and the AOH Nationalist Games, and picnics and smaller versions of this style of leisure appeared all over the city. Even the Catholic Total Abstinence Union held games in fall 1889, at Pastime Park in North Philadelphia.[51] Baseball was played at the Company H Hibernian Rifles picnic in the Falls of Schuylkill, between the many neighborhood teams of this working-class district; this time, the Actives of Manayunk defeated the Bellevues of East Falls, 16–11.[52] Such was

IRISH GAMES

Under the Auspices of the

CLAN-NA-GAEL

—AT—

THE GROVE WASHINGTON PARK

ON THE DELAWARE

FRIDAY, JULY 4, 1902

$2,000 IN PRIZES Owing to the extended programme presented this year noted athletes from Ireland, Scotland, Canada, and the United States have announced their intention to compete.

Irish Jigs, Reels, and Hornpipes danced to Irish Music TWO BANDS of MUSIC DAY and EVENING

TICKETS Including Fare on Boat Both Ways and Admission to Games **40 CENTS**
Admission at Gate 25 cents.

Boats Leave Arch street Wharf every 15 minutes

PROGRAMME OF SPORTS

1 Running Long Jump	$12 $8 $5		
2 Throwing 16 lb. Hammer from 7-ft. circle, Irish style, (under 90 ft, no prize	12 8 5		
3 Running Hop, Step and Jump	12 8 5		
4 220 yds. Flat Race	12 8 5		
5 Pushing 56 lb. Weight from the shoulder, stand and follow	12 8 5		
6 Sack Race, over hurdles and through barrels once around the ring	12 8 5		
7 220 yds. Hurdle Race	12 8 5		
8 Two-mile Amateur Bicycle Race. Gold and Silver Medals			
9 Boy's Race, handicap, under 14 years, once around the ring	$6 4 3 2		
10 Half-mile Race	$20 12 8		
11 Irish Jig contest, for Ladies	12 8 5		
12 Irish Hornpipe for Gentlemen	12 8 5		
13 Three-mile Bicycle Race, professionals	15 10 5		
14 One-mile Race	25 15 8		
15 Running High Jump	15 10 5		
16 Irish Reel for Ladies	12 8 5		
17 Irish Reel for Gentlemen	12 8 5		
18 Pole Vault	12 8 5		
19 Two-mile Race	30 20 10		
20 Five-mile Bicycle Race, professionals	20 12 8		
21 Boxing Contest	Special prize		
22 Five-mile Race	$75 40 20		

MANAGER of GAMES ....Harry McCarney   REFEREES........................Jerry Bennett and George Keogan
JUDGES ....Felix Brown, Joseph McGarrity and Patrick Broderick   CLERK........................James McKernan

ENTRANCE FEE, 50 cents for each event, except No. 9, which is free.   Entries can be made at the Irish-American Club, 726 Spruce Street, or on the grounds on July 4th.

TICKETS can be procured at the CLUB HOUSE, or at ARCH STREET WHARF JULY 4th.

Advertisement and program of the 1902 Clan na Gael Games, held on the Fourth of July. Source: Digital Library@Villanova University.

the eclectic nature of Irish American sport and leisure in the 1890s as it spread itself across the Irish American associations of Philadelphia; yet, for Irish American cultural nationalists, the choice of sport was hurling or Gaelic football.

THE DARWINISTIC LEANINGS OF NINETEENTH-CENTURY SPORT

Donna Gabaccia writes, "In the United States, Social Darwinism rooted consensual citizenship not just in whiteness . . . but in the Anglo-Saxon race,"[53] a social fact the Irish Americans reacted to and confronted to invent their own racial type. Thus, the ancient Celtic warrior wed to the soil, embattled and often defeated but never vanquished, appeared in the 1890s to be set aside a morally inferior British type, an urban dweller with materialistic goals and values. Gaelic sport was often portrayed as race combat, and the Irish took pride in their manly events involving the rural strength of the Celt working the land and the militaristic show on a Sunday afternoon that became modern hurling, all in contrast to the Anglo sport derided by Irish observers as more suited for a restrained, urban civility.

All these racialized slogans and images of Irish manly vigor in hurling and Irish football resonated in Diaspora Philadelphia, creating an ideal type, an image of the Irish sportsman as a militant warrior for a nation in waiting, willing and able to drop the hurling stick and pick up the rifle when called on. Sport embodied much more of a martial spirit than the other attendant expressions of the Gaelic revival, the language movement for example, and inspired a connection to an emerging pride in Gaelic masculine achievement; as McDevitt states, the GAA in these years combined "manhood, patriotism and resistance."[54] In an era of Social Darwinism when nation, sport and war all blended together to produce a national heroic type, these phrases of Celtic ideology rolled easily off the tongues of the Irish in Philadelphia, communicative beacons in the Gaelic public sphere.

The GAA offered the Irish their own national games restored to resemble the shape and form of established British games like soccer and rugby but rougher and more traditional with the skilled use of the Irish caman or hurling stick invoking ancient Gaelic martialism. As Richard Holt states, GAA sport was a "unique blend of the traditional and the modern" eventually adapting to a public demand for speed, skill, and open play visible to a mass audience in an enclosed space.[55]

The GAA made political and social statements with its public style, its popularity among rural and town workers, and its active opposition to British Victorian sport and came to eventually place its own GAA ban on British games altogether.[56] GAA ideology was total in its opposition to British modernism, as McDevitt writes that hurling "associated the games with violence and violence

Ticket to an 1891 ball hosted by a division of the AOH Hibernian Rifles.
Source: CHRC.

with manhood. Any fear of bodily harm was deemed a sign either of encroaching British influence or effeminacy."[57]

MANLY SPORT AND IRISH MILITARISM

AOH president of Division 34 in Philadelphia's Old Southwark just south of the central city, Jeremiah Sheehan, stated in 1895, "... there should be 35,000 armed and disciplined Irishmen in this country . . . no organization is more worthy to foster the military spirit than the A.O.H."[58] The attraction of sport and its Irish revival, in hurling and Irish football, resonated in the association meeting halls and ethnic press combining a resurgent Irish masculinity with Celtic racial nationalism, made more vital by displays of military bearing.

The martial presentation of Philadelphia's Irish athletes tapped into a popular version of Irish Social Darwinism that reinvented the Celtic race as the true bearer of Irish masculinity and the martial expression of the coming Irish nation—John O'Dea, an officer in AOH 49 and the chief organizer of Irish sport in the city and a fixture at every Irish sports picnic, revered the Irish athlete in Philadelphia as "an excellent type of the Irish race."[59] O'Dea crossed his sporting allegiance with political nationalism, serving on the 1919 Philadelphia committee to host Éamon De Valera's reception and address at the Academy of Music in 1919.[60] Irish joined multiple ethnic organizations and, as a result, the image of the militant hurler and the defiant Hibernian rifleman often merged in the same individual as he moved in and out of Irish societies in the 1890s, adjusting roles and uniforms as he constructed a Celtic masculinity suitable for the 1890s.

PHILADELPHIA'S HIBERNIAN RIFLES: PARAMILITARY SHOW

Irish paramilitarism had an early history in Philadelphia where there were few restrictions on the display of arms in public. The Hibernian Rifles of Philadelphia's AOH were organized in the 1880s "to encourage the formation and maintenance among citizens of Irish birth or descent of an independent body of citizen soldiers."[61] The Rifles were an auxiliary organization attached to the AOH, and its warriors assembled in uniform, drilled, marched, and even went out on maneuvers, holding an occasional encampment in the Pennsylvania woods and readying themselves for the ultimate test to defend their nation of descent.

The Irish-American Military Union was established in 1884; the real associational energy of this martial society was confined to the branch societies in various cities of high Irish concentration, such as Philadelphia. The Irish-American Military Union vowed to bring together "the best and ablest men of our race . . . men of Irish descent, in whose hearts burn that love for the military art."[62] The union advanced an ideology of Irish racial supremacy to contrast with the "Anglo-Saxon pirates" and organized encampments and instruction on how to use arms.[63] As with most of the Irish American paramilitary associations, there seems to have been much play-acting at war in mock battles with imagined historical enemies.

In 1890 the Hibernian Rifle Clubs of Philadelphia mustered out for their nationalist sports and picnic on Easter Monday. The Frankford and Manayunk Hibernians squared off in a rough game of football in which one of the Manayunk "boys . . . was carried from the field."[64] Across the Delaware River, in Camden's Stockton Park, the New Jersey Hibernian Rifles Company C sponsored its field day of sports and cultural events in May 1890; Philadelphia Hibernians crossed the Delaware by taking the ferry from Market Street in Philadelphia.[65]

At the 1889 Irish Nationalist Games sponsored by the Clan na Gael, the featured event was a tournament in "hurling by the leading Irish American clubs" as well as the military drill exhibition by the Hibernian Rifles.[66] Public order during the nationalist games and gatherings of the Hibernian Rifles was also an opportunity for martial display, and during the 1899 games "a detachment of the Irish Volunteers were on duty, under the command of Captain McGuiness . . . but the Irish Volunteers whose duty it was to maintain order had scarcely anything to do."[67]

By the turn of the century the Irish American societies and clubs of Philadelphia were well schooled in the detailed organization and advance planning by an assortment of the committees for the presentation of large cultural events in Philadelphia. These were public galas that were opportunities for the display of an Irish martial bearing within the context of a communal Celtic racial pride. The Hibernian Rifles, First Regiment, under Colonel James H. Murphy, followed the tradition of Irish militarism on St. Patrick's Day 1890, marching through the streets of Philadelphia while displaying "soldierly bearing and excellent discipline."[68] These maneuvers by the Philadelphia Hibernian Rifles were apparently not all that threatening a military presence in Philadelphia: U.S. Army Colonel Wendell P. Bowman observed the Rifles on this occasion and reported: "When I saw this gang of buccaneers, who call themselves the First Infantry, Hibernian Rifles, or something of the sort, parading down the street, I thought they were as harmless, as well as badly disciplined, a set of young fellows one could meet with."[69]

Such public disrespect of Irish military valor naturally motivated a public defense in the Irish American zone of communication, its ethnic press: "At Gettysburg, Fredericksburg, Malvern Hill and Antietam, when the rebels saw the Irish Brigade advancing with the green flag of their motherland and the Stars and Stripes, they did not regard them as 'harmless boys.' Neither Sheridan, Meagher, Corcoran, Shields, McClellan, nor Grant spoke of them as 'buccaneers.'"[70]

The Hibernian Rifles missed few opportunities to appear at Irish American public gatherings in the 1890s, promoted as "exhibition drill by Irish American Military Companies." At the Clan na Gael Games in 1890, Company F of the Rifles entered the drill contest, and they "gave an exhibition drill" for the large crowd gathered for the day's athletics.[71] The combined camps of the Hibernian Rifles, at the St. Patrick's Day celebrations in 1894, "paraded in the afternoon" and held a reception in the evening at Horticultural Hall."[72] At the 1895 Irish Nationalist Gaelic Games at Rising Sun Park, there was "an exhibition drill by the Emmet Guards . . . each company went through a series of military evolutions in a way that drew cheers from the spectators."[73]

The Hibernian Rifles of Philadelphia saw themselves as ideal public defenders of the Celtic race as well as American freedoms: "The Hibernian Rifles are no tax upon the state. They clothe themselves, pay for the rent of their drill rooms and buy their own guns . . . [if] a call came tomorrow for troops to defend the State of Nation, no body of men in Pennsylvania would more quickly respond than the Hibernian Rifles. The race of which they form a part has proven beyond all question its devotion to this Republic."[74]

At the Clan na Gael Games in the summer of 1899, on July 4th, "a detachment of the Irish Volunteers were on duty . . . to maintain order."[75] The Irish nationalist Luke Dillon was the celebrity referee for the games. After the athletic contests were completed,

the Irish Volunteers gave an exhibition drill under the command of Captain McGuiness. The efficiency and general conduct of this military body of Clan-na-gael men merits the highest encomiums. For such meritorious duty . . . the "Irish Volunteers" ought to be supported in every possible way and encouraged, and every true Irishman . . . should enlist in this regiment and learn how to use the rifle and the day will come when they will have to use it "In freedom's righteous cause."[76]

The Hibernian Rifles of the AOH established a central board to monitor the branch associations, the various military "camps." The board met at the Sheares' Club on Sunday afternoons, and the organization kept up a military bearing in all things. In 1890, Lieutenant Colonel O'Brien called "the quartermaster to the chair" for Sunday meetings and the board decided to take part in a flag-raising ceremony in nearby Bryn Mawr for Decoration Day. "Colonel O'Brien issued orders from headquarters to the captains of the various companies to assemble . . . for the train ride to Bryn Mawr."[77] Such was the exalted vernacular of Irish American militarism in late-nineteenth-century Philadelphia.

Colonel O'Brien of the Philadelphia Hibernian Rifles was also the treasurer of the Irish American Military Union of Philadelphia. The Irish American Military Union held its monthly meetings at 8th and Walnut and in 1890 had an "encampment" for three straight nights at Rising Sun Park for July Fourth, presenting a massive, open display of Irish American militarism that coincided with the Irish nationalist picnic and athletic sport scheduled for that site at that time.[78] Six hundred tents were ordered for the many Irish associations expected to join the open-air encampment, and Irish American paramilitary units from as far away as Brooklyn, Boston, Hartford, and Scranton signed on, amounting to a total of 2,000 Irish American "soldiers" expected for the four-day event, a show complete with prizes for the contests in military march, formations, and weapons drill.[79]

The Knights of the Red Branch, which revived the martial legends of the Ulster Red Branch Knights, was another Philadelphia Irish American paramilitary association with at least fourteen divisions spread across Philadelphia in the late nineteenth century. It called its divisions "commands," and its leader was known as a "grand chief."[80]

The penetration of the Irish American public sphere by militaristic images and mock preparation for war was all part of the renewal of a defiant Irish masculinity, attaching itself to cultural forms and gathering momentum in the late nineteenth century. The distinctive uniforms, the marching and military order drill, the overnight encampments, the public marshaling of weapons, the rhetoric of warfare, and even the choice of Irish hurling over American baseball were propaganda, set pieces in open display in the streets and gathering places of Philadelphia's Irish, and part of a forming identity that eschewed integrative complacency for images of militant opposition.

THE IDEOLOGY OF MILITANT OPPOSITION

The Rifles, the Guards, and the Red Knights were an extension of the construction of historical memory parlayed in the ethnic press and gatherings of the ethnic associations, a vital link that served to bolster a battered image of past military defeats in Ireland and failed military excursions in Canada. Irish association meetings tapped into the reservoir of martial discourse generated by Irish service in the American Civil War, a record that generated more battlefield success. This was noted at an AOH meeting of Kensington's Branch 21, when guest speaker Colonel O'Reilly rose and "spoke of the gallant deeds of the 69th Pennsylvania during the Civil War."[81]

The following few lines from the poem "At Gettysburg" based on the exploits of the Irish Brigade during the Civil War were read at a Clan na Gael dinner in 1891, to celebrate Robert Emmet's birth:

Hancock is sullen and Meade is in anger;
Chivalrous Lee cometh on with the South;
Thunder on thunder the maddening clangor
Bellows from cannon and battery's mouth,
Fierce is the shock—in the red gap of danger,
Dire is the need of a stubborn blade;
Golden and green comes the flag of the stranger—
Forward to glory, the Irish Brigade![82]

Men of the various camps of the Hibernian Rifles of Philadelphia were appreciated for their martial militancy, their status among their peers elevated during these years of martial posturing. John Flanagan, an officer in Command 13, was described as being from the "Irish liberating army that went to Canada years ago," a reference to the Fenian "invasion" of Canada in the late 1860s.[83] "Captain" Thomas O'Neill was president of AOH Division 35, of South Philadelphia, a title he earned as the leader of a Hibernian Rifle company in Philadelphia. "While never seeking a fight in civil life, O'Neill is full of it as a soldier, and his sword is ready to leap from its scabbard at the first call for Irish volunteers or defenders of the American flag."[84]

England's loss was always seen as Ireland's gain in the circulating vernacular of the Irish public sphere, and Britain's struggles in the late-century Boer War were not lost on the Irish American associations in Philadelphia. Philadelphia's AOH Division 64 produced this resolution during one of their monthly meetings in 1899: "This Division of the Ancient Order of Hibernians does express its entire sympathy with the brave Boers in their just and righteous war against their invader, and hopes that the God of Justice and Right will continue to aid them until final victory shall crown their gallant fight."[85]

Close to a thousand Irish Americans gathered at Philadelphia's Industrial Hall in 1900, representatives of the more than ninety branches of the city's AOH, forty camps of the Clan na Gael, the Abstinence associations, and other Irish societies to register support for the Boers in their "struggle against British aggression."[86] The associations made it clear that Philadelphia would not be sending an Irish American brigade to fight in the Transvaal but did admonish the mainstream press to stop printing sensationalist stories of Irish American adventures that suggested "proposed invasions of Canada, equipment of alleged volunteers" and Irish American weapon ships headed to South Africa.[87]

Across town, the Anglo-Saxon Brotherhood held its own meeting in a hall on Poplar Street to express support for the British cause in the Transvaal, boasting to place "200,000 men at the disposal of the British Empire" to be transported by the British Navy.[88] The outpouring of symbolic support for the Boers and military posturing among Philadelphia's Irish Americans thus became part of a dueling war of hyperbolic words with native Protestant support for Britain in Philadelphia.

The discourse of opposition and discontent punctuated the public space of the Irish American association at the monthly meetings in the late nineteenth century, and a cultural consensus among Philadelphia's Irish Americans arrived to confirm that they were a diaspora nation, victims of an Anglo tyranny, exiled by the forces of Famine and landlordism, with a special mission to help set Ireland free. Even the loss of the Irish language was presented as a British ploy: "The English government relied to crush the Irish nation by breaking the symbol of their civilization, the embodiment of their glorious and fond traditions, so elegantly set in the chaste and beautiful form of the Irish language."[89]

The Irish community also enjoyed a degree of cross-fertilization among the various nationalist movements and associations, and so if you were a member of the Gaelic League you might be attracted to other traditional Gaelic arts, dance, music and, naturally, Irish sport. At the post-match banquet, when the Gaelic Club of New York visited Philadelphia to play a hurling match with the Limerick Guards of Philadelphia, the president of the New York team rose and addressed the group: "hurling was only one feature of the work their association had commenced, and that literary excellence was by no means lost sight of in the desire for greater physical prowess. A study of the Gaelic language is . . . the principal matter of a literary nature that engages the attention of the members of the club."[90]

At the Irish Nationalist Games in 1895, sponsored by the Clan na Gael, it was observed that "there were several interesting contests between tug-of-war teams from the different Irish American literary clubs, for a handsome banner."[91] Various currents of ethnic identity and Irish nationalist fervor were constantly colliding and overlapping in the complex and broad cultural life that was Irish Philadelphia in the 1890s.

Irish American Sport as Cultural Revival

The men and women of the Irish community, inspired and influenced by an ethnic press and a vibrant communal interaction that included monthly society
meetings, annual balls, summer Gaelic games, and the will and initiative to create a distinct diaspora Irish public sphere did not seem to distinguish between
political and cultural nationalism. Instead, they more often embraced a united
front of oppositional images and slogans, a rhetoric of defiance and masculine
resolve merged in the image of the Irish hurler.

The choice of Irish sport as it emerged in the Gaelic cultural revival in the
1880s and 1890s was part of this stance, a cultural revival that instilled pride and
purpose among the Irish searching for meaning and connections in late-century
Philadelphia. As David Fitzpatrick writes, "The Gaelic revival served a further
purpose for immigrants by encouraging a belief in the community of Celtic
peoples . . . feelings of abstract solidarity flourished in the absence of chilling
first-hand acquaintance. The mystique of race helped ameliorate the immigrants'
sense of alienation."[92]

Philadelphia was a good test of the ability and drive of the late-nineteenth-
century Irish to reach beyond the fragmenting obstacles the industrial city presented to construct an ethnic consciousness. The city was a vast workshop in the
late nineteenth century that required labor, and, as the Irish followed the prospect of employment, they were dispersed to all corners of the urban landscape—
no neighborhood or urban area emerged as a special zone of Irish influence.

The Irish found homes in multiple, ethnically heterogeneous neighborhoods
and naturally established local ties to home blocks and responded to neighborhood cues. Yet Philadelphia's late-century Irish, constricted geographically, did
not let the cost and inefficiency of the urban transport system interfere with
building an Irish American community, a public sphere, and instead used the
trolley lines to establish unity, reaching beyond a neighborhood parochialism
to construct an impressive, vibrant cultural community. In their late-nineteenth-
century ethnic associations, hurling clubs, Gaelic-language societies, ethnic
press, and loyalty to Anglo opposition, the late-century Irish in Philadelphia
overcame the fragmentation and potential isolation of urban life to create a
vibrant, rich, united ethnic consciousness.

Conclusion

A GAELIC PUBLIC SPHERE—ITS RISE AND FALL.

This study found that the Irish Americans of Philadelphia in a specific historical time, those who exposed themselves to the contents of the surge of late nineteenth-century Gaelic culture in their diaspora city, were transformed into citizens armed with a mission, emboldened by a self-instructed knowledge and reasons to be proud of their Irish heritage. The late-nineteenth-century Irish were more than a collection of migrated rural, city, and town folk intent on improved life chances—more than the scattered "exiles" of a land in crisis; they indeed belonged to a diaspora community but extended the physical boundaries of a given urban neighborhood, the material facts of work in the industrial city, to construct a public sphere of Irish meaning.

Habermas defined a public sphere as a neutral social space for discussion and opinion formation, insulated from the impact of large, impersonal social systems, and thus the ideal forum for open thought using reason as a guide. Eventually, Habermas's bourgeois public sphere succumbs to the pressure from commercial interests and "uncouples" from its original form and liberal intentions, becoming absorbed as commercialized public opinion.

Habermas posits the public sphere of his idealized bourgeois intellectuals and aesthetics in the early 1800s as a rare episode of enlightenment, a subculture of men on the rise with a half-life of short duration, communicating and acting in modernizing settings. Similarly, the vibrant life world of Irish Philadelphia, with its rich record of associationalism and its active defense of Gaelic culture and language in the 1890s and early 1900s, became a forward-looking subsociety with a limited life span activated by a vision of the past.

The Irish community of Philadelphia of the late 1800s and early 1900s eventually retreated from its Gaelic purity as it came into contact with competing forces and grappled with the complexity of its dual roles in America. America's entry into World War I on the side of England represented one such moral dilemma, which threw Irish Americans into hard debate and a difficult choice of national allegiance, which was eventually made on the side of American democracy and war. The birth of the Irish national state and the end of the Irish Civil War in the 1920s deflated the energy and impulse for Irish nationalism, defusing the mechanism of conflict that binds ethnic groups in diaspora settings. Eventually, the modernist supports of the Irish public sphere, which were located in the economic structure of the industrial city, withered away as suburbanization and deindustrialization proceeded in the twentieth century.

It has been suggested that the stifling localized life of the Irish isolated in neighborhood settings prevented the forging of a citywide Irish American collective consciousness. If the Irish Americans were merely satisfied with having a life world within walking distance, the dynamic cultural life of ethnic difference that they constructed would not have occurred in the Philadelphia of the 1890s and early 1900s. Instead, this ethnic group reached beyond the confines of immediate residence and simple wants to ride the electric trolleys that brought them together to meetings and Irish festivals outside their neighborhood, into a public sphere of their own creation.

SOCIAL LEARNING, SOCIAL CLASS

The transportable nature of social learning accounted for the ease with which the Irish established their own associations in Diaspora Philadelphia. This study puts forward in a comparative historical methodology the proposition that life experiences in Ireland, passed along as cultural learning, were the original reference points for the explosion of civic enlightenment in their new home. The men and women of Cavan and Donegal, for example, had plenty of prototypes and models within their midst from formal associations to sporting clubs to cooperatives, precursors of democratic institutions that were easily applicable in Diaspora Philadelphia.

Much has been made of social class in the study of the Irish in America and the fact that the Irish were the first mass proletariat in the nation's transformation to an urban, industrial social order. In an ideal rendering of the public sphere, status hierarchies are conceded as facts of social existence but excluded as a basis of discussion and argument, as irrelevant to deciding the outcomes in debate in public settings. The Gaelic public sphere could not set aside the modest hierarchies of status indigenous to modern society, but, like Habermas's bourgeois agents, they did not allow social rank to settle arguments, set rules, or establish hegemony.

It has been noted that those who joined Irish American mutual aid societies in the late 1800s and early 1900s were primarily of the working class, generally skilled artisans and laborers, many of whom were recent immigrants and who had found work in the industrial workshops of Philadelphia. Yet when it came to setting the agenda for gatherings of Irish Americans in their public institutions, the social facts of labor were crowded out in favor of Irish culture, Irish remembrance, and nationalist fervor for an independent Ireland. Culture overwhelmed social class as a medium for discussion and identity in Gaelic Philadelphia and did not combine with a defense of labor in a united front of opposition.

THE CLOUDED GAELIC VISION

The Irish of Philadelphia constructed a public sphere of Irish meaning using a variety of communicative practices available in their time and location, print media, the ethnic press but also a broad array of circulating pamphlets, reprinted speeches, letters, posters and handbills. This communicative network was supplemented by individuals of influence, journalists, traveling priests, neighborhood orators, and association officers, all enhanced by the informal conversations of the Irish as they gathered in public places.

The monthly meeting of the Irish American association was a location for social learning the disciplinary codes of belonging to a formal ethnic association as well as an opportunity to mold the cast of mind required for debate in public settings; it was backed by an expressive order in which symbols of Irish resurgence were prominent, supplemented by traditional Irish songs, poems, and humor, comprising a complex social setting bound by an instrumental and affective ritual code.

The Philadelphia Irish in the 1890s were remarkable in the civic life they constructed, allowing reason to flourish in debate and in business matters promoting savings, calculation, and the acquisition of property. Their public lives were also full of gaiety and a largess of spirit, their gatherings expansive and often expensive, their oratory sentimental and bellicose, yet their communal achievements were also reflective of the confidence of their era and their status in Philadelphia. These achievements in the civic arena were all the more impressive because the Irish Americans relied on their own internal sources of guidance and inspiration, in the absence of an extensive, deep exposure to American civic institutions.

This study has isolated a core of Gaelic activists of the 1890s and early 1900s, Irish Americans saturated by the inherited script of nationalism bequeathed to those of Catholic Irish descent, an 1890s nationalism of cultural reconstruction and language preservation, and a "counterpublic" of committed action. The Gaelic activists were a sizable group but a minority of Irish Philadelphians, as the majority population was absorbed by the normative demands of work, family, and community and many were active members of neighborhood Catholic parishes; by the 1890s this was an American citizenry of the working class attracted to assimilationist impulses.

But as much as Philadelphia's mass of Irish American men and women may have preferred to ignore the pervasive messages and imagery of Irish nationalism, they often bumped into its ideological pull in the normal course of living. When joining a parish mutual aid society, casually reading the *Irish American Review and Celtic Literary Advocate*, attending a summer's ethnic picnic, even thumbing through the pages of a local parish calendar, the reminders of late-century Gaelic reconstruction and rebirth were unavoidable. Parish and its expansive community, its pantry of educational options and opportunities for neighborly interaction and leisure, its clubs and seminars, were subject to fragments of the discourse and text of Irish national redemption.

The Irish in Philadelphia found a steely rationality in the creation and running of their voluntary associations and deviated from reason only when it came to a historical rendering of an Irish past; for all the analytic skills they demonstrated in their building of solid institutions of working class support, they preferred an emotional, simplistic interpretation of Irish history laden with villains and victims. Forever on the losing side of multiple failed risings, initial bottom dwellers of an American labor hierarchy requiring the exertion of hard physical effort, and victims of nativist oppression, Irish Americans, by the 1890s, had fostered a clarity of vision peering upwards through the contradictions of the American experience.

Richard Sennett writes, "Clarity is what a humane Marx meant by alienation, the unhappy disassociated consciousness which reveals, however, things as they are and where a person stands."[1] For the Irish Americans of Philadelphia, looking up through the established status and occupational hierarchy of Philadelphia, ethnic and religious separatism became a clear and reasoned choice of adapting to nativist pressures. Historical clarity was marginally clouded by an ideology of nationalism and the redemptive hope of a past of distinction; the real achievement of the Gaelic public sphere was the archive of organizational effort spent and recorded, the deeds of the Philo-Celtic Society of Philadelphia, the highly orchestrated feiseanna sponsored by the city's branch of the Gaelic League, the sporting exploits of the Limerick Guards hurlers, and even the mock displays of the Hibernian Rifle regiments of Philadelphia.

Finally, industrial society eventually chips away at ethnic and national solidarity as E. J. Hobsbawm writes: "Urbanization and industrialization, resting as they do on massive and multifarious movements, migrations and transfers of people, undermine the other basic nationalist assumption of a territory inhabited essentially by an ethnically, culturally and linguistically homogeneous population."[2] This, of course, was the eventual outcome for Philadelphia's Irish community in the mid-twentieth century, a slow effacement of the supports of an ethnonational community, but for a few decades, from the 1880s through World War I and Irish Independence in the early 1920s, the Irish Diaspora nation in Philadelphia was alive and flourishing in its Gaelic public sphere.

Acknowledgments

A book starts with an idea or a question and sends the author on a journey, a long expedition of the mind. It seems like a solitary trek, but along the way you discover you are not alone but surrounded by people who help in multiple and surprising ways. I'd like to acknowledge those individuals, the debts owed, and the gratitude deserved for the many large and small acts of kindness, research assistance, mentorship, and encouragement exhibited in the completion of this book project.

I started rather late in life acquiring the skills and mentality required in the discipline of history. My fellow grad students at Temple University in Philadelphia, an eclectic but tight band of committed disciples, welcomed an older entry to their group, and we supported ourselves in our studies. Temple University Professors Susan Klepp, Wilbert Jenkins, and Jay Lockenour as well as the departed Russell Weigley all instructed me, and I learned from them and was inspired by their breadth of scholarship, commitment to students and their compassion. But it was Professor Herb Ershkowitz, with his love of the historical potential of Philadelphia, who found and nurtured an acolyte; Herb discovered what was good, ignored the bad, and through doses of mild motivation, humor, and critical judgments pushed me, and this project forward.

Let me also recognize Enrico Dal Lago, professor of history at the National University of Ireland, Galway, for his insights and advice on the value and nuanced application of comparative history.

At Swarthmore College, my college of the past forty-two years, colleagues shared their appraisals of my work and offered critical opinions, opening up new ways of looking at problems. Debts of gratitude are offered to Professors Phil Weinstein, Steve O'Connell, and my colleagues in the Sociology/Anthropology Department, Braulio Munoz, Farha Ghannam, and Sarah Willie-LeBreton. Professor Richard Valelly, my friend and tennis partner, always saw the promise of my central concept, read my work, and with a kind word redirected the author to the right path.

Let me acknowledge two individuals at Swarthmore: Marian Fahy for her stories of Cavan, Ireland, and Adam Hertz, director of Athletics, who must have wondered how he inherited a coach sometimes more interested in intellectual matters than athletics, but who always, always supported my scholarship.

Also, Derek Van Rheenan, professor of education and director of the Athletic Study Center at the University of California, Berkeley, was an inspirational model for balancing a life of the mind with important work in university athletics. And thanks go to Mark Fallati, my research assistant, and Will Chung, my technical assistant, both of whom are former students, for their work in the final stages of manuscript preparation and for their friendship.

Answers to the mysteries of past cultures are often housed in material structures—archives—guarded by committed professionals eager to share knowledge. Shawn Weldon is one. The manuscript curator of the Catholic Historical Research Center of the Archdiocese of Philadelphia, he was tireless in his search for relevant and interesting material and is himself a committed student of Philadelphia's past. And Sarah Elichko, social science librarian at Swarthmore, always found time and energy to direct me in the search for source material. Michael Foight, director of Distinctive Collections at Villanova's Falvey Library, assisted with digital imaging. This book was supported by multiple grants of the Swarthmore College Research Fund administered by Marcia Brown, associate provost for administration.

Let me offer recognition from a grateful author to my editor at Rutgers University Press, Peter Mickulas, who took a chance on a writer with a novel perspective and through the many steps of publication guided the work forward. Let me also praise the work of Professor Dermot Quinn of Seton Hall University and his generous colleague, the original reviewers of my manuscript, ever critical, but so purposeful and honest in the support of a fresh interpretation on an old topic.

Authors, researchers, all of us have families that sustain us emotionally, provide stability and comfort and so let me acknowledge mine, my sister and colleague Kathleen Harris Mullan, my two sons Conor and Brendan, who may have asked themselves from time to time why their Dad read so many books and, of course, my dear wife Marsha Nishi Mullan who, after 43 years of marriage, knows more than she ever bargained for about a "Gaelic public sphere." And finally, my parents, Richard and Peggie Mullan, present in spirit and in the heart, now given up to the world having provided so much.

Notes

INTRODUCTION

1. Brian Cowan, "Mr. Spectator and the Coffeehouse Public Sphere," *Eighteenth-Century Studies* 37, no. 3 (2004): 345–366. In the years preceding the French Revolution, the availability of multiple print options in British coffeehouses attracted a crowd that was intent on discussion.

2. Joanna Brooks, "The Early American Public Sphere and the Emergence of a Black Print Counterpublic," *William and Mary Quarterly* 62, no. 1 (January 2005): 67–92.

3. Ibid., 70. Geoff Eley also notes that the ideal social setting for the flowering of Habermas's ideal is elusive; in its place exist multiple public spheres acknowledging differentiation in society, ethnic groups, gender associations—in essence, "a variety of public spheres." Geoff Eley, "Nations, Publics, and Political Cultures: Placing Habermas in the Nineteenth Century," in *Habermas and the Public Sphere*, ed. Craig Calhoun (Cambridge, Mass.: MIT Press, 1992), 289–339, 306.

4. John L. Brooke notes, "The public sphere is a permanent fixture in modern society—plural, anarchic, wild, unregulated, and fluid with time and space." John L. Brooke, "Reason and Passion in the Public Sphere: Habermas and the Cultural Historians," *Journal of Interdisciplinary History* 29, no. 1 (July 1998): 43–67, 61.

5. Harold Mah, "Phantasies of the Public Sphere: Rethinking the Habermas of Historians," *Journal of Modern History* 72, no. 1 (March 2000): 153–182, 181.

6. Peter O'Neill, "The Racial State and the Transatlantic Famine Irish," in *Re-Framing the Transnational Turn in American Studies*, ed. Winfried Fluck et al. (Hanover, N.H.: Dartmouth College Press, 2011), 117–137, 127.

7. Michel Foucault, *The Order of Things: An Archaeology of the Human Sciences* (New York: Random House, 1966), xviii.

8. E. P. Thompson, "Time, Work-Discipline, and Industrial Capitalism," *Past & Present*, no. 38 (December 1967): 56–97, 93.

9. Peter Kolchin, *A Sphinx on the American Land: The Nineteenth-Century South in Comparative Perspective* (Baton Rouge, La.: LSU Press, 2003), 3, 75.

10. *The Hibernian* (Philadelphia), December 14, 1893, Catholic Historical Research Center of the Archdiocese of Philadelphia (CHRC).

CHAPTER 1 — OUTLINES OF A GAELIC PUBLIC SPHERE

1. Jürgen Habermas, *The Theory of Communicative Action, Volume 1: Reason and the Rationalization of Society,* (Boston, MA: Beacon Press, 1984), ix.

2. Thomas Bender, *Community and Social Change in America* (New Brunswick, N.J.: Rutgers University Press, 1978), 5, 7.

3. Marco Cenzatti, "Heterotopias of Difference," in *Heterotopia and the City: Public Space in a Postcivil Society,* ed. Michiel Dehaene and Lieven De Cauter (London: Routledge, 2008), 75–84, 76.

4. J. Matthew Gallman, *Receiving Erin's Children: Philadelphia, Liverpool, and the Irish Famine Migration, 1845–1855* (Chapel Hill: University of North Carolina Press, 2000), 32. Gallman recounts that in a single week in spring 1847. five ships deposited over 1,500 Irish immigrants in the port of Philadelphia.

5. *The Freeman and Irish American Review,* December 7, 1889, Catholic Historical Resource Center of the Archdiocese of Philadelphia (CHRC).

6. "Constitution, Rules, Bylaws and Rules of Order of the True Sons of Ireland Benevolent Society of San Jose, California," 1863, F87016 T7, Bancroft Library, University of California, Berkeley (hereafter cited as Constitution of the True Sons of Ireland), 8.

7. Ibid.

8. Jürgen Habermas, *The Theory of Communicative Action,* trans. Thomas McCarthy (Boston: Beacon Press, 1984).

9. Michel Foucault, "Des espace autres, Une conference inedited de Michel Foucault," trans. Jay Miskowiec, *Architecture Mouvement Continuité,* no. 5 (October 1984): 46–49, 47.

10. Dennis Clark, *Erin's Heirs: Irish Bonds of Community* (Lexington: University Press of Kentucky, 1991), 3.

11. *The Clan-na-Gael Journal,* Joseph McGarrity Collection, Falvey Memorial Library, Villanova University, June 25, 1916.

12. *Hibernian,* October 5, 1895.

13. Nathaniel Burt and Wallace E. Davies, "The Iron Age, 1876–1905," in *Philadelphia: A 300-Year History,* ed. Russell Weigley (New York: W. W. Norton, 1982), 471–523, 488.

14. Ibid.

15. Walter Licht, *Getting Work: Philadelphia, 1840–1950* (Cambridge, Mass.: Harvard University Press, 1992).

16. Dale B. Light Jr., "Class, Ethnicity and the Urban Ecology in a 19th Century City: Philadelphia's Irish, 1840–1890" (Ph.D. dissertation, University of Pennsylvania, 1979), 42.

17. Philip Scranton, *Figured Tapestry: Production, Markets, and Power in Philadelphia Textiles, 1885–1941* (Cambridge: Cambridge University Press, 1989).

18. Stuart M. Blumin, "Residential Mobility within the Nineteenth-Century City," in *The People of Philadelphia: A History of Ethnic Groups and Lower-Class Life, 1790–1940,* ed. Allen Davis and Mark Haller (Philadelphia: Temple University Press, 1985), 37–51.

19. "Minute Book of the Cavan Catholic, Social, and Beneficial Society of Philadelphia, 1907–1926," Cavan Society of Philadelphia (hereafter cited as Cavan Society Minute Book), July 13, 1919.

20. Theodore Hershberg et al., "The 'Journey-to-Work': An Empirical Investigation of Work, Residence, and Transportation, Philadelphia, 1850 and 1880," in *Philadelphia: Work, Space, Family, and Group Experience in the Nineteenth Century,* ed. Theodore Her-

shberg (New York: Oxford University Press, 1981), 140. This was the lesson of the Philadelphia Social History Project, which concluded that "there were no massive and distinctly defined ethnic ghettoes" among the Irish in Philadelphia.

21. U.S. Census Bureau, 1910, National Archives at Philadelphia.

22. Malcolm Campbell, *Ireland's New Worlds: Immigrants, Politics, and Society in the United States and Australia, 1815–1922* (Madison: University of Wisconsin Press, 2008), 137.

23. Ibid.

24. Jürgen Habermas, *The Structural Transformation of the Public Sphere: An Inquiry into a Category of Bourgeois Society*, trans. Thomas Burger (Cambridge, Mass.: Polity Press, 1989).

25. The reference to "counterpublics" is from Brooks's study of a public sphere in early American Black communities. Brooks, "Early American Public Sphere," 70.

26. *Public Ledger* (Philadelphia), February 29, 1876, microfilm, McCabe Library, Swarthmore College.

27. D. Clark, *The Irish Relations: Trials of an Immigrant Tradition* (East Brunswick, N.J.: Associated University Presses, 1982); D. Clark, *The Irish in Philadelphia: Ten Generations of Urban Experience* (Philadelphia: Temple University Press, 1973).

28. Anna Clark, *The Struggle for the Breeches: Gender and the Making of the British Working Class* (Berkeley: University of California Press, 1995), 3.

29. E. P. Thompson, "Time, Work-Discipline, and Industrial Capitalism," *Past & Present*, no. 38 (December 1967): 56–97, 96.

30. *Freeman and Irish American Review*, December 14, 1889.

31. Robert D. Putnam, *Bowling Alone: The Collapse and Revival of American Community* (New York: Simon & Schuster, 2000), 385.

32. Geoff Eley, "Nations, Publics, and Political Cultures: Placing Habermas in the Nineteenth Century," in *Habermas and the Public Sphere*, ed. Craig Calhoun (Cambridge, Mass.: MIT Press, 1992), 289–339, 297.

33. Jason Kaufman and Steven J. Tepper, "Groups or Gatherings? Sources of Political Engagement in 19th Century American Cities," *Voluntas: International Journal of Voluntary and Nonprofit Organizations* 10, no. 4 (1999): 299–332, 312.

34. *Hibernian*, October 6, 1893.

35. Howard Wach, "Civil Society, Moral Identity and the Liberal Public Sphere: Manchester and Boston, 1810–40," *Social History* 21, no. 3 (October 1996): 281–303, 283.

36. Ira Katznelson, "Working-Class Formation: Constructing Cases and Comparisons," in *Working-Class Formation: Nineteenth-Century Patterns in Western Europe and the United States*, ed. Ira Katznelson and Aristide R. Zolberg (Princeton, N.J.: Princeton University Press, 1986), 3–40, 23.

37. Rowland Berthoff, *An Unsettled People: Social Order and Disorder in American History* (New York: Harper & Row, 1971), 446.

38. David S. Shields, *Civil Tongues and Polite Letters in British America* (Chapel Hill: University of North Carolina Press, 1997), xv.

39. Alexis de Tocqueville, *Democracy in America*, trans. Henry Reeve (New York: Schocken Press, 1967), 596.

40. Max Weber, *Economy and Society: An Outline of Interpretive Sociology* (Berkeley: University of California Press, 1978), 385.

41. *Hibernian*, March 5, 1895.

42. D. Clark, "Urban Blacks and Irishmen: Brothers in Prejudice," in *Black Politics in Philadelphia*, ed. Miriam Ershkowitz and Joseph Zikmund II (New York: Basic Books, 1973), 22.

43. Gary B. Nash, *Forging Freedom: The Formation of Philadelphia's Black Community, 1720–1840* (Cambridge, Mass.: Harvard University Press, 1988).

44. V. P. Franklin, "The Philadelphia Race Riot of 1918," in *African Americans in Pennsylvania: Shifting Historical Perspectives*, ed. Joe W. Trotter Jr. and Eric L. Smith (University Park: Pennsylvania State University Press, 1997), 287–315; Clark, "Urban Blacks and Irishmen," 18–29.

45. Kevin Kenny, *Making Sense of the Molly Maguires* (New York: Oxford University Press, 1998), 6.

46. Raymond Williams, *Problems in Materialism and Culture* (London: Verso, 1980), 37.

47. Appeal letter from the All Hallows Missionary Fathers, 1895, RG 40-1-4, CHRC.

48. Quoted in Bryan P. McGovern, *John Mitchel: Irish Nationalist, Southern Secessionist* (Knoxville: University of Tennessee Press, 2009), 224.

49. John Mitchel, *An Apology for the British Government in Ireland* (Dublin, 1903), Bancroft Library, University of California, Berkeley, 49.

50. Ibid.

51. Rev. John Hughes, "A Lecture of the Antecedent Causes of the Irish Famine in 1847," 1847, box 1, Irish American Materials, CHRC.

52. "Proposed Constitution of the American Association for the Recognition of the Irish Republic," 1920–1922, MSS 87/91, box 1, Bancroft Library, University of California, Berkeley.

53. 1921–1922, Irish American Pamphlet Collection, Bancroft Library, University of California, Berkeley.

54. *Oration Delivered at the Request of the Fenian Brotherhood*, July 4, 1867, F870 I6D4, Bancroft Library, University of California, Berkeley.

55. Ibid.

56. Herbert Marcuse, *One Dimensional Man: Studies in the Ideology of Advanced Industrial Society* (Boston: Beacon, 1964), 97.

57. Ibid., 101.

58. David M. Doolin, "Exploring Textures of Irish America: A New Perspective on the Fenian Invasion of Canada," *Irish Studies Review* 23, no. 2 (2015): 154–165, 154.

59. E. P. Thompson, *The Making of the English Working Class* (New York: Pantheon Books, 1964), 9.

60. Sean Wilentz, *Chants Democratic: New York City and the Rise of the American Working Class, 1788–1850* (New York: Oxford University Press, 1984), 18.

61. Friedrich Engels, "The Condition of the Working-Class in England," in Karl Marx and Friedrich Engels, *Ireland and the Irish Question*, ed. R. Dixon, trans. Angela Clifford et al. (New York: International Publishers, 1972), 33–43, 33.

62. "Rules and Regulation of the Northumberland Society," 1874, in *British Parliamentary Papers* 5, 72.

63. Ibid., 74.

64. Constitution of the True Sons of Ireland, 15.

65. *Hibernian*, October 15, 1895.

66. *Hibernian*, May 5, 1894.

67. Thomas N. Brown, *Irish-American Nationalism, 1870–1890* (Philadelphia: J. B. Lippincott, 1966), 180.

68. "Minute Book of the Clan na Gael, 1889–1923," MSS 37, box 1, Historical Society of Pennsylvania (HSP) (hereafter cited as Clan na Gael Minute Book), June 5, 1889.

69. "Letter to Affiliated Societies," Irish Catholic Benevolent Union, 1889, box 1, Irish American Materials, CHRC.

70. Kenny, *Molly Maguires*, 10.

71. Ibid., 18.

72. *The Irish American Review and Celtic Literary Advocate*, September 30, 1899, CHRC.

73. Cavan Society Minute Book, July 9, 1911.

74. Mary Daly, *Dublin, the Deposed Capital: A Social and Economic History, 1860–1914* (Cork, Ireland: Cork University Press, 1984).

75. D. Clark, "The Irish in the American Economy: The Industrial Period," in *The Irish in America*, ed. P. J. Drudy (Cambridge: Cambridge University Press, 1985), 234–242, 240.

76. "Constitution, Bylaws and Rules of Order of the Irish-American Benevolent Society," 1869, F870 1617, Bancroft Library, University of California, Berkeley, 5.

77. Brown, *Irish-American Nationalism*, 37.

78. "St. Patrick's Day Grand Celebration and Ball," AOH Woodward's Gardens Branch, March 17, 1893, Irish American Pamphlet Collection, F870 I6P, Bancroft Library, University of California, Berkeley.

79. *Irish American Review and Celtic Literary Advocate*, June 3, 1899.

80. Clan na Gael Minute Book.

81. *Freeman and Irish American Review*, November 23, 1889.

82. *Hibernian*, September 7, 1895, October 12, 1895.

83. Mitchel, *An Apology*, 89.

84. *Irish American Review and Celtic Literary Advocate*, September 30, 1899.

85. *Hibernian*, September 2, 1893.

86. *Hibernian*, July 13, 1895.

87. Brown, *Irish-American Nationalism*, 45.

88. *Hibernian*, March 16, 1895.

89. *Irish American Review and Celtic Literary Advocate*, August 12, 1899.

90. "Constitution & Bylaws of the Ancient Order of Hibernians," 1872, P007.01, CHRC.

CHAPTER 2 — INSERTING THE GAELIC IN THE PUBLIC SPHERE

1. A. C. Hepburn, "Language, Religion and National Identity in Ireland since 1880," *Perspectives on European Politics and Society* 2, no. 2 (2001): 197–220, 204.

2. Úna Ní Bhroiméil, "The Creation of an Irish Culture in the United States: The Gaelic Movement, 1870–1915," *New Hibernia Review* 5, no. 3 (2001): 87–100, 88.

3. Ní Bhroiméil, *Building Irish Identity in America, 1870–1915: The Gaelic Revival* (Dublin, Ireland: Four Courts Press, 2003), 31.

4. Timothy McMahon, *Grand Opportunity: The Gaelic Revival and Irish Society, 1893–1910* (Syracuse, N.Y.: Syracuse University Press, 2008).

5. Open letter from the Philo-Celtic Society of Philadelphia, 1920, RG 40-1-4, CHRC (hereafter cited as Philo-Celtic open letter, 1920).

6. *Catholic Standard and Times*, April 25, 1903.

7. *Clan-na-Gael Journal*, June 27, 1914.

8. *Doctor Douglas Hyde and the Gaelic Revival*, 1902, MB80B, Association Pamphlets, CHRC.

9. "Constitution and Bylaws of the Philo-Celtic Society of Philadelphia," 1884, P008.917, CHRC.

10. Philo-Celtic Society, "Devoted to the Language, Literature, History, Music, Sports and Pastimes of the Gael," *Irish Echo* 4, no. 3 (June 1893): 34, CHRC.

11. "Handbill of the Philo-Celtic Society of Philadelphia," 1901, RG 40-1-4, Irish American Materials, CHRC (hereafter cited as Philo-Celtic Society handbill, 1901).

12. Ibid.

13. *Irish American Review and Celtic Literary Advocate*, June 24, 1899.

14. *Catholic Standard and Times*, March 21, 1903.

15. Ibid., March 24, 1894.

16. *Irish American Review and Celtic Literary Advocate*, September 23, 1899.

17. Ibid., October 14, 1899.

18. *Catholic Standard and Times*, June 20, 1903.

19. Ibid.

20. Philo-Celtic open letter, 1920.

21. Ní Bhroiméil, *Building Irish Identity*, 41.

22. *Philadelphia Inquirer*, June 11, 1888.

23. Ibid.

24. *Catholic Standard and Times*, June 6, 1903.

25. *Catholic Standard*, May 24, 1890.

26. *Philadelphia Inquirer*, December 16, 1892.

27. Philo-Celtic open letter, 1920.

28. Ibid.

29. John Hutchinson, *The Dynamics of Cultural Nationalism: The Gaelic Revival and the Creation of the Irish Nation State* (London: Allen & Unwin, 1987), 4.

30. *Catholic Times*, January 20, 1894; *Catholic Standard and Times*, November 3, 1900.

31. *Hibernian*, June 17, 1890.

32. *Irish American Review and Celtic Literary Advocate*, October 13, 1900.

33. Ibid.

34. *Catholic Standard and Times*, November 14, 1903.

35. Ibid., March 21, 1903.

36. Ibid., June 27, 1903.

37. Ibid., November 12, 1900.

38. *Philadelphia Inquirer*, July 6, 1902.

39. Tom Garvin, "The Anatomy of a Nationalist Revolution: Ireland, 1858–1928," *Comparative Studies in Society and History* 28, no. 3 (July 1986): 468–501, 498.

40. *Philadelphia Inquirer*, November 24, 1903.

41. 1901, MB80B, Association Pamphlets, CHRC.

42. "The Celtic Revival: An Address Delivered by Robert Ellis Thompson, S.T.D., President of the Celtic Association of Philadelphia," scrapbook, November 7, 1901, CHRC.

43. "Address at the *Feis* in the Academy of Music, By Robert Ellis Thompson," December 5, 1902, MB80B, Association Pamphlets, CHRC.

44. Philo-Celtic Society, "Devoted to the Language."

45. *Philadelphia Inquirer*, March 9, 1919.

46. Ibid. St. Enda's was the school that Patrick Pearse developed in Ireland around Gaelic culture, history and language.

47. McMahon, *Grand Opportunity*, 182.

48. Ibid., 183.

49. *Clan-na-Gael Journal*, June 27, 1914.

50. *Hibernian*, July 14, 1895.

51. *Philadelphia Inquirer*, December 15, 1912.

52. Ibid., October 7, 1912.

53. Ibid., February 2, 1913.

54. Scrapbook, 1913, 2010.19, CHRC.

55. Ibid.

56. McMahon, *Grand Opportunity*, 185.

57. *Irish American Review and Celtic Literary Advocate,* November 18, 1899.

58. 1913, MB80B, Association Pamphlets, CHRC.

59. *Philadelphia Inquirer,* October 5, 1902.

60. Ibid., July 6, 1902. It was announced in this meeting that the Gaelic League branch of Philadelphia contained 1,000 members.

61. Ibid., October 4, 1902.

62. Ibid., October 7, 1902.

63. Ibid.

64. Ibid., October 4, 1902.

65. Ibid., August 14, 1902.

66. Ibid., November 20, 1910.

67. Ibid.

68. 1913, MB80B, Association Pamphlets, CHRC.

69. Ibid.

70. *Irish American Review and Celtic Literary Advocate*, June 24, 1899.

71. Ibid., August 8, 1899.

72. *Philadelphia Inquirer,* January 14, 1913.

73. Ibid., December 15, 1912.

74. Ibid., January 14, 1913.

75. Ibid., October 29, 1923.

76. *Irish American Review and Celtic Literary Advocate*, November 18, 1899.

77. Ibid.

78. *Philadelphia Inquirer,* December 11, 1905.

79. Ibid. Attendance at his speech at the Academy of Music was reported to have been over 2,000.

80. *Philadelphia Inquirer,* March 6, 1908.

81. Garvin, "Nationalist Revolution."

82. Ibid., 485.

83. McMahon, *Grand Opportunity*, 103.

84. Ibid., 113.

85. Ibid., 112.

86. Ibid., 138. All of Catholic Ireland was not supportive of this measure as it meant closing public houses on a Sunday.

87. Hutchinson, *Cultural Nationalism.*

88. E. P. Thompson, "Patrician Society, Plebeian Culture," *Journal of Social History* 7, no. 4 (1974): 382–405, 388.

89. Hutchinson, *Cultural Nationalism*.

90. Ibid., 14.

91. Ibid., 30.

92. *Philadelphia Inquirer*, November 24, 1903.

93. Ibid.

94. Ibid.

95. *Philadelphia Inquirer*, January 24, 1912.

96. *Clan-na-Gael Journal*, February 22, 1912, November 21, 1914.

97. *Philadelphia Inquirer*, January 24, 1912.

98. Ibid.

99. McMahon, *Grand Opportunity*, 11.

CHAPTER 3 — IRISH PHILADELPHIA IN AND OUT
OF THE GAELIC SPHERE

1. Kathleen Gavigan, "The Rise and Fall of Parish Cohesiveness in Philadelphia," *Records of the American Catholic Historical Society of Philadelphia* 86 (1975): 107–131, 108.

2. "Annual Report of the Superintendent of the Parochial Schools of the Archdiocese of Philadelphia, PA.," 1898, CHRC.

3. Ní Bhroiméil, *Building Irish Identity*, 41.

4. U.S. Census Bureau, 1890.

5. *Philadelphia Inquirer*, July 6, 1902. The membership of the Gaelic League was recorded at 1,000.

6. "History of St. Anne's Church: Grand Souvenir," 1920, PH0010, CHRC.

7. Ibid.

8. "Sesquicentennial of St. Anne's Parish," 1995, PH0010, CHRC.

9. *Clan-na-Gael Journal*, June 25, 1916.

10. Ibid., November 14, 1914.

11. *Evening Public Ledger* (Philadelphia), November 23, 1920, microfilm, McCabe Library, Swarthmore College.

12. "Constitution & Bylaws of the St. Anne's Total Abstinence Benevolent Society," 1873, P007.01, CHRC.

13. "St. Anne's One Hundred Years, 1845–1945," Falvey Memorial Library, Villanova University.

14. "St. Anne's Parish Kalendar," 1902, PH0010, CHRC.

15. Ibid.

16. Ibid.

17. "Ascension Parish Register, 1910–11," PH0014, CHRC.

18. "Handbill of St. Agatha's Grand Concert of Music," scrapbook, 1892, MB58, CHRC.

19. "Ascension Parish Register, 1909–10," PH0014, CHRC.

20. Ní Bhroiméil, *Building Irish Identity in America, 1870–1915: The Gaelic Revival* (Dublin, Ireland: Four Courts Press, 2003), 134.

21. Philo-Celtic Society handbill, 1901.

22. "Broadside from Our Lady of Mercy Catholic Church," scrapbook, 1891, CHRC.

23. "Minute Book of the St. Charles Catholic Beneficial Society, 1868," 1993.016, CHRC.

24. "Letter to I.C.B.U. Delegates of Philadelphia," scrapbook, June 1, 1872, MB97, CHRC.

25. "Invitation to St. Agatha's I.C.B.U. Branch," 1891, MB97, CHRC.

26. ICBU journal, scrapbook, 1891, MB97, CHRC; Gavigan, "Parish Cohesiveness," 116.

27. Scrapbook, 1890, MB97, CHRC.

28. Meeting announcement of the St. Joseph's Society of the ICBU, October 1891, MB97, CHRC.

29. Letters from ICBU president Edward Murphy, March 1, 1890; November 6, 1891, MB97, CHRC.

30. "Constitution and Bylaws of the Father Mark Crane Beneficial Society of Philadelphia," 1883, P007.01, CHRC.

31. "Constitution and Bylaws of the Kensington Catholic Benevolent Society of the Irish Catholic Benevolent Union," 1873, AC0127C, CHRC (hereafter cited as Kensington Society Constitution, 1873).

32. "Constitution and Bylaws of the St. Augustine Beneficial Society of Philadelphia," 1844, P007.01, CHRC.

33. "Constitution and Bylaws of the Bishop Hughes Beneficial Society of the City of Philadelphia," 1865, P007.01, CHRC.

34. Ascension Parish Register, 1910–1911.

35. "Circular of the Cardinal Gibbons Benevolent Society," 1888, AC0127C, CHRC.

36. "Constitution and Bylaws of the Rev. M. Filan Catholic Male and Female Beneficial Society," 1883, AC0127C, CHRC.

37. Ibid.

38. "Constitution and Bylaws of the St. Regina Beneficial Association of Philadelphia," 1870, P007.01, CHRC.

39. "Constitution and Bylaws of Our Lady of Lourdes Catholic Beneficial Society," 1877, P007.01, CHRC; "Constitution and Bylaws of St. Catherine's Beneficial Society of Philadelphia," 1869, P007.01, CHRC.

40. "Constitution and Bylaws of St. Veronica's Female Beneficial Society of Philadelphia," 1889, P007.01, CHRC.

41. "Charter, Constitution and Bylaws of the Saint Vincent's Beneficial Society of Frankford," 1871, P007.01, CHRC.

42. "Constitution and Bylaws of St. Veronica's Female Beneficial Society of Philadelphia," 1871, P007.01, CHRC.

43. "Constitution and Bylaws of the Ladies Catholic Union No. 1 of Philadelphia," 1886, AC0127C, CHRC.

44. "Constitution and Bylaws of the St. Agnes Ladies Benevolent and Social Association of Frankford," 1869, AC0127C, CHRC.

45. Ibid.

46. Ascension Parish Register, 1910–1911.

47. Gavigan, "Parish Cohesiveness," 116.

48. "National Directory of the Ancient Order of Hibernians in America," 1901–02, AC0013, CHRC; U.S. Census Bureau, 1900.

49. "14th Annual Report, Our Lady of Lourdes Female Beneficial Society," 1891, P007.01, CHRC.

50. Daniel H. Mahony, Historical Sketches of the Catholic Churches and Institutions of Philadelphia (Philadelphia, 1895), xlix.

51. Ibid.

52. Noel Ignatiev, How the Irish Became White (New York: Routledge, 1995), 1.

53. "Constitution and Bylaws of the Southwark Beneficial Society," 1870, P007.01, CHRC.

54. "Charter, Constitution and Bylaws of the Premium Loan Association of Philadelphia," 1855, P007.01, CHRC; "Constitution and By-Laws of the St. Charles Catholic Beneficial Society of Philadelphia," 1867, P007.01, CHRC, 329.

55. Ignatiev, *Irish Became White*.

56. Quoted in Ibid., 165.

57. "Constitution and Bylaws of the Robert Emmet Beneficial Society of Germantown," 1889, AC0127C, CHRC.

58. "Constitution and Bylaws of the St. Monica Male and Female Catholic Benevolent Association of Philadelphia," 1881, AC0127C, CHRC.

59. "Constitution and Bylaws of the St. Anne's Total Abstinence Benevolent Society of Philadelphia," 1873, PC07.01, CHRC.

60. "Announcement of the Philadelphia I.C.B.U. Convention," 1882, AC0127C, CHRC.

61. Mahony, *Historical Sketches of the Catholic Churches*.

62. Kensington Society Constitution, 1873.

63. Mahony, *Historical Sketches of the Catholic Churches*.

64. Ibid, xxiv.

65. Gavigan, "Parish Cohesiveness," 118.

66. Letter to the Presidents of the Branches of the Total Abstinence Society of Philadelphia, scrapbook, 1874, 2010.019, CHRC.

67. "Manual of the Young Men's Temperance Society and Association of Prayer of St. John's Parish, Manayunk," 1881, P007.01, CHRC.

68. "Constitution and Bylaws of the Workingmen's Beneficial Society of Philadelphia," 1867, P007.01, CHRC.

69. "Catholic Young Men's Archdiocesan Union (C.Y.M.A.U.), 1895–1910," scrapbook, 1901, MB80B, CHRC (hereafter cited as CYMAU scrapbook).

70. Ibid.

71. *Irish American Review and Celtic Literary Advocate*, November 11, 1899.

72. *Clan-na-Gael Irish Patriot Martyrs Anniversary Magazine*, April 24, 1917, Joseph McGarrity Collection, Falvey Memorial Library, Villanova University.

73. General report of the Irish National Land League of America, 1882, AC01301, CHRC (hereafter cited as Land League report, 1882).

74. "Constitution and Bylaws of the Philadelphia Municipal Council of the Irish Land League of America," 1882, AC01301, CHRC.

75. *Catholic Standard*, August 21, 1886.

76. Ibid., May 19, 1894.

77. Ibid., November 17, 1894.

78. Land League report, 1882. Michael Davitt partnered with Parnell to provide leadership for the Land League.

79. Scrapbook, 1892, 2010.019, CHRC.

80. *Advocate* (Philadelphia), February 1, 1890, CHRC.

81. *Irish American Review and Celtic Literary Advocate*, September 16, 1899.

82. *Advocate* (Philadelphia), February 1, 1890.

83. "Constitution and Bylaws of St. Patrick's Beneficial Society, No.197 I.C.B.U.," 1892, AC0127C, CHRC.

84. Mahony, *Historical Sketches of the Catholic Churches*, xvi.

85. "Constitution and Bylaws of the Catholic Young Men's Archdiocesan Union (C.Y.M.A.U.), 1895–1910," 1908, AC0085, CHRC.

86. "Program of the Reception of the Catholic Young Men's Archdiocesan Union of Philadelphia," 1895, CYMAU scrapbook.

87. CYMAU scrapbook.

88. *Public Ledger*, September 18, 1891.

89. "Souvenir of the Forty-Third Annual Convention, Catholic Young Men's National Union of America, Philadelphia," 1917, PO13.099, CHRC.

90. *Irish American Review and Celtic Literary Advocate*, September 2, 1899.

91. "Souvenir of the 27th Annual Convention of the Catholic Young Men's National Union, Philadelphia," 1901, PO13, CHRC.

92. *Clan-na-Gael Journal*, July 4, 1917.

93. "Handbill of C.Y.M.A.U. Field Day," 1901, CYMAU scrapbook.

94. Letter to clubs of the CYMAU, 1906, CYMAU scrapbook.

95. *The North American*, September 2, 1904, CHRC.

96. *Irish American Review and Celtic Literary Advocate*, September 8, 1899.

97. "Program of the Reception of the Catholic Young Men's Archdiocesan Union of Philadelphia," 1899, CYMAU scrapbook.

98. *The North American*, April 26, 1899.

99. CYMAU Banquet, March 2, 1905, CYMAU scrapbook.

100. "The Helper," 1905, CYMAU scrapbook.

101. CYMAU scrapbook.

102. Ibid.

103. "Constitution and Bylaws of the De Sales Institute of Philadelphia," 1870, P007.01, CHRC.

104. Program of the "Grand Musical Celebration" of the Clan na Gael, Philadelphia, 1891, box 1, Irish American Materials, CHRC.

105. Ibid.

CHAPTER 4 — TRANSATLANTIC ORIGINS OF IRISH AMERICAN VOLUNTARY ASSOCIATIONS

1. R. F. Foster, *Modern Ireland, 1600–1972* (New York: Allen Lane Penguin Press, 1988), 348.

2. Ruth-Ann M. Harris, *The Nearest Place That Wasn't Ireland: Early Nineteenth-Century Irish Labor Migration* (Ames: Iowa State University Press, 1994), xv.

3. Cormac Ó Gráda, *Ireland: A New Economic History, 1780–1939* (Oxford, U.K.: Clarendon Press, 1994), 213.

4. David Brundage, *Irish Nationalists in America: The Politics of Exile, 1798–1998* (New York: Oxford University Press, 2016).

5. Between 1783 and 1798, 60 percent of ships heading from Dublin to America docked in Philadelphia, Newcastle, or Wilmington. Maurice Bric, *Ireland, Philadelphia and the Re-Invention of America, 1760–1800* (Dublin: Four Courts Press, 2008).

6. Quoted in ibid., 35. Bric estimates that 18,600 Irish came from the northern ports of Ireland to the Delaware Valley by the mid-1700s. Ibid., 40.

7. Ibid., 42.

8. J. Matthew Gallman, *Receiving Erin's Children: Philadelphia, Liverpool, and the Irish Famine Migration, 1845–1855* (Chapel Hill: University of North Carolina Press, 2000).

9. Ibid., 45–46.

10. Joel Mokyr, *Why Ireland Starved: A Quantitative and Analytical History of the Irish Economy, 1800–1850* (London: Allen & Unwin, 1983), 249.

11. Harris, *Nearest Place*.

12. Ibid, 163. Handley estimates almost 38,000 seasonal migrants annually left Ireland for Britain between 1880 and 1900. James E. Handley, *The Irish in Modern Scotland* (Cork, Ireland: Cork University Press, 1947), 213.

13. Patrick Blessing, "Irish Emigration to the United States, 1800–1920: An Overview," in *The Irish in America*, ed. P. J. Drudy (Cambridge: Cambridge University Press, 1985), 11–38, 19.

14. The original Friendly Sons of St. Patrick, as Brundage notes, was populated by "wealthy Protestant merchants." Brundage, *Irish Nationalists*, 44.

15. James R. Barrett, *The Irish Way: Becoming American in the Multiethnic City* (New York: Penguin Press, 2012), 4.

16. Alexis de Tocqueville, *Democracy in America*, trans. Henry Reeve (New York: Schocken Press, 1967), 198–199.

17. Mary P. Ryan, *Civic Wars: Democracy and Public Life in the American City during the Nineteenth Century* (Berkeley: University of California Press, 1997), 80.

18. Mary Ann Clawson, *Constructing Brotherhood: Class, Gender, and Fraternalism* (Princeton, N.J.: Princeton University Press, 1989), 21.

19. *The Irish World and American Industrial Liberator*, February 8, 1890. Workers' consumer and producer cooperatives of ship carpenters, leather workers, machinists, blacksmiths, weavers, and printers surfaced in Philadelphia in the 1870s and 1880s in the wake of a labor movement involving the Irish and other immigrant groups. Judith Goldberg, "Strikes, Organizing and Change: The Knights of Labor in Philadelphia, 1869–1890" (Ph.D. dissertation, New York University, 1985).

20. *Clan-na-Gael Journal*, February 22, 1913.

21. Mary Ryan notes the distinction and class separation of the early nineteenth-century, pre-Famine, elite Irish associations in New York; she writes that these "were elite clubs set apart from the poor émigrés of the 1840s." Ryan, *Civic Wars*, 82.

22. *British Parliamentary Papers* 5, 1871.

23. "Reports of the Assistant Commissioners on Friendly and Benefit Building Societies with Indices," 1864, in *British Parliamentary Papers* 8 (Shannon, Ireland: Irish University Press, 1970), 2.

24. David A. Fleming, "Clubs and Societies in Eighteenth-Century Munster," in *Clubs and Societies in Eighteenth-Century Ireland*, ed. James Kelly and Martyn Powell (Dublin: Four Courts Press, 2010), 427–446, 444–445.

25. *British Parliamentary Papers* 5, 1872, 25.

26. "Rules and Regulations of the Emerald Society," 1886, R.F.S. 480, National Archives of Ireland, Dublin (hereafter cited as Emerald Society Rules, 1886), 10.

27. *British Parliamentary Papers* 5, 1874.

28. Ibid., 377.

29. John Campbell, "Tontine and Benefit Society Records in the National Archives and in the Registry of Friendly Societies, Dublin," *Saothar* 17 (1992): 3.

30. *British Parliamentary Papers* 5, 1872, 25.

31. Emerald Society Rules, 1886.

32. Ibid.

33. Ibid., 11.

34. John H. Campbell, *History of the Friendly Sons of St. Patrick and of the Hibernian Society* (Philadelphia: Hibernian Society, 1892), 31.

35. Emerald Society Rules, 1886, 47.

36. Ibid.

37. Ibid., 15.

38. Ibid., 13.

39. "Friendly Societies Building Societies and Industrial and Provident Societies," 1886–1899, in *British Parliamentary Papers* 10 (Shannon, Ireland: Irish University Press, 1971), 225.

40. Ibid.

41. Daly, *Dublin, The Deposed Capital*, 108.

42. *British Parliamentary Papers* 5, 1872, 27.

43. Daly, *Dublin, The Deposed Capital*, 322.

44. Ibid.

45. Michael L. Mullan, "The Devolution of the Irish Economy in the Nineteenth Century and the Bifurcation of Irish Sport," *International Journal of the History of Sport* 13, no. 2 (August 1996): 42–60.

46. *British Parliamentary Papers* 5, 1874, 27.

47. Ibid., 38.

48. Ibid., 48.

49. "Rules of the Amicable Society," 1874, in *British Parliamentary Papers* 5, 56–58.

50. Ibid.

51. Ibid., 56–58.

52. Ibid.

53. Appendix to "Report by E. Lynch Daniell, Esq., on Friendly Societies in Ireland," 1874, in *British Parliamentary Papers* 5 (hereafter cited as "Friendly Societies in Ireland," 1874), 94.

54. McGovern, *John Mitchel*, 40.

55. T. C. Barnard, "Sites and Rites of Associational Life in Eighteenth-Century Ireland," in *Associational Culture in Ireland and the Wider World*, eds. R. V. Comerford and Jennifer Kelly (Dublin: Irish Academic Press, 2010), 11–26, 11.

56. Anthony Buckley, "'On the Club': Friendly Societies in Ireland," *Irish Economic and Social History* 14 (1987), 39–58, 56.

57. *British Parliamentary Papers* 5, 1874, 46.

58. "Minute Book of the Donegal Beneficial, Social and Patriotic Association of Philadelphia, 1905–1925," Irish Center of Philadelphia (hereafter cited as Donegal Association Minute Book).

59. Ibid., March 21, 1915.

60. *The Ballyshannon Herald*, September 16, 1882, Central Library, Letterkenny, Ireland.

61. Harris, *Nearest Place*, 23.

62. Simone Wegge, Tyler Anbinder and Cormac Ó Gráda, "Immigrants and Savers: A Rich New Database on the Irish in 1850s New York," *Historical Methods: A Journal of Quantitative and Interdisciplinary History* 50, no. 3 (May 2017): 144–155, 154.

63. Ibid.

64. Foster, *Modern Ireland*, 351.

65. The Dublin model was derived from the financial reports of fourteen mutual aid societies in 1874. "Friendly Societies in Ireland," 1874, 112.

66. Mary Daly, *Dublin, the Deposed Capital: A Social and Economic History, 1860–1914* (Cork, Ireland: Cork University Press, 1984), 121.

67. Ibid., 122.

68. Ibid.

69. Mary E. Daly, "Social Structure of the Dublin Working Class, 1871–1911," *Irish Historical Studies* 23, no. 90 (November 1982): 121–133.

70. Emerald Society Rules, 1886, 8.

71. Daly, *Dublin, The Deposed Capital.*

72. Emerald Society Rules, 1886, 8.

73. "Rules and Regulations of the Independent Branch of the Andrean Christian Burial Society," 1871, in *British Parliamentary Papers* 5, 100–102.

74. "Rules of Saint Columbanus's Society," 1874, in *British Parliamentary Papers* 5, 105–106.

75. John Campbell, "Tontine and Benefit Society Records," 2.

76. "Rules and Regulations of the Independent Burial Society," 1874, in *British Parliamentary Papers* 5, 100.

77. "Rules and Orders of the St. Bridget's Burial Society," 1874, in *British Parliamentary Papers* 5 (hereafter cited as St. Bridget's Society Rules, 1874), 103–106.

78. John Campbell, "Tontine and Benefit Society Records," 5.

79. Emerald Society Rules, 1886, 12.

80. Ibid., 27.

81. St. Bridget's Society Rules, 1874, 103–104.

82. Daly, *Dublin, The Deposed Capital*, 36.

83. *British Parliamentary Papers* 5, 1874, 73.

84. "Amended Rules and Regulations to be observed by the Members of the Inchicore Friendly Society," 1874, in *British Parliamentary Papers* 5, 73–75, 74.

85. Ibid.

86. "Rules of the Friendly Brothers of the Harp and Shamrock Tontine Society," 1874, in *British Parliamentary Papers* 5, 77–79.

87. Ibid., 77.

88. "Bylaws of the Friendly Brothers of the Harp Society," 1874, in *British Parliamentary Papers* 5, 79.

89. St. Lawrence Society Rules, 1874.

90. Ibid.

91. "Rules of the Friendly Brothers of St. Luke's Society," 1874, in *British Parliamentary Papers* 5, 68–70.

92. St. Lawrence Society Rules, 1874.

93. *Irish American Review and Celtic Literary Advocate*, September 28, 1889.

94. This society collected its dues and turned them over to the Post Office for safekeeping; the Post Office acted as a dispenser of burial monies. *British Parliamentary Papers* 5, 1874, 360.

95. *British Parliamentary Papers* 5, 1874, 355–356.

96. "Rules & Regulations of the Dublin General Post Office Letters Carriers' Friendly Beneficial Society," 1860, R.E.F. 249, National Archives of Ireland, Dublin, 4.

97. Ibid., 1.

98. Ibid., 4–9.

99. *British Parliamentary Papers* 5, 1872, 412.

100. Ibid., 412.

101. Ibid., 413.

102. Ibid.

103. Ibid., 415.

104. Ibid., 420.

105. Ibid., 413.

106. Ibid., 412.

107. "Reports of the Assistant Commissioners on Friendly and Benefit Building Societies with Indices," 1864, in *British Parliamentary Papers* 8, 6.

108. Ibid., 407. "The respectable middle class of tradesmen, who want to build a country house for themselves; they take a piece of ground, and they build a little country residence."

109. Ibid., 405.

110. Ibid., 406.

111. Donegal Association Minute Book, June 14, 1906.

112. Cavan Society Minute Book, April 13, 1925.

113. Donegal Association Minute Book, August 21, 1910.

CHAPTER 5 — A MICROANALYSIS OF IRISH AMERICAN CIVIC LIFE

1. Rudolph Vecoli, "Are Italians Just White Folks?" *Italian Americana* 13, no. 2 (Summer 1995): 149–161, 156.

2. David Brundage, *Irish Nationalists in America: The Politics of Exile, 1798–1998* (New York: Oxford University Press, 2016), 157.

3. John T. Ridge, "Irish County Societies in New York, 1880–1914," in *The New York Irish*, ed. Ronald H. Bayor and Timothy J. Meagher (Baltimore, Md.: Johns Hopkins University Press, 1996), 276–300, 297.

4. D. Clark, *The Heart's Own People: A History of the Donegal Beneficial, Social, Charitable and Patriotic Association of Philadelphia* (Newtown Square, Pa.: Harrowood Books, 1988), 24.

5. Ibid., 26.

6. "Minute Book of the Donegal Beneficial, Social and Patriotic Association of Philadelphia, 1905–1925," Irish Center of Philadelphia (hereafter cited as Donegal Association Minute Book), 1905.

7. Ibid.

8. Ibid., May 1, 1905.

9. Ibid.

10. Donegal Association Minute Book.

11. U.S. Census Bureau, 1910.

12. Ibid.

13. Donegal Association Minute Book.

14. Ibid.

15. Ibid.

16. Ibid.

17. Ibid., 1906.

18. Ibid.

19. Ibid., 1910.

20. Clark, *The Heart's Own People*, 29.

21. Donegal Association Minute Book, 1906.

22. Clark, *The Heart's Own People*, 28–29.

23. Donegal Association Minute Book, 1906.

24. Ibid.

25. Ibid., 1905.

26. Seamus Deane, "Dumbness and Eloquence: A Note on English as We Write It in Ireland," in *Ireland and Postcolonial Theory*, ed. Clare Carroll and Patricia King (Cork, Ireland: Cork University Press, 2003), 109–121, 113.

27. Donegal Association Minute Book, July 1914.

28. *Slater's Directory*, 1890, Donegal Public Library, Letterkenny, Ireland.

29. *Ballyshannon Herald*, January 17, 1880.

30. Ibid., March 21, 1883.

31. *Derry Journal*, April 8, 1885.

32. Ibid.

33. Ibid., January 15, 1890.

34. Ibid., January 1, 1890.

35. Ibid., January 30, 1885.

36. Richard McElligott, *Forging a Kingdom: The GAA in Kerry, 1884–1934* (Cork, Ireland: Collins Press, 2013), 376.

37. *Liberator* (Donegal), January 10, 1906.

38. Conor Curran, *The Development of Sport in Donegal, 1880–1935* (Cork, Ireland: Cork University Press, 2015), 253.

39. Ibid.

40. *Ballyshannon Herald*, March 13, 1880.

41. Ibid., October 29, 1881.

42. Ibid.

43. Ibid., March 15, 1886.

44. Ibid., January 30, 1885.

45. *Rules of the Killybegs Agricultural Cooperative* (Dublin: Sealy, Bryers and Walker, 1900), Donegal County Archives, Lifford, Ireland.

46. Ibid., 15.

47. Ibid., 25.

48. Ibid., 8, 24.

49. "Annual Report for the Letterkenny Cooperative Flax Society, 1915," RFS R803, National Archives of Ireland, Dublin.

50. "Report to the Department of Industry and Commerce," Registry of Friendly Societies, Michael Davitt Branch, January 18, 1915, RFS R605, National Archives of Ireland, Dublin.

51. "Minute Book of the Cavan Catholic, Social, and Beneficial Society of Philadelphia, 1907–1926," Cavan Society of Philadelphia (hereafter cited as Cavan Society Minute Book).

52. Max Weber, *Economy and Society: An Outline of Interpretive Sociology* (Berkeley: University of California Press, 1978), 395.

53. *The Anglo-Celt*, March 1, 1890, microfilm, Johnston Central Library, Cavan, Ireland.

54. Cavan Society Minute Book.

55. Ibid., June 11, 1922.

56. Ibid.

57. Ibid.

58. *Anglo-Celt*, October 24, 1903.

59. Walter Licht, *Getting Work: Philadelphia, 1840–1950* (Cambridge, Mass.: Harvard University Press, 1992), 231.

60. Cavan Society Minute Book, August 8, 1915.

61. E. P. Thompson, *The Making of the English Working Class* (New York: Pantheon Books, 1964).

62. Cavan Society Minute Book, May 9, 1920.

63. *Anglo-Celt*, March 28, 1903.

64. Ibid.

65. Paul Bew, *Conflict and Conciliation in Ireland, 1898–1910: Parnellites and Radical Agrarians* (New York: Clarendon Press and Oxford University Press, 1987).

66. *Anglo-Celt*, March 28, 1903.

67. Ibid.

68. "Cavan County Agricultural Association Friendly Societies Registry Form," 1912, R.F.S. R677, National Archives of Ireland, Dublin.

69. Ibid.

70. *Anglo-Celt*, June 27, 1903.

71. Ibid., May 14, 1903.

72. Ibid., 1903.

73. Ibid., July 25, 1908.

74. Ibid., February 13, 1892.

75. Ibid., March 8, 1890.

76. Ibid., January 17, 1903.

77. Ibid.

78. Ibid.

79. Ibid.

80. Ibid., January 11, 1890.

81. Ibid.

82. Ibid., January 24, 1903.

83. Ibid.

84. Ibid., July 5, 1903.

85. Ibid., June 6, 1903.

86. "Anniversary Program and Souvenir," Cavan Society Minute Book, 1912.

87. Kerby Miller, *Emigrants and Exiles: Ireland and the Irish Exodus to North America* (New York: Oxford University Press, 1985), 25.

88. Cavan Society Minute Book, October 10, 1920.

89. Ibid.

90. Ibid., July 14, 1907.

91. It has been estimated that an unskilled laborer in the early 1880s had trouble earning $400 per year. Eudice Glassberg, "Work, Wages, and the Cost of Living: Ethnic Differences and the Poverty Line, Philadelphia, 1880," *Pennsylvania History* 66 (1979): 17–58.

92. Cavan Society Minute Book, March 14, 1926.

93. Ibid.

94. Ibid., December 13, 1914.

95. Ibid.

96. Ibid., May 11, 1913.

97. Ibid., May 9, 1915.

98. Ibid., November 8, 1914.

99. *Hibernian*, September 30, 1895.

100. Cavan Society Minute Book, April 9, 1916.

101. Ibid.

102. Ibid., November 11, 1923.

103. Ibid., November 11, 1911.

104. Ibid.

105. Ibid., June 11, 1916.

106. Ibid., April 3, 1915.

107. Ibid., August 11, 1907.

108. Ibid., May 13, 1917.

109. *Irish American Review and Celtic Literary Advocate*, August 13, 1899.

110. *Hibernian*, January 6, 1894.

111. Clan na Gael Minute Book, July 17, 1892.

112. *Hibernian*, March 16, 1895.

113. Cavan Society Minute Book, July 9, 1911.

114. Ibid.

115. Ibid., August 12, 1917.

116. Ibid., January 13, 1918.

117. Ibid., August 12, 1917.

118. Ibid., May 11, 1919.

119. Ibid., September 18, 1916.

120. Ibid., August 13, 1916.

121. Ibid., March 9, 1919.

122. Ibid., November 14, 1920.

123. Ibid., July 11, 1920.

124. Ibid., November 10, 1919.

125. Ibid., January 21, 1921.

126. Ibid., March 14, 1920.

127. Ibid., September 12, 1920.

128. Ibid., June 9, 1918.

129. Ibid., April 13, 1919.

130. E. J. Hobsbawm, *Primitive Rebels: Studies in Archaic Forms of Social Movement in the 19th and 20th Centuries* (New York: Praeger, 1959), 126.

131. Donegal Association Minute Book, December 17, 1905.

132. Ibid., December 15, 1907.

133. Miller, *Emigrants and Exiles*, 458.

134. Clark, *The Heart's Own People*, 27.

135. *Freeman and Irish American Review*, June 10, 1899.

136. *Irish American Review and Celtic Literary Advocate*, September 17, 1899.

137. Cavan Society Minute Book, October 11, 1925.

138. Ibid., May 15, 1916.

139. *Anglo-Celt*, January 1, 1890.

140. Ibid., May 19, 1914.

141. Ibid., December 10, 1922.

142. Ibid., January 14, 1923.

143. Thompson, *English Working Class*, 194.

CHAPTER 6 — THE FORGING OF A COLLECTIVE CONSCIOUSNESS

1. *Hibernian*, April 15, 1894.

2. David Brundage, *Irish Nationalists in America: The Politics of Exile, 1798–1998* (New York: Oxford University Press, 2016), 85.

3. *Hibernian*, July 14, 1893.

4. *Freeman and Irish American Review*, March 15, 1890.

5. Frank Beito, *From Mutual Aid to the Welfare State: Fraternal Societies and Social Services, 1890–1967* (Chapel Hill: University of North Carolina Press, 2000), 3.

6. *Hibernian*, September 2, 1893.

7. Dale B. Light Jr., "Class, Ethnicity and the Urban Ecology in a 19th Century City: Philadelphia's Irish, 1840–1890" (Ph.D. dissertation, University of Pennsylvania, 1979), 155.

8. *Irish American Review and Celtic Literary Advocate*, September 2, 1899.

9. Kerby Miller, *Emigrants and Exiles: Ireland and the Irish Exodus to North America* (New York: Oxford University Press, 1985), 422.

10. Bryan P. McGovern, *John Mitchel: Irish Nationalist, Southern Secessionist* (Knoxville: University of Tennessee Press, 2009), 102.

11. "John Mitchel, The Irish Patriot and Exile," The Library Company of Philadelphia.

12. Miller's description of the Famine exodus as exile has penetrated Irish American historical discourse: "a morbid perception of themselves as involuntary exiles, passive victims of English oppression." Miller, *Emigrants and Exiles*, 7.

13. E. P. Thompson, *The Making of the English Working Class* (New York: Pantheon Books, 1964), 194.

14. *Hibernian*, June 24, 1898.

15. Miller, *Emigrants and Exiles*, 390.

16. *Hibernian*, March 30, 1895.

17. *Irish American Review and Celtic Literary Advocate*, September 9, 1899.

18. Jim Smyth, *The Men of No Property: Irish Radicals and Popular Politics in the Late Eighteenth Century* (London: Macmillan, 1992), 162.

19. Max Weber, *Economy and Society: An Outline of Interpretive Sociology* (Berkeley: University of California Press, 1978), 390.

20. *Irish American Review and Celtic Literary Advocate*, August 19, 1899.

21. Ibid., December 7, 1889.

22. *Philadelphia Inquirer*, February 27, 1911.

23. *Hibernian*, September 7, 1895.

24. Ibid., July 5, 1895.

25. Renato Rosaldo, "Celebrating Thompson's Heroes: Social Analysis in History and Anthropology," in *E. P. Thompson: Critical Perspectives*, ed. Harvey J. Kaye and Keith McClelland (Philadelphia: Temple University Press, 1990), 101–124, 101.

26. *Irish American Review and Celtic Literary Advocate*, September 10, 1899.

27. Ibid., September 2, 1899.

28. *Hibernian*, May 5, 1894.

29. "Why the Catholic Church Cannot Accept Socialism," 1913, AC0196, Association Pamphlets, CHRC.

30. Scrapbook, 1891, 2010.092, CHRC.

31. *Irish American Review and Celtic Literary Advocate*, June 24, 1899.

32. *Hibernian*, September 2, 1895.

33. Ibid., October 26, 1895.

34. Kevin Kenny, *Making Sense of the Molly Maguires* (New York: Oxford University Press, 1998).

35. *Irish American Review and Celtic Literary Advocate*, September 2, 1899.

36. *Hibernian*, December 7, 1895.

37. Ibid., July 12, 1890.

38. Ibid., October 4, 1893, May 5, 1894.

39. Ibid., May 4, 1894, October 19, 1895; *Irish American Review*, September 2, 1899.

40. *Irish American Review and Celtic Literary Advocate*, September 2, 1899.

41. *Freeman and Irish American Review*, August 10, 1889.

42. *Irish American Review and Celtic Literary Advocate*, July 29, 1899.

43. *Freeman and Irish American Review*, July 12, 1890.

44. *Hibernian*, May 11, 1895.

45. *Freeman and Irish American Review*, July 12, 1890.

46. *Irish American Review and Celtic Literary Advocate*, December 16, 1899.

47. Ibid., July 29, 1899.

48. *Hibernian*, September 30, 1895. Division 3, 2nd and South Street, and Division 13, 38th and Haverford in West Philadelphia, were both active AOH divisions for women.

49. *Hibernian*, February 2, 1895.

50. Ibid.

51. Ibid.

52. *Philadelphia Record*, February 2, 1895, Free Library of Philadelphia.

53. *Hibernian*, February 9, 1895.

54. The Philo-Celtic Society of Philadelphia sponsored lectures such as "The Celt in History" delivered by Rev. Joseph V. O'Connor in 1895. *Hibernian*, May 11, 1895.

55. Ibid., February 3, 1898.

56. Ibid., September 7, 1895; ibid., October 12, 1895.

57. Ibid., September 2, 1893.

58. Ibid., June 10, 1899.

59. Ibid.

60. *Irish American Review and Celtic Literary Advocate*, September 22, 1899.

61. Ibid., August 20, 1899.

62. Ibid., September 9, 1899.

63. *Hibernian*, November 2, 1889.

64. Ibid., October 5, 1895.

65. Ibid., July 8, 1898.

66. Ibid.

67. *Irish American Review and Celtic Literary Advocate*, July 29, 1899.

68. Ibid., April 17, 1899.

69. Ibid., September 22, 1899. Wolfe Tone, United Irish leader, was also an icon of heroic Irish remembrance in Philadelphia. Jim Smyth writes of "that heroic idea, reiterated in ballads . . . publicly commemorated in 1898, carried into the twentieth century in the shape of Wolfe Tone." Smyth, *No Property*, 182.

70. *Irish American Review and Celtic Literary Advocate*, September 22, 1899.

71. Ibid., July 14, 1898.

72. Ibid., June 24, 1898. This building was eventually purchased and became the headquarters of the AOH in Philadelphia.

73. Ibid.

74. Ibid.

75. Weber, *Economy and Society*, 391.

76. *Irish American Review and Celtic Literary Advocate*, August 19, 1899.

77. D. Clark, "Militants of the 1860's: The Philadelphia Fenians," *The Pennsylvania Magazine of History and Biography* 95, no. 1 (January 1971): 98–108, 102.

78. "Minute Book of the Clan na Gael, 1889–1923," MSS 37, box 1, Historical Society of Pennsylvania (HSP) (hereafter cited as Clan na Gael Minute Book).

79. *Public Ledger* (Philadelphia), February 29, 1876, microfilm, McCabe Library, Swarthmore College, March 14, 1859.

80. Clan na Gael Minute Book.

81. Clark, "Militants of the 1860's."

82. Ibid.

83. R. V. Comerford, "The Land War and the Politics of Distress, 1877–82," in *A New History of Ireland, Volume 6: Ireland under the Union, II: 1870–1921*, ed. W. E. Vaughan (Oxford, U.K.: Clarendon Press, 1996), 22.

84. Clan na Gael Minute Book.

85. Ibid., July 5, 1891.

86. Bric, "Ireland, Irishmen, and the Broadening of the Late-Eighteenth-Century Philadelphia Polity" (Ph.D. dissertation, Johns Hopkins University, 1990), 526.

87. Clan na Gael Minute Book, September 16, 1888.

88. Ibid.

89. Ibid., November 4, 1888.

90. Ibid., April 27, 1904.

91. Ibid.

92. Ibid., May 22, 1892.

93. Ibid., December 6, 1891.

94. *Freeman and Irish American Review*, November 23, 1889.

95. *Anglo-Celt*, October 24, 1903.

96. *Freeman and Irish American Review*, March 7, 1891.

97. Ibid.

98. Michel Foucault, "Des espace autres, Une conference inedited de Michel Foucault," trans. Jay Miskowiec, *Architecture Mouvement Continuité*, no. 5 (October 1984): 46–49, 48.

99. Beer was easily obtained for the Irish American Club from any number of breweries, bottlers and purveyors in Philadelphia, from Pat Doherty's on 20th and Ridge and Robert Walsh's at 8th and South to Joseph McGurk's in Kensington. On one advertising page of *The Freeman and Irish American Review*, twenty-nine different breweries, bottlers and merchants for beer were listed. *Freeman and Irish American Review*, August 9, 1890.

100. Clan na Gael Minute Book, January 19, 1917; ibid., April 12, 1917; ibid., May 31, 1918.

101. Ibid., March 16, 1894; ibid., January 19, 1922; ibid., March 9, 1922.

102. *Freeman and Irish American Review*, August 14, 1890.

103. *Irish American Review and Celtic Literary Advocate*, July 24, 1899.

104. E. J. Hobsbawm, *Primitive Rebels: Studies in Archaic Forms of Social Movement in the 19th and 20th Centuries* (New York: Praeger, 1959), 152.

105. Clan na Gael Minute Book, March 30, 1894.

106. Ibid., August 17, 1904.

107. Appendix to "Report by E. Lynch Daniell, Esq., on Friendly Societies in Ireland," 1874, in *British Parliamentary Papers* 5 (hereafter cited as "Friendly Societies in Ireland," 1874)," 112.

108. Clan na Gael Minute Book, September 16, 1888.

109. Ibid.

110. Ibid., December 11, 1919.

111. Ibid., April 27, 1904.

112. Ibid., March 20, 1892.

113. Ibid., July 5, 1923.

114. *Hibernian*, September 2, 1895.

115. Clan na Gael Minute Book, September 16, 1888; ibid., November 27, 1892; ibid., February 12, 1893; ibid., March 19, 1893.

116. *Irish American Review and Celtic Literary Advocate*, August 19, 1899.

117. Ibid.

CHAPTER 7 — SPORT, CULTURE, AND NATION AMONG THE IRISH OF PHILADELPHIA

1. E. J. Hobsbawm, *Nations and Nationalism since 1780: Programme, Myth, Reality* (Cambridge: Cambridge University Press, 1990), 142–143.

2. Benedict Anderson, *Imagined Communities: Reflections on the Origin and Spread of Nationalism* (London: Verso, 1991).

3. Richard Peterson, "Slide, Kelly, Slide: The Irish in American Baseball," in *New Perspectives on the Irish Diaspora* (Edwardsville: Southern Illinois University Press, 2000), 176–188.

4. Mike Cronin, *Sport and Nationalism in Ireland: Gaelic Games, Soccer and Irish Identity Since 1884* (Dublin: Four Courts, 1999), 30.

5. Ernest Gellner, *Nations and Nationalism* (Ithaca, N.Y.: Cornell University Press, 1983).

6. John Hutchinson, *The Dynamics of Cultural Nationalism: The Gaelic Revival and the Creation of the Irish Nation State* (London: Allen & Unwin, 1987), 9.

7. Patrick F. McDevitt, "Muscular Catholicism: Nationalism, Masculinity and Gaelic Team Sports, 1884–1916," *Gender & History* 9, no. 2 (1997): 262–284, 266.

8. Cronin, *Sport and Nationalism*, 38.

9. Marcus de Búrca, *The G.A.A.: A History* (Dublin: Macmillan, 1980).

10. Eoin Kinsella, "Riotous Proceedings and the Cricket of Savages: Football and Hurling in Early Modern Ireland," in *The Gaelic Athletic Association, 1884–2009*, ed. Mike Cronin et al. (Dublin: Irish Academic Press, 2009), 15–33, 29.

11. Kerby Miller, *Emigrants and Exiles: Ireland and the Irish Exodus to North America* (New York: Oxford University Press, 1985).

12. *Hibernian*, July 20, 1895.

13. Cronin, *Sport and Nationalism*; W. F. Mandle, *The Gaelic Athletic Association and Irish Nationalist Politics, 1884–1924* (Dublin: Macmillan, 1987).

14. Mandle, *Gaelic Athletic Association*.

15. De Búrca, *The G.A.A.*

16. Paul Rouse, "Michael Cusack: Sportsman and Journalist," in *Gaelic Athletic Association*, ed. Cronin et al., 47–60, 47.

17. *Freeman's Journal*, April 15, 1880.

18. Ibid., November 2, 1885.

19. Mandle, *Gaelic Athletic Association*, 155.

20. Rouse, "Sport and Ireland in 1881," in *Sport and the Irish: Histories, Identities, Issues*, ed. Alan Bairner (Dublin: University College Dublin Press, 2005), 7–21, 20.

21. *Public Ledger*, April 8, 1908.

22. Paul Darby, *Gaelic Games, Nationalism and the Irish Diaspora in the United States* (Dublin: University College Dublin Press, 2009).

23. *Freeman and Irish American Review*, May 31, 1890.

24. *Hibernian*, May 11, 1895.

25. Ibid., May 18, 1895.

26. Ibid., May 11, 1895.

27. Ibid., March 16, 1895.

28. Ibid., December 7, 1889.

29. Ibid.

30. Ibid.

31. *Freeman and Irish American Review*, December 7, 1889.

32. Ibid., December 14, 1893.

33. Ibid., November 23, 1893.

34. Ibid.

35. *Clan-na-Gael Journal*, November 14, 1914.

36. *Hibernian*, July 4, 1895.

37. Ibid., June 22, 1895.

38. The expansive grounds of Pastime Park in North Philadelphia, which were accessible by trolley, became the venue of choice. Holding crowds of 40,000 or more for their nationalist games, this became an example of Foucault's heterotopia, in which the private citizen enters a public territory for an excursion into another world. Foucault, "Des espace autres, Une conference inedited de Michel Foucault," trans. Jay Miskowiec, *Architecture Mouvement Continuité*, no. 5 (October 1984): 46–49.

39. *Hibernian*, September 14, 1895.

40. *Freeman and Irish American Review*, August 2, 1890.

41. Ibid., June 28, 1894.

42. *Hibernian*, May 5, 1894.

43. Ibid., September 14, 1895.

44. Ibid.

45. *Freeman and Irish American Review*, August 17, 1889.

46. Ibid., August 7, 1889.

47. Ibid., August 17, 1889.

48. Ibid., August 14, 1890.

49. Ibid.

50. Ibid.

51. Ibid., October 26, 1889.

52. Ibid., April 12, 1890.

53. Donna Gabaccia, "Race, Nation, Hyphen: Italian-Americans and American Multiculturalism in Comparative Perspective," in *Are Italians White? How Race Is Made in America*, ed. Jennifer Guglielmo and Salvatore Salerno (New York: Routledge, 2003), 57.

54. McDevitt, "Muscular Catholicism," 265.

55. Richard Holt, "Ireland and the Birth of Modern Sport," in *Gaelic Athletic Association*, eds. Cronin et al., 25–46, 32.

56. Mullan, "Opposition, Social Closure, and Sport: The Gaelic Athletic Association in the 19th Century," *Sociology of Sport Journal* 12, no. 3 (September 1995): 268–289.

57. McDevitt, "Muscular Catholicism," 273.

58. *Hibernian*, July 13, 1895.

59. Ibid., August 17, 1889.

60. Letter from the President De Valera Reception Committee of Philadelphia, 1919, RG 40-1-4, box 1, Irish American Materials, CHRC.

61. "Constitution of the First Regiment of Hibernian Rifles of Philadelphia," 1886, Recording Group 103, Box 34, CHRC.

62. The goals of the Union were stated: the dissemination of "knowledge of the military art . . . through encampments, conventions, lectures, official communications, and the formation of small bodies into regiments and brigades." "Constitution of the Irish-American Military Union," 1889, recording group 103, box 36, CHRC.

63. Ibid.

64. *Freeman and Irish American Review*, April 12, 1890.

65. Ibid., May 31, 1890.

66. Ibid., August 10, 1889.

67. Ibid., July 24, 1899.

68. Ibid., March 22, 1890.

69. *Freeman and Irish American Review*, March 29, 1890. Bowman had a fear of public disorder, referring to the display of the Hibernians on St. Patrick's Day, 1919, "while this free organization is allowed to continue there would be nothing to prevent a large band of socialists to arm themselves in the same way by loaded weapons and by a sudden and overwhelming onslaught exterminate the municipal police force."

70. *Freeman and Irish American Review*, March 22, 1890.

71. Ibid., August 14, 1890.

72. *Hibernian*, March 22, 1894.

73. Ibid., September 14, 1895.

74. Ibid., March 22, 1890.

75. Ibid., July 24, 1899.

76. Ibid.

77. Ibid., May 24, 1890.

78. Ibid., June 14, 1890.

79. Ibid., May 24, 1890.

80. Ibid., September 30, 1895.

81. Ibid., September 21, 1889.

82. Ibid., March 7, 1891.

83. *Hibernian*, May 5, 1894.

84. Ibid.

85. *Irish American Review and Celtic Literary Advocate*, December 16, 1899.

86. *Philadelphia Inquirer*, January 8, 1900.

87. Ibid.

88. Ibid., January 22, 1900.

89. *Hibernian*, February 3, 1898.

90. *Freeman and Irish American Review*, December 7, 1889.

91. *Hibernian*, August 11, 1895.

92. David Fitzpatrick, *Politics and Irish Life 1913–1921: Provincial Experience of War and Revolution* (Dublin: Macmillan, 1977), 677.

CONCLUSION

1. Richard Sennett, *The Corrosion of Character: The Personal Consequences of Work in the New Capitalism* (New York: W. W. Norton, 1998), 70.

2. E. J. Hobsbawm, *Nations and Nationalism since 1780: Programme, Myth, Reality* (Cambridge: Cambridge University Press, 1990), 159.

Index

Page numbers followed by *t* refer to tables.

About the Author

Michael L. Mullan is a professor of sociology at Swarthmore College in Pennsylvania. In addition to teaching sociology, he was the head coach of the men's tennis team at the college for forty years. Coach Mullan's teams at Swarthmore won three national NCAA Division III team championships during his time; he maintains his love of tennis and is active on the international veteran's tennis circuit. Professor Mullan holds PhDs in both sociology and history.